Jewelry
MAKING MANUAL

Jewelry
MAKING MANUAL

Sylvia Wicks

BRYNMORGEN
PRESS

A *Quill* BOOK

© Quill Publishing Limited 1985

This edition published in 1990 by
Brynmorgen Press
33 Woodland Road
Cape Elizabeth, Maine 04107
207-767-6059

ISBN 0 9615984 2 5

Reprinted 1991, 1995

This book was designed and produced by
Quill Publishing Limited
The Old Brewery, 6 Blundell Street
London N7 9BH

Senior editor Patricia Webster
Project editor Jane Laing
Editor Emma Foa
Designer Alex Arthur
Illustrators Fraser Newman Ray Brown Mick Hill
Photographer Rose Jones
Picture researcher Veneta Bullen
Paste-up artist Carol McCleeve
Indexer Elizabeth Rolfe
Also thanks to Atlas Photography Mark Frankel R Holt & Co Ltd
Tim McCreight Paul Owens Eva Ratanakul Patrizio Semproni
Elizabeth Sloan H S Walsh & Sons Ltd Chris Walton

Art director Nigel Osborne
Editorial director Jim Miles

Consultant Peter Gainsbury

The author would like to thank the following for their contributions to the projects illustrated:
David Blow, Sheelagh Burch, Marlon Campbell, Lawrence Cohen, Alan Craxford,
Roy Flewin, Georgina Follet, Susan Fortune, Jayne Hierons, Ralph Hollingdale, Tony Laws,
Selina Preece, David Reid, Setsu Sato, Roger Taylor, Dana Tinsley, Len Wilcox, Heidi Yeo.
Thanks are also due to the staff and students of the Jewellery and Silversmith Department,
Sir John Cass Faculty of Arts, City of London Polytechnic.

Filmset by Leaper & Gard Ltd, Bristol and QV Typesetting, London
Color origination by Hong Kong Graphic Arts Ltd, Hong Kong
Printed and bound by Leefung-Asco Printers Ltd, China

CONTENTS

JEWELRY TODAY

People are drawn to making jewelry for several reasons: they may be eager to try out design ideas; they may enjoy constructing pieces; or they may simply be keen to have a finished piece of their own making. Whatever the reason, the jeweler today is able to use a number of methods and work with a variety of interesting materials. Facilities may be severely limited or extensive; the main principle to remember is to work with integrity, continually aiming to expand personal skills and understanding.

WHAT IS JEWELRY?

Over the last two decades, jewelry designers and technicians have questioned the validity of past values, traditions and techniques, both in their work and in the way they have spoken about the subject. This questioning has not led to the discarding of earlier principles, but to the broadening of them. Jewelry is no longer definable simply in terms of its materials, its status associations, or its decorative role. There are no longer any hard or fast rules or restrictions.

Probably the most generally agreed guideline is that the jewelry should be wearable. Wearable does not necessarily mean comfortable for 24 hours a day. In the same manner that wearers of high-heeled shoes adjust their walk, stance and distance to be covered to suit the shoes they are wearing, so jewelers are now suggesting that wearers adjust their movement or stance to suit different types of jewelry.

Today, classical, contemporary and experimental jewelry items are displayed side by side. One individual may, at the same time, wear an old family ring and an avant-garde neck ornament. The clothing fashions of any group of people might conform, but the jewelry worn is likely to vary widely in period, style and material. One person might wear a fashionable aluminum necklace; another might prefer antique crystals; and someone else might display a varied assortment of stones, both real and imitation. Every item of jewelry whether precious metal or plastic has a valid place in jewelry today.

So jewelry can be made of anything wearable, and is certainly individual. Not everything made under the title of "jewelry" is good simply because it is made, but it is worth continuing to experiment — researching new materials, developing new techniques and constantly improving skills. In time, good pieces will result.

Sarah Osborn, who was a selector for the major jewelry exhibition of 1982 at the British Crafts' Centre entitled "Jewelry Redefined," wrote the following words in the introduction to the catalog:

A welter of 'whacky' materials cannot elevate a derivative, weak or uninspired idea or clumsy unsympathetic making. It is really what the jewellery maker makes of, or makes with the material that counts. It can be so sweetly simple. The rubberiness of rubber; the plasticity of plastic; the paperiness of paper. When it's right there is no mistaking the fact.

All types of jewelry are worn today, from antique to contemporary. And while the decorative qualities of the piece are likely to reflect the age in which it was constructed, the choice usually rests on the fact that it goes well with what one is wearing, that it suits the occasion, or, more simply, because it is pleasing.

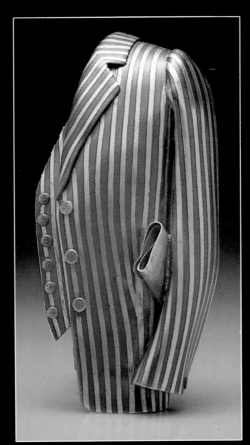

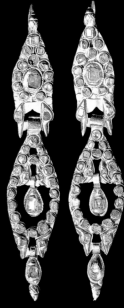

The pin (left) by Sophie Chell (UK) is made of anodized silver and gold, and is 6cm high. Some of the stones have been replaced in the antique gold suspended earrings set with emeralds (above).

WHAT ATTRACTS JEWELERS?

Many jewelers wear very little jewelry. For it is not a █ the possession of the end product that is important; perhaps it is the development of the design, the challenge of the construction, or the need to explain an idea or express a point of view. Alternatively, it may be the scale of the work, the nature of the materials or the fascination of the technology that attracts the beginner jeweler to this fascinating craft.

Some █ welers are inspired by the end product or by the fact that the jewelry is personal and likely to be treasured, or by the undeniable mystique that jewelry sometimes acquires. And there are intangible attractions, too. Some people begin by dabbling, find that they are drawn to jewelry making and eventually find the subject totally compelling.

WHO MAKES JEWELRY?

Anyone who wants to! Many of today's jewelers were trained in other disciplines, or had no formal training at all. Jewelry remains one of the █ fields in which the talented individual working alone and with limited facilities, can make a significant contribution. All it takes is commitment, practice and perseverance.

Neither does jewelry have to be a full-time occupation. There are so many different facets of the subject that those people with less time can concentrate on acquiring skills in one or two specialized aspects. For example, after the stone has been cut, a diamond ring is constructed by three specialists: the mounter makes the metal section and sends the ring to the polisher; after a preliminary polish it goes to the setter, who secures the stones in the metal; then back to the polisher for the final finish.

At the moment, some highly skilled hand processes are being practiced by amateur jewelers who are happy to spend a great deal of time on work that does not have to be sold at a profit. Professionals are generally under pressure to reduce labor costs and therefore are no longer able to take time needed for some manual techniques. For instance, until quite recently, as well as mass-produced chains, various unusual hand-made chains were available. Chain making is not difficult, only time-consuming; refer to the advanced section for chain-making suggestions.

Measurements

In the late 1960s, the measurements by which precious metals were sold were standardized, and by the early 1970s, all dealers were selling metals by metric measurement.

Because the metric system has now operated for so long in the precious metal trade, dealers and craftsmen normally use only metric measurements for specifying both the length and weight of all tools and materials, and this convention has been adhered to throughout the book, with one exception. Hammers continue to be sold, by the weight of the head, in avoirdupois ounces, and so, when specifying the weight of hammers, imperial measurements have been given, together with their metric equivalents.

Many of the metric measurements given when describing a technical process are necessarily minuscule but accurate. Since precision is essential in completing these processes, no approximate imperial equivalents have been provided.

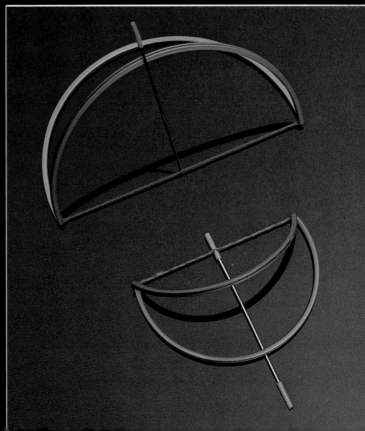

The anodized aluminum brooches (below) were made by Eric Spiller in 1984. Jewelry is not the exclusive preserve of women. Some men like to decorate their jacket lapels, shirt collars and sweaters. The rich colors and strong lines of these pieces are worn by both sexes.

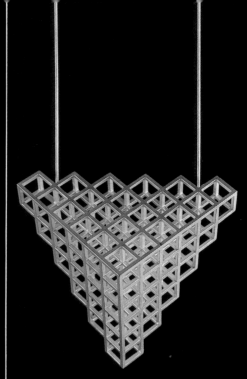

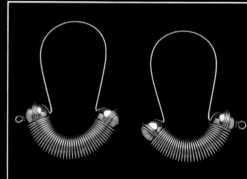

The neckpiece (above) by Wendy Ramshaw (UK) is entitled "Circle of Blue Feathers." It is made of silver with gilding and the brilliant blue, purple and turquoise feathers are actually pale emu feathers dyed.

Arline Fisch (USA) has become known for her extensive use of techniques involving textiles. She weaves metal strips into jewelry and crochets and knits wire into neckpieces and bracelets, which echo the textile characteristics of collars and cuffs. This brooch (right) is made of silver.

The gold pendant (top) by Frank Bauer (Australia) was constructed by hand. Delicate work of this kind requires an enormous amount of patience and skill. The earrings (above) by Shula Nitzani-Laws (UK) are made of steel springs that terminate in silver balls; they are held in place with steel ear wires.

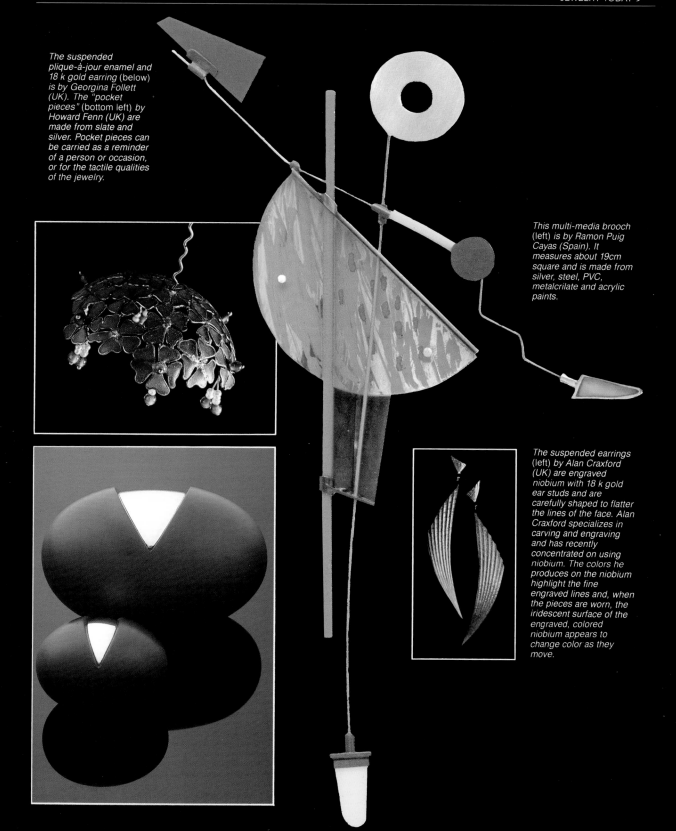

The suspended plique-à-jour enamel and 18 k gold earring (below) is by Georgina Follett (UK). The "pocket pieces" (bottom left) by Howard Fenn (UK) are made from slate and silver. Pocket pieces can be carried as a reminder of a person or occasion, or for the tactile qualities of the jewelry.

This multi-media brooch (left) is by Ramon Puig Cayas (Spain). It measures about 19cm square and is made from silver, steel, PVC, metalcrilate and acrylic paints.

The suspended earrings (left) by Alan Craxford (UK) are engraved niobium with 18 k gold ear studs and are carefully shaped to flatter the lines of the face. Alan Craxford specializes in carving and engraving and has recently concentrated on using niobium. The colors he produces on the niobium highlight the fine engraved lines and, when the pieces are worn, the iridescent surface of the engraved, colored niobium appears to change color as they move.

The necklace and bracelet (below) by Goudji (France) are made from 18 k gold. The stone is lapis lazuli.

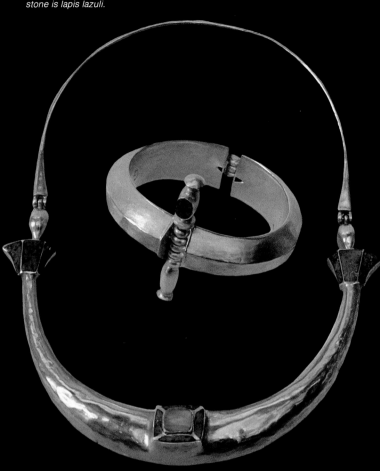

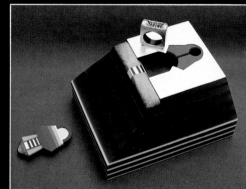

Both the watches (right) by Gordon Burnett (UK) were especially commissioned. The left-hand watch has a lacquered, oxidized brass case and a gold face decorated with an oxidized brass square. The other watch has a stainless steel body with a silver face and the numbers are represented by 18 k white gold dots. Both watches contain quartz movements.

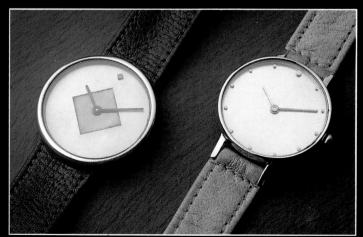

The pendant (top) by Dominique Favey (France) is made of bronze, a material more usually associated with monuments and sculptures. The metal is easily cast and has a rich surface color. Some jewelers are interested in the display of jewelry even when it is not being worn. Roger Morris (UK) designed the ring, brooch and stand (above right) so that, when not worn, the pieces can be combined to form a small sculpture. The materials used are silver and acrylic.

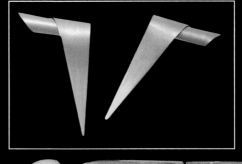

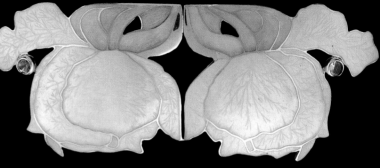

The neckpiece (far left) by David Watkins (UK) is entitled "Torus Minos" and is made of paper, gold leaf and stainless steel. The gold and tin earrings (left) are by Fritz Maierhofer (Austria). Because tin is such a soft metal, the earrings can be unrolled. The champlevé enamel belt buckle (below left) is by Setsu Sato (UK).

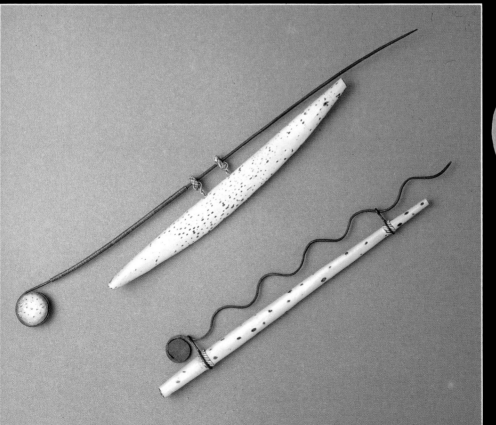

In the ring (above) by Joel Degen (UK), coral beads are set in silver, with black oxidized silver decoration, titanium washers and stainless steel screws. The brooches (left) by Cynthia Cousens (UK) are about 10cm long and are made from copper, steel and silver.

THE BEGINNER'S WORKSHOP

Simple jewelry is easily made in a limited space from a wide range of materials and using few tools. This chapter shows how to set up a work-bench, and takes a broad look at the kinds of tools and materials that the beginner may use.

A PLACE TO WORK

Many people begin making jewelry at the kitchen table. The kitchen is easily adapted for this purpose by clamping a wooden support called a bench pin to the edge of the table, ensuring that there is adequate light on the work surface and adjusting the height of the working surface, where possible.

The bench pin is an essential item of equipment used to steady and support the work. The pin, which is wedge-shaped, is fitted with its sloping side facing upwards, and must be firm and secure.

The working area needs to be brightly and directly lit. An adjustable reading lamp clamped to the back, left-hand corner of the bench (for a right-handed person) is ideal. No shadows cast by the jeweler or tools should fall across the work.

The work surface should be about 1m high. This is higher than a standard table to allow for easy use of tools, particularly the jeweler's saw, and a clear view of the work. The right height can be achieved by standing the table on a platform. Alternatively, leave the table as it is and use a low seat when working. As a guide, when sitting upright at the table, the work surface should be at about mid-chest level. A tray can be placed across the knees to catch metal filings, called lemmel.

The traditional jeweler's bench is made of solid wood about 5cm thick. The bench is fixed firmly to a wall or stands rigidly on a solid floor. This is important, as a rickety bench leads to inaccurate work. The bench has a large, curved section cut out from the edge. A leather skin is hung under this gap to catch metal filings, and the bench pin is wedged securely in the center of the cut-out. Bench pins eventually wear out and therefore need to be replaced from time to time, so it is not a good idea to glue them in place. Over the years, the leather skin will become impregnated with metal; when worn out, it may be sent with the floor sweepings to a metal refinery. There the material will be burnt and the metal recovered.

Ideally, the wooden surface should be sealed with a wax polish to prevent metal filings from penetrating the surface. It is easily cleaned and maintained with regular re-waxing. A varnished or plastic surface can be used instead; these surfaces are easy to clean but they do not withstand heat and are therefore unsuitable for use as soldering supports (*see page 30 for suitable soldering supports*).

Traditionally, the hemispherical piece of wood cut from the bench was fitted with three legs to make a stool. However, a hard stool is uncomfortable when used for long periods, so it is better to use a soft seat with a back rest. A typist's chair is ideal.

SELECTING TOOLS AND MATERIALS

The household repair and maintenance kit generally includes several tools that are suitable for the construction of jewelry. Anyone who has fixed a picture hook to a wall is likely to own a ball-pein hammer, and anyone who has wired an electric plug will probably own a pair of snipe-nose pliers and some wire cutters. Moreover, some common household materials, such as copper piping, wood offcuts and plastic containers, are useful for initial experiments with basic jewelry techniques.

In the engraving of a sixteenth-century goldsmith's workshop (below left) *bow drills, pliers and hammers hang along the wall. Many of the tools in a contemporary jeweler's kit* (below) *have hardly changed at all.*

Basic tool kit

Piercing saw and 2/0 blades	crossing, barrette	Steel block	Brass tweezers
Jeweler's shears for fringing solder	Parallel pliers	Ring mandrel	Buff sticks with flour-grade sandpaper, emery
Hand files: three-square, crossing	Chain-nose pliers	Blow torch	polishing paper and suede
	Flat pliers	Soldering surface	Polishing motor and buffs
	Round-nose pliers	Flux (borax, borax dish, brush)	Steel rule
Needle files: square, three-square, round,	Large half-round pliers	Steel tweezers	Dividers
	Ball-pein hammer	Pickle	Scriber
	Wooden mallet		

Tools

In addition to the common tools, a wide range of specialized tools has been developed especially for the jeweler. Beginners should buy their tools a few at a time, as the need arises, because the tools required depend so much on the type of work to be done. Consequently, if you begin by buying a wide range of tools you will probably find that many of them remain unused, and yet you still need to purchase more. Some common jewelry tools are shown in the photograph on page 13 to give an idea of the kind of equipment involved. A detailed look at the tools suitable for each task is given in conjunction with the various techniques described later in the book.

Materials

Jewelers need to select their materials with great care, bearing in mind the requirements of the piece to be made. A wedding band must last a lifetime, and at the same time retain its attractive appearance throughout. It must resist corrosion and survive temperature changes. Also, since it will be in contact with the skin for long periods, the band must be made of a material that is unlikely to irritate the skin. Gold and platinum fit all these requirements and are also valuable and therefore suitable for jewelry.

Fashion jewelry, on the other hand, is designed to reflect trends, and is likely to be discarded with the fashionable clothes it matches. Materials that are cheap and easy to color are most suitable for fashion jewelry. For example, for large, brightly colored earrings, the designer might choose plastics, or use light metals such as aluminum or titanium. These metals may be colored very effectively by using an electrical process called anodizing.

When selecting materials for a piece of jewelry, be prepared to experiment. In this way, you may find new uses for materials, and give the jewelry you produce an individual look. Soon you may develop a preference for working with certain materials, and this may lead you to specialize in a particular type of jewelry or technique. For example, some jewelers prefer to work with non-metals, such as wood or plastics. Others specialize in particular finishing techniques, such as enameling. The illustrations on this page show just a few of the many uses of traditional and modern materials.

Materials for making jewelry
A selection of attractive, imaginative and unusual pieces of jewelry can be seen on this and the two following pages. A wide variety of materials has been used, from the traditional gold and silver to the colorful refractory metals and from plexiglass to paper. Experiment with all sorts of materials, however unorthodox, until you find one that suits your design; you may break new ground!

Silver *The bracelet and ring* (right) *are made from fine silver and are by Yasuki Hiramatsu (Japan).*

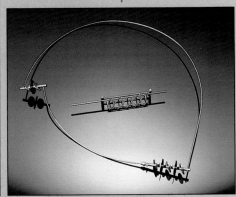

Gold *Leonard Smith (UK) made the neckpiece and brooch* (right) *from yellow and white golds.*

Gold *Reema Pachachi (UK) constructed the necklace and matching earrings* (below) *from three colors of gold*

Gold *The unusual 18 k gold brooch* (below) *by Jacqueline Mina (UK) is heat and rolling mill textured with a mokumé center.*

Steel *The steel and silver earrings (below) are by Susan Fortune (UK).*

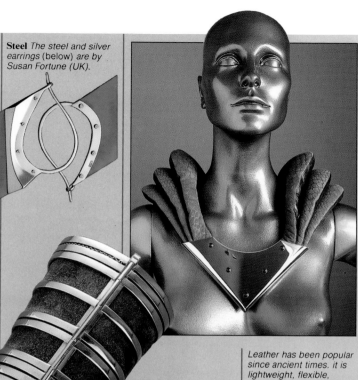

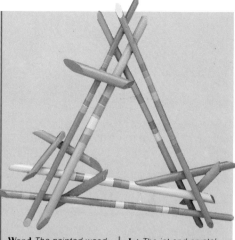

Wood *The painted wood brooch (above) is by Marjorie Schick (USA).*

Jet *The jet and crystal earrings (below) are by Fortini Kafiri (UK).*

Leather has been popular since ancient times. it is lightweight, flexible, comfortable to wear and takes dye well.

Leather *Susan Fortune (UK) made the leather and silver armband (left), and Karla Moon (UK) made the leather and metal neckpiece (above).*

Beads *Beads come in an enormous range of colors, shapes and materials (below).*

Refractory metals *The niobium pendant (below) is by Barry and Sally Milburn (UK). Refractory metals can be brightly colored, but they are not easy to join by soldering.*

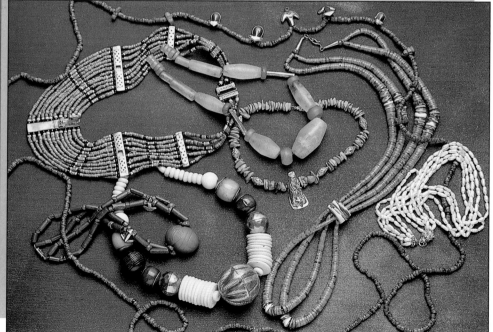

Synthetic resins *The four silver and polyester resin earrings (below) by Susan Heron (UK) are from the Crafts Council collection.*

Textiles *The fabric neckpiece (below) is by Jenny Sedgwick (UK).*
Paper *The paper pins (bottom) are by Julie Wallis (UK).*

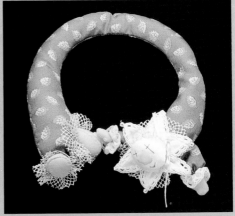

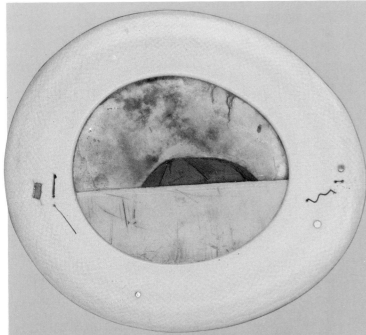

Glass *The bracelets (below) by Svatopluk Kasaly (Czechoslovakia) are made of glass and silver and glass.*

Ivory *The ivory and bone brooch (above) by Ann Brownsworth (Australia) is called "The Rock."*

Plexiglass *The neckpiece in steel and plexiglass (below) is by Maria Lugossy (Hungary)*

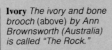

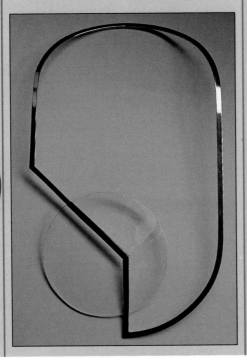

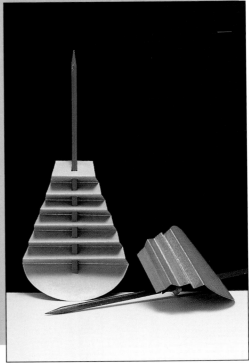

METALS FOR JEWELRY

METAL	COLOR	APPROXIMATE MELTING TEMPERATURE	ANNEALING DETAILS	SPECIFIC GRAVITY (approx)	GENERAL INFORMATION	SOLDERS AND APPROXIMATE MELTING TEMPERATURES
Fine gold	Rich yellow	1945°F	Annealing not required	19.5	Fine gold is known as a "noble" metal because of its durability and the fact that it is unaffected by oxygen and most chemicals. Fine or pure gold (24 k) must be alloyed with other metals before it is hard enough to be used for jewelry.	High karat gold solders
18 k gold	Yellow, red, white, sometimes green	Yellow — 1652°F, white — 1832°F, red — 1607°F	Yellow and red — 1202°F, white — 1382°F	15.58	18 k gold contains 18 parts in 24 of fine gold (750 parts in 1000) and has good working properties.	18 k solder: hard 1436°-1526°F; med 1346°-1409°F; easy 1175°-1301°F
14 k gold	Yellow, red, white	Yellow — 1760°F, white — 1832°F, red — 1580°F	Yellow and red — 1202°F, white — 1382°F	13.4	14 k gold contains 14 parts in 24 of fine gold (585 parts in 1000) and has good working properties.	14 k solder: hard 1382°-1445°F; easy 1310°-1346°F
9 k gold	Yellow, red, white	1652°F	1202°F	11.3	9 k gold contains 9 parts in 24 of fine gold (375 parts in 1000), has good working properties and may be harder than 18 k gold.	9 k solder: hard 1391°-1463°F; med 1355°-1391°F; easy 1202-1328°F
Fine silver	Lustrous white	1762°F	Annealing not required	10.53	Fine silver has a highly reflective surface and is malleable and ductile. It tarnishes in contact with air containing sulfur.	Silver solders
Sterling silver	White	About 1634°F	1112°-1202°F	10.4	Contains 925 parts of fine silver in 1000. Sterling silver is not as strong as gold but has good working properties. During heating, black copper oxide penetrates the surface, creating a black stain known as fire stain.	Silver solders: enameling 1346°-1472°F; hard 1373°-1436°F; med 1328°-1409°F; easy 1292°-1337°F
Platinum	Grey-white	3191°F	1652°-1832°F	21.4	Malleable, ductile, and good tensile strength. Very fine wires can be used and it takes a bright polish. Platinum has an exceptional resistence to corrosion.	Platinum solder: hard 2588°-2633°F; med 2156°-2228°F; easy 1850°-1886°F
Copper	Red	1981°F	1202°F	8.94	Good working qualities. Copper does not retain a polished surface.	Silver solders
Brass	Pale yellow	1724°F	1112°-1202°F	8.5	An alloy of copper and zinc. Brass does not retain a polish.	Silver solders
Nickel silver (German silver)	Grey-white	2093°F	1202°-1256°F	Varies	Nickel silver is an alloy of nickel, copper, and zinc but its appearance is similar to silver. It has good working properties but work hardens quickly.	Silver solders
Aluminum	Blue-white	1220°F	542°-662°F	2.70	Aluminum can be colored by anodizing and dyeing. As a guide to annealing, cake soap rubbed on the surface turns black when the metal reaches the right temperature.	Special solders containing no lead
Titanium	Grey	3047°F	Annealing requires a high vacuum chamber	4.5	Titanium can be colored by anodizing — best colors are achieved if the surface is etched. Difficult to shape or bend.	Cannot be soldered in the usual way
Zirconium	Grey	3366°F	Annealing requires a high vacuum chamber	6.4	Zirconium can be colored by anodizing and can be shaped and bent.	Cannot be soldered in the usual way
Niobium	Grey	4532°F	Annealing requires a high vacuum chamber	8.4	Niobium can be colored by anodizing — the colors are bright and the surface does not have to be etched. Easy to shape and bend.	Cannot be soldered in the usual way

BASIC TECHNIQUES

Making jewelry is an ancient craft: many basic techniques and tools that were developed thousands of years ago are still in use today and the modern jeweler often cuts, drills, files, solders and bends metal using traditional techniques. Advances in metallurgy, however, have led to great improvements in the quality of some tools, and the introduction of electrically powered equipment has helped to speed up some manufacturing processes.

CUTTING

Many different tools can be used to cut metal for making jewelry. A Roman process of cutting metal with a chisel was exploited by Byzantine jewelers, who chiseled out elaborate and delicate patterns in gold. This technique is not now generally used by Western jewelers, probably because it is suitable only for fairly thin metal, but the characteristic chiseled edge is highly decorative, and can still be seen on much jewelry originating from the Middle East.

Shears can be used to cut sheet metal, but they are unsuitable for accurate work, as the edge left after cutting is stretched and distorted. A guillotine gives a good, straight cut, but this, too, distorts the edge of the metal. So, like shears, it is used mainly for cutting sufficient material for a single job from a large stock sheet of metal.

For intricate cutting, jewelers use saws. The backsaw is like a miniature tenon-saw, and is used mainly for sawing long, straight lines. However, it is not a popular tool as it has limited uses. By far the most common cutting tool used by jewelers is the more versatile piercing saw.

The piercing saw

The piercing saw resembles a small fretsaw. Wing-nut clamps, one at each end of the saw frame, hold the blade in position. The frame is made of springy steel and keeps the blade at the right tension for sawing. Because the blade is extremely thin, the piercing saw is suitable for making intricate cuts in sheet metal and other materials. With experience, a jeweler can cut accurate straight lines with it, too.

The tool is called a piercing saw because of the way it is used to cut out holes. The blade has to be threaded through a pilot hole, made by drilling through the material. So the blade, in effect, pierces the material,

The use of the cutting technique opus interrasile *can be clearly seen in the section of the Byzantine gold necklace* (above), *made in the ninth century. The pattern is chiseled out of sheet metal. Patterns similar to that shown in the Roman bronze ring* (left) *are easily cut from sheet metal and the ends bent to form a ring.*

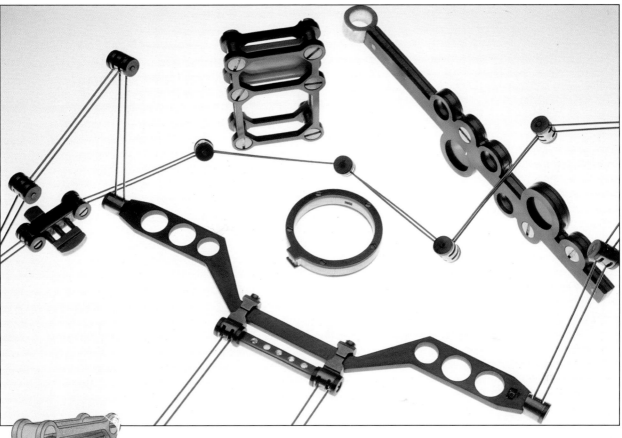

Joel Degen pierced the component parts for this jewellery (above and top) from titanium. Sections were assembled mechanically for design and practical reasons: mechanical devices suit mechanical shapes, and steel is hard to join in any other way.

and the piece that is then cut out is said to be pierced out.

The saw is described by its depth (the distance from the blade to the back of the frame), and whether or not it is adjustable. Adjustable frames enable you to use up short bits of broken blades. However, this is usually unsatisfactory, as cutting is quicker and more accurate when sawing with the full length of the blade. A non-adjustable saw frame with a depth of 8cm is the most convenient and, therefore, the most common.

Blades for the piercing saw
The blades available for this saw range from coarse to very fine (*see page 21*). The most useful general purpose blade is size 2/0. As a general guide, cutting is most efficient when there are at least $2\frac{1}{2}$ teeth to the thickness of the material. With more widely spaced teeth, the material may tend to jam between them.

For cutting metal, the teeth of the blade should lie in a straight line. Blades with offset teeth, as on a woodworker's saw, are suitable for soft materials, such as plastics, wood and shells. The offset teeth allow for clearance of sawdust and other debris and help prevent the blade from jamming in the soft material. The offset blade is capable of cutting metal, but the cut will be wider than is necessary and some material will be wasted. This can prove expensive when working in precious metals.

Piercing saw blades are sold by the bundle (12) or by the gross (144).

Securing the blade
Sit at the work-bench and support the saw frame between the edge of the bench and your chest, with the wooden handle toward you and the blade clamps uppermost. This leaves both hands free to insert the blade. Clamp the blade at the far end of the frame, with the teeth along the top edge and pointing toward you. Lean gently against the

wooden handle and the steel bow will flex slightly. With the frame flexed, tighten the other wing-nut to secure the blade in the frame.

Pluck the blade to test the tension. If it "pings" the tension is correct. A dull "plunk" indicates a slack blade, which will soon break when sawing. To readjust the blade, undo the handle-end clamp, lean on the frame to compress it further, and then re-tighten the wing-nut.

Marking the metal

Before cutting, the required shape must be marked on the material. It is difficult to draw a design directly on a smooth metal surface, so jewellers normally use tracing paper to transfer drawings onto the metal.

To transfer the design, first trace the drawing. On the back of the tracing paper, pencil over the lines again. Then roll a ball or sausage of plasticine over the metal so that it leaves a coating onto which the pattern can be transferred easily.

Position the tracing on the metal so that the amount wasted in cutting will be as small as possible. Run a pencil over the traced line. The pencil line on the back of the tracing will transfer to the surface of the material. Carefully lift off the tracing paper and lightly score over the faint pencil line with a sharp point. A marking tool called a scriber is the best implement for this task.

Basic sawing

Sit at the work-bench and hold the marked material on the bench pin. Aim to cut on the outside edge of the lines rather than inside them as it is best to have too much material rather than too little. Rest the saw blade on the edge of the material and gently draw the blade downward across the edge. The blade should then begin to cut. If it does not, check that the blade is the right type for the thickness of material and is correctly fitted in the frame. If the blade sticks, tilt the frame to one side so that the edge of the blade bites into the metal, and gradually move the frame back to an upright position as you continue sawing. Another way to overcome sticking is to lubricate the blade with oil or beeswax.

Because the teeth point toward the handle, the blade cuts on the downstroke. The upward stroke simply repositions the blade for the next cutting stroke. The jeweler's low sitting position facilitates such

SAWING PROJECT

The letter "J" includes straight and curved lines. Saw cuts in the "swan" suggest shape, like lines in a drawing. First sawing efforts may be less than accurate and the beginner might like to start with the abstract shape which allows discrepancies in the sawing to be disguised or even used to advantage. End lugs allow a cord or ribbon to be attached by a simple slip knot.

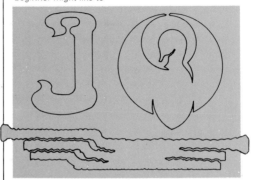

Tools and materials

Piercing saw with frame 80mm deep
Blades: size 2/0 saw blades for metal, size 1 for plastic or wood
Tracing paper and pencil
Plasticine
Scriber
Metal sheet: silver, gold, nickel silver, gilding metal, copper or brass (it is probably wise to practice on non-precious metals first) 1mm-thick sheet sufficient for the design chosen
Plastic: 2mm-thick sheet
Wood: 2mm-thick 3-ply

a sawing action. It is not necessary to apply great pressure, nor to saw frantically. If you draw the full length of the blade slowly up and down, cutting should be easy.

To saw straight lines, tilt the saw forw slightly so that the cut already made helps tⱼ guide the blade. To saw around curves, keep the blade upright. To turn corners, raise and lower the blade, gradually turning the frame until the blade faces in the new direction, then saw on.

So far, we have dealt only with sawing at right angles to the surface of the material. But a beveled edge can be made by simply tilting the frame to the required angle. If necessary, you can change the cutting angle while sawing by gradually altering the tilt of the frame.

It is important to hold the material firmly. Movement of the material is liable to result in a crooked line and a broken blade. It is also good work practice to hold items in the hand, rather than in a vise or with pliers, as the material is less likely to be marked if you do this. At first, your hand may quickly become tired, but the muscles soon strengthen.

Sawing holes

The jeweler often needs to cut holes of various shapes in sheet metal. To do this, first mark the shape of the hole to be cut and then drill a hole through the waste material within the marked lines. The drilled hole should be

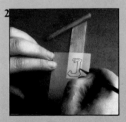

1 *Trace the pattern. With a pencil, retrace the lines on the back of the tracing paper. The design will not transfer to the smooth surface of materials like metal or*

Basic cutting tools
Jeweler's piercing saws are available with either adjustable or non-adjustable frames. Piercing saw blades are purchased in bundles of 12 or by the gross (144): *begin with size 2/0. The jeweler's backsaw has a strong support along the top of the deep blade, which is for sawing straight lines through thick material. A scriber marks the lines.*

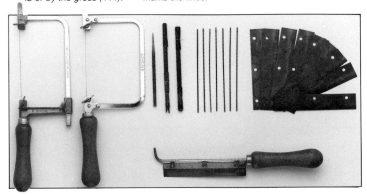

just big enough to take the piercing saw blade, and should be close to the marked line. Undo the blade clamp nearest to the handle and thread the blade through the hole from the top. Then re-tension the frame and secure the blade in the clamp again. Now cut out the hole, keeping to the inside of the lines.

The finishing touch
After using the piercing saw, a beginner usually has to resort to the use of a file to remove odd bits of unwanted metal from the work. With experience, the jeweler will be able to cut right up to the line marked on the material. The saw itself is then used like a file, just to remove sharp edges. This is done by stroking the edge of the material with the blade. After finishing in this way, the cut is clean and requires no further work.

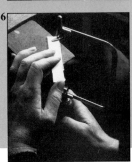

plastic. This can be overcome by rolling plasticine across the surface.
2 Position the tracing on the material as economically as possible and pencil over the traced line. The pencil line on the back of the tracing will transfer to the surface of the material.
3 Scratch over the faint pencil line with a scriber.
4 Lean gently against the handle to secure the blade in the saw frame. The teeth should point out from the frame and toward the handle. Check the tension by plucking the blade.

5 Hold the work firmly on the bench pin and begin sawing.
6 Saw carefully along the marked lines, erring on the waste side of the line. Remember to leave room to turn corners. File the edge of the material with the saw blade to finish.

DRILLING

Round holes are made by drilling. They can be functional, for example, to provide access for the piercing saw, or decorative and arranged in a pattern. The size of the hole depends on the size of the tools used.

Drills

For several thousand years, jewelers have bored holes with a tool called a bow drill. It is extremely easy to use as it is operated with only one hand, leaving the other hand free to hold the material. Also, the direction of the hole and the pressure on the drill are easily controlled.

Alternatives include the Archimedian drill, which is a small device, usually about 10cm long. It is worked by sliding a handle up and down a twisted steel shaft. Operation of this tool requires both hands. The common hand drill has the same disadvantage.

Flexible shaft drills are suspended, electrically operated motors with flexible drive shafts. Drill presses are also electrically operated but fixed to a stand or bench. Work to be drilled is supported on a horizontal platform and the drill is moved down in a vertical column. Both these electric drills are very useful, but they are an unnecessary expense for beginner jewelers.

Bits and chucks

The bit is the part of the drill that does the cutting. It is held in place by a chuck. The chuck may be variable, taking any size of drill bit, or interchangeable, requiring a change of chuck with a change of drill size. Standard bits range is size from 0.3mm upward. The most common type of bit is called a twist drill. It cuts only when it rotates in a clockwise direction (viewed from above). A twist drill can be used in a bow drill, but is inefficient as it rotates first one way, then the other. Better results are obtained by using a needle drill — a special bit that cuts whichever way it turns. Jewelers grind steel needles to make these special bits. Instructions for doing this are given opposite.

(a bow drill illustrated on page 24)

MAKING A NEEDLE DRILL
1 *Hold the needle with two pairs of pliers and snap it in two. Look away from the needle so that fragments of steel do not fly into your eyes. The needle should break cleanly; if it only bends, the steel is too soft.*
2 *Secure the needle in a pin vise with the broken end protruding. Grind two flat faces so that the end of the needle becomes wedge-shaped.*
3 *Hold the wedge upright on a carborundum stone. Tilt the needle toward you and roll it onto the right-hand tip. Grind the first cutting edge with about three strokes. Without lifting the needle from the stone, roll it onto the other tip, and repeat.*

Tools and materials

Pin vise
Carborundum or India stone
Two pairs of pliers
Packet of top-quality steel embroidery needles

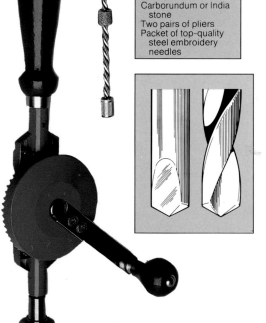

Types of drill
The fixed drill press (above) facilitates the drilling of vertical holes. Support the work either on wood or in an engineer's vise. The flexible shaft drill (right) is usually controlled from a foot pedal. Switch on and gently depress the pedal to start the motor turning. Apply greater pressure to increase the speed of the drill. Do not race the motor, though — a sharp drill cuts easily without requiring high speed. A small hand drill, such as the Archimedian drill (far right), allows access to awkward or recessed places. However, a bow drill (illustrated on page 24) is more useful.

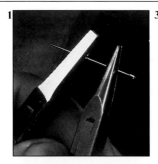

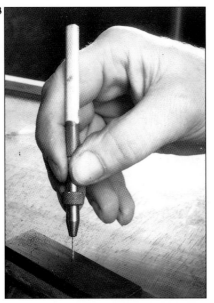

Using the bow drill

Select the drill bit and match it with the correct size of chuck. The drill should slide easily into the chuck. Do not force the jaws of the chuck outward as this will change their alignment and prevent them from gripping properly. Screw down the chuck head to secure the drill.

Clearly mark the point to be drilled with a scriber. Locate the drill on the mark and hold the bow section upright. Then twist the shaft, winding the string around it and so drawing up the handle. Using one hand, rest two fingers on each side of the handle and push it down gently. The flywheel (the heavy disk at the base of the shaft) will keep the drill turning and once the handle has traveled as far as the string will permit, it will begin to rise back up the shaft. Allow your hand to rise with the handle. Push down again as soon as the handle reaches its starting position at the top of the shaft. Build up speed as the drill begins to turn more easily. This skill is easily acquired.

The tools and materials itemized in the box (left) are all you need to make a needle drill. Needle and twist drill heads (below left) are not interchangable. The needle drill shown is sharpened to cut in one direction but a needle can be sharpened to cut whichever way it turns and a needle drill head is, therefore, suitable for use in a bow drill. The commercially produced twist drill cuts in only one direction, allowing swarf to escape down the recessed twist.

Tunisian women wear a variety of beautiful hair ornaments and decorated medallions (right). By using the simple processes of drilling and piercing, you can make similar jewelry.

USING A BOW DRILL

After completing this project you should be accustomed to using the bow drill. There is also the opportunity to improve sawing skills.

Tools and materials

Tracing paper, pencil and plasticine
Scriber
Bow drill and drill bits
Piercing saw and blades
Metal sheet: 1mm thick and sufficient for the pattern chosen

1 *Trace, transfer and scribe the pattern. Lightly tap the scriber to mark each point to be drilled; this is called spotting and should prevent the drill from skidding across the surface.*
2 *Drill all the holes. Then rest the work on the bench pin.*
3 *Loosen the handle-end clamp of the piercing saw and thread the blade through the drilled hole from the front.*
4 *Carefully saw out each hole.*

Drilled holes can be functional or decorative. The numbers on the faces of the die (below) are indicated by the holes that are drilled into them. The die was sawn from a 6mm square rod of silver. The hole for the jump ring that allows the die to be worn as a pendant or charm is made by drilling deep holes on two adjoining faces. The disks of the necklace (right) are decorated with an arrangement of holes of varying size and depth. Holes are also made to attach the cord.

FILING

Filing removes small quantities of material at a time. The jeweler files an item to shape it, and to even out rough surfaces or edges to make them smooth.

Files

Files are described by their shape, cut (arrangement of teeth) and length. The most useful cut for the jeweler is a medium cut, known as cut 2, although it can also be helpful to have one fine cut (called the smooth cut or cut 4) and one coarse cut (called the bastard cut or cut 0).

Needle files and hand files are the two types most commonly used in jewelry making. Needle files come in lengths of 10cm, 14cm, 16cm and 20cm. Initially, choose the 14cm size, cut 2, and the following shapes: round, square, three-square, crossing and barrette.

For hand files, select a length of 15cm in the following shapes and cuts: three-square, cut 2; barrette, cut 4; crossing, cut 2; equalling, cut 0.

Handles

The handle of a needle file is an integral part of the tool. Hand files have separate handles. Choose a handle that feels comfortable, and then follow the step-by-step instructions for fitting it (*see below*).

Needle files are normally used without handles. Although hand files are sold without handles, the rough tang end is liable to dig into the hand or wrist, making it uncomfortable to use. So fit handles to suit both your hand and the file.

1 Hand file
2 Pillar file
3 Three-square file
4 Round file
5 Knife-edge file
6 Joint or gapping file
7 Safety-back file
8 Half-round file
9 Barrette file
10 Crossing file

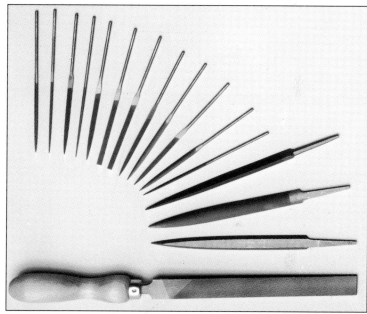

FITTING A FILE HANDLE

1 Hold the file upright. With a blow torch, heat the tang end until it is red hot. Direct the flame upward so that the rest of the file does not heat.

2 As soon as the tang is red, push it into the wooden handle. Continue pushing, allowing the hot metal to burn into the wood.

3 Secure the file in a vise. Protect the file by covering the jaws of the vise with aluminum or copper. Jewelers normally use jaw protectors when a vise is used for gripping tools. Tap the handle with a wooden mallet until it is secure.

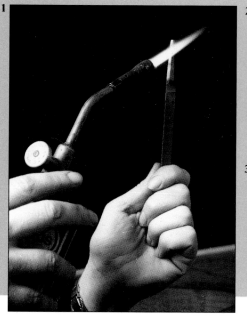

Castle-tower shapes like these (right) can be filed from solid rods of metal. This silver pendant is by Robin Kyte (UK).

How to file

Always choose the largest file possible for the job to give a smoother finish. This will normally be a hand file. The cut should be appropriate to the task: if the surface is very rough, or a large quantity of material is to be removed, the coarse file (bastard cut) is the most suitable. Conversely, for removing only small amounts of material, the fine cut (cut 4) is appropriate. Filing with a cut 2 file eliminates the marks left by the bastard file and, similarly, the cut 4 file removes the marks of the cut 2 file.

Support the article to be filed firmly on the bench pin (the file should be the only moving object as unstable work leads to inaccurate filing). To file a straight edge, rest the file diagonally across the material and move it back and forth, without lifting it from the work. The cutting stroke is the push stroke, which should be long and even in pressure. The pull stroke simply returns the file to the start position, ready for the next cutting stroke. Work with steady, even strokes; frantic, aggressive filing is unlikely to be accurate.

File around curves with long strokes of the file. Short, broken strokes may destroy the continuity of the curve.

FILING A TRIANGULAR EARRING

1 Transfer the pattern and pierce out the triangle. Wedge the triangle against the bench pin. File all sawn edges with a hand file.
2 Hold the edge of a ruler against the filed edge. If light can be seen between the two edges, refile the triangle.
3 Mark a bevel on each side of the earring.
4 File the bevel. Drill a hole for the ear-wire.

Tools and materials

Equipment for
  transferring pattern
Piercing saw and blades
Dividers
Three-square hand file,
  cut 2
Barrette hand file, cut 4
  for finer filing
Metal sheet, wood or
  plastic: 2mm thick

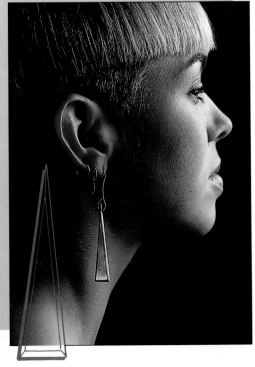

SOLDERING

Soldering is the process most used by jewelers for joining metal, and solder is the material that makes the join. Solder is also metal, but it is a special alloy designed to melt at a lower temperature than the metal it is to join. On heating, the solder melts and flows between the pieces of metal. On cooling, the solder solidifies to form a strong bond.

Hard soldering and soft soldering are the two common soldering processes. Soft soldering is used mainly in electronic, electrical and plumbing work. The solder used is a lead alloy, but this is inappropriate for most jewelers' requirements because it forms a relatively weak join. It also tends to spread over the work, adding an undesirable impurity to pieces made from precious metal. Hard soldering is the joining process preferred by jewelers. Hard solder contains a high proportion of the precious metal it is to join (for example, silver solder contains mostly silver), and consequently makes a stronger bond. Additives reduce the melting point of the solder, so that it is workable.

Hard soldering gives a strong, permanent and, when finished, invisible join. The technique, which is quick and easy to carry

Tools for soldering
1 *Composition soldering block.*
2 *Reverse-action tweezers with insulated handles.*
3 *Brass tweezers.*
4 *Borax cone and dish.*
5 *Gas-air torch for use with compressed air.*
6 *French blow torch for*
gas and mouth-blown air.
7 *Charcoal block.*
8 *Soldering wig.*
9 *Reverse-action wire soldering tweezers.*
10 *A small spirit burner can be placed beneath an acid container to provide a gentle heat. Soldering is an ancient process. Sumarian*
jewelers made the gold pieces (above) circa 2500 BC. The filigree decoration in the roundels is soldered to the round wires.

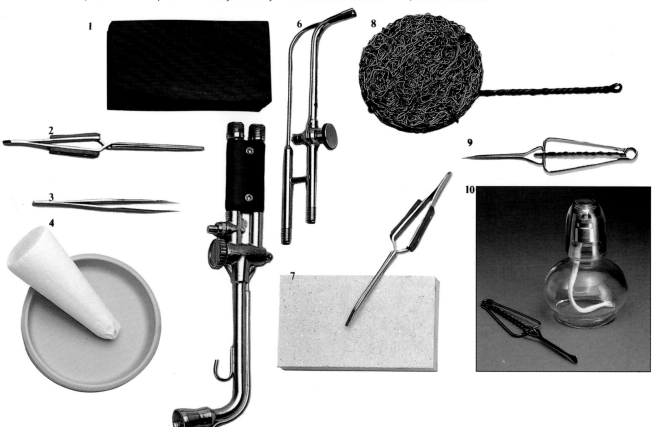

out, is suitable for many metals, including copper, brass, German silver, gilding metal, silver, gold and platinum.

The metal to be soldered is cleaned and aligned so that it touches where it is to be joined. A form of metal protection called flux is painted around the join to keep it clean. The solder is placed in contact with the work and then heat is applied. This causes the solder to melt and join the metal. After the metal has cooled, it is cleaned in an acid solution called pickle. Any excess solder is then removed from the area around the join by filing.

Tools and materials

The main items needed to carry out hard soldering are as follows: a blow torch to heat the work; a means of supporting the work; tools to hold the hot metal; solder, flux and pickle. These and related items are discussed in detail below.

Blow torches

A blow torch is a device in which air or oxygen is mixed with a combustible gas, such as natural gas or propane. The mixture is burnt to provide heat for various jewelry processes. The combustible gas is obtained from the main supply or from a cylinder or canister. Air can be blown in by mouth, or pumped in by means of a bellows or compressor. If oxygen is used, this is usually obtained from a cylinder. The choice of blow torch is mainly a matter of tradition and personal preference.

Mouth blow torches Some jewelers favor a mouth blowpipe used with an open flame, such as that from a Bunsen burner. Others prefer the French blow torch, which is easier to master. It is a gas-air torch, with the user supplying the air through a mouthpiece and hose connected to the torch. With local gas company approved installation, this torch is connected to the main gas supply, or via a suitable pressure regulator to a bottle of gas. A French blow torch, such as the "Dutch E-type" is light to hold and has a widely variable flame size. These features make it a popular choice.

Compressed air torches Compressed air torches are used for large-scale work, or

The projects on this and the following four pages provide practice in soldering three types of join. The buttons *(below)* have T-joins, the daisy pendant *(see pages 30-31)* has overlapping joins, and butt joins are used in the earring *(see pages 32-33)*. The post ear wire on the earring

SOLDERING T-JOINS

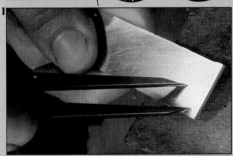

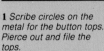

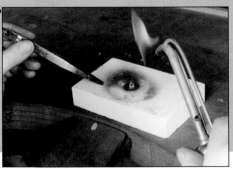

4 Fringe the end of a strip of hard silver solder. Support the end of the fringe on the forefinger and snip off as many small pieces (pallions) of solder as you need to make the join. The small pallions of solder are prevented from flying across the room by the position of the finger.
5 For this join, two pallions, each approximately 1mm square, are sufficient.
6 Heat the whole button with a soft flame until the solder flows.
7 When the metal is cool

1 Scribe circles on the metal for the button tops. Pierce out and file the tops.
2 Transfer the patterns for the backs (shanks) to a strip of metal. Drill all the holes before cutting the shanks as the strip is easy to hold.
3 Grind the borax cone in the dish with a little water until the liquid is a creamy consistency.

allows the jeweler to gain experience in soldering small, delicate pieces of metal to larger, bulky ones. To solder successfully, the metal must be clean and the joins well fitted. If light can be seen through the two pieces of metal, the join must be refitted.

suede shoe brush will do
Buttons: metal sheet 1.5mm thick
Daisy pendant: metal sheet 1mm thick
Earring: sheet metal 1mm thick, sheet metal 1.5mm thick, round wire 0.8mm in diameter
Purchase sufficient metal for the pattern chosen. Silver, gold, nickel silver, gilding metal, copper or brass are all suitable metals. Solder is needed for each project. Purchase one length each of hard, medium and easy silver solder. Or, if using gold, match the solder to the karat gold chosen.

when a higher temperature is required. This type of torch burns gas at a fast rate, and it is not possible to provide sufficient air by mouth. So a foot-operated bellows or an electrically driven compressor is used to force air into the torch. Foot bellows supply air for most torches burning coal gas; a compressor is used with natural gas and larger coal gas torches.

Bottle gas torches Torches of this kind operate directly from pressurized bottles of propane or butane gas and draw in their own air supply through holes in the burner nozzle. In compact bottle gas torches, the burner is fitted to the top of a small gas cylinder, which also acts as the handle of the tool. The cylinder may be either refillable or disposable. In larger bottle gas torches, the burner is connected to the bottle of gas via a hose and regulator.

Any one of these torches can be used for soldering jewelry. But whichever torch you choose, it must have a small burner so that the heat can be applied precisely where it is needed.

How to use a blow torch There are two main types of flame — a soft flame and a hard flame. A soft flame is blue and slightly bushy with yellow tips. A flame is described as hard when it is bright blue and focused to a point. A soft flame suits most tasks, and a hard flame is needed only when a very small area is to be heated.

Much of the oxygen in the gas-air mixture of a soft or reducing flame is consumed, and so the metal engulfed by the flame is unlikely to oxidize. Conversely, the metal heated by a hard or oxidizing flame does oxidize. Oxide forms in the presence of the oxygen in the air surrounding the metal, as the pin-point flame heats small sections of the metal.

To light a hand-held bottle gas torch, turn on the gas a little and light it at the burner. Once the flame is alight, adjust it by turning the on/off knob. The gas burns with a soft flame when the knob is adjusted to about the middle of its range; the highest setting gives a hard flame.

The French blow torch is held in one hand and the control knob is adjusted with the forefinger and thumb. Once you have lit the gas, the pilot light should stay on even when

remove the oxide and borax by immersing it in pickle.
8 Wash thoroughly under running water to remove all traces of acid.
9 To finish the button, file away excess solder and sharp or misshapen edges on both the front and the shank. Then,

either leave it plain or decorate the button by scalloping or beveling the edge with a file: a cut 4 file leaves a pattern of fine lines on the surface. Scrub the filed surface under running water with a brass brush and detergent to produce a mat finish.

the control knob is turned to its minimum setting. With the knob in the middle of its range, the flame should be yellow and bushy. On blowing gently down the air hose, the flame will turn blue with only tips of yellow; this is the soft flame. Keep the gas at the same setting and blow harder to obtain a hard, pointed flame.

To find the hottest part of a flame, move it up and down over the soldering surface and note when the hot spot is brightest. This will be when the surface is about 2cm from the tip of the light blue part of the flame. It is important to be familiar with the characteristics of the flame so that it can be used efficiently.

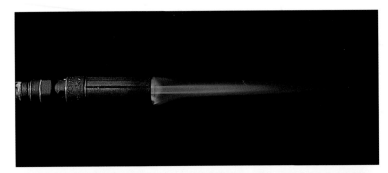

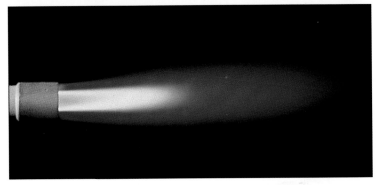

Supporting the work
Various substances and accessories are available for supporting work while soldering. They are all designed to withstand high temperatures. Asbestos blocks were once used, but are now known to be a health hazard and therefore should not be used under any circumstances.

The main types of soldering supports now used are detailed below. With accurate, controlled soldering, any of these surfaces can be stood directly on the wax-polished work-bench. Do not stand the support blocks directly on varnished, painted, laminated or plastic surfaces. Such surfaces must be protected with a steel plate, or a revolving soldering stand. Stands are available in a wide variety of sizes.

Soldering blocks These blocks are available in both natural and compressed charcoal. Natural charcoal is suitable for most soldering operations. It lasts longer than compressed charcoal, which is inclined to continue burning after use and quickly crumbles to powder.

Magnesium soldering blocks have been developed to replace the asbestos blocks previously used. These new types of block last well and retain a flat working surface. Although they are inclined to dissipate heat, they are probably the most convenient and inexpensive type of block for the amateur jeweler to use.

Soldering wig This circular mat of twisted iron wire 10cm in diameter allows heat to flow all around the work with a minimum of dispersion. Grasp firmly by the handle.

Charcoal chips Fine charcoal grains give all-round support to work that is being heated. The charcoal grains sold for fish tank filters are suitable for this purpose. Store and use them in any old small, flat steel box that you can find.

Tools for handling hot metal
Excess heat will soften pliers and brass tweezers, so hold hot metal with steel tweezers or soldering tongs *(see page 27)*. Size AA tweezers are strong and have fine points and are recommended for the beginner. Reverse action tweezers have points that grip when the handles are released. These tweezers can provide a convenient means of clamping the work while you are soldering it, thus leaving your hands free to apply the flame.

Solder
There are three main grades of solder used for hard soldering — hard, medium and easy. Easy solder melts at the lowest temperature, medium solder requires more heat to melt it, and hard solder requires further heat to melt it. Grades other than these have specialist uses and will be dealt with where relevant.

Always match the solder to the metal

SOLDERING OVERLAPPING JOINS
1 *Prepare the separate elements. Clean each section thoroughly and balance the middle daisy on top of the other two.*
2 *Borax along both joins. With the wet borax brush, position pallions of solder every 3mm.*
3 *Gently heat the whole piece. Concentrate the flame on one join and make the solder flow. Solder the other join. Note: Never balance pieces precariously: they are bound to topple, since metal and borax move when heat is applied.*

Two types of flame
A hard flame (above left) appears blue and is pointed like a sharpened pencil. It has no yellow tips at the point. The hottest part of the flame is in front of the light blue section. To find the hot spot in the flame of the torch you are using, direct the flame onto the charcoal block, varying the distance between it and the flame, and watch the red patch: it appears brightest where the flame is hottest. A soft flame (left) is bushy with yellow tips; it is the flame most used for soldering operations. Since solder flows only when the metal it is touching reaches the melting point of the solder, the whole object usually needs to be heated: a soft, engulfing flame heats evenly.

being joined. Thus, when soldering gold, match the solder to the karat and color of the gold, for example solder 10 karat yellow gold with 10 karat yellow-gold solder, solder 14 karat white gold with 14 karat white-gold solder, and so on. Solder platinum with platinum solder, and silver with silver solder. Silver solder also solders copper, gilding metal and brass; so start with silver solder, buying one strip of each grade, to suit the various tasks.

Flux

Solder will not flow unless the metal surface is clean. When heated in air, metal forms a surface "skin" called oxide that inhibits the flow of solder. Flux prevents this happening by providing a coating which excludes air.

The most common flux is borax. This is sold compressed into a cone and is ground, as needed, in a ceramic dish. Liquid flux is also favored by some jewelers. Both types of flux are suitable for use with all solders. Other fluxes have specialized uses and are described where relevant. Apply all types of flux with a small, soft-haired brush.

Cleaning solutions

After soldering, a cleaning solution called a pickle is used to remove flux and oxide from the metal. Proprietary, so-called safety pickles can be purchased, but most jewelers prefer to use alum solution or dilute sulfuric acid. Alum is safe to use at home. It works a little more slowly than acid and must be used hot.

Sulfuric acid at 10 per cent dilution can be purchased for use as pickle. Alternatively, concentrated acid can be diluted with water in the ratio of one part acid to nine parts water. However, concentrated acid is extremely corrosive, and the mixing process can be dangerous if carried out incorrectly. For these reasons, it is advisable to buy the acid already diluted. If you do decide to dilute the concentrated acid yourself, carefully read the instructions given below before you start.

Acid pickle works best when warm. But the heat causes it to give off pungent fumes, so ensure that there is adequate ventilation when using acid pickle.

Store the acid in a glass bottle with a ground glass stopper. NOTE: *For safety reasons do not use or store sulfuric acid in a kitchen or where children or animals may have access to it.*

Diluting acid When concentrated acid is mixed with water, heat is generated. Adding water to some concentrated acids can release heat rapidly and may cause a violent spurting. To avoid this danger, *pour the acid slowly into the water while stirring.* Diluting in this way ensures that the heat is released much more slowly. Use one volume of the concentrated acid to nine volumes of water.

Soldering techniques

It is most important to ensure that metal to be joined fits well before soldering, as solder flows by capillary action between closely fitting pieces of metal. This effect decreases as the gap between the surfaces increases, thus making the solder less likely to flow. As a general guide, if you can see light through the gap, then soldering will be difficult. Because solder relies on capillary action in order to flow, it cannot be used to bridge noticeable gaps between surfaces.

When metal is soldered, it passes through six basic stages: cleaning, fluxing, the application of solder, heating, cooling, and cleaning. Though this sounds complicated, the process is extremely simple and quick to carry out.

Cleaning the metal
Metal to be soldered must be clean, that is, free of both grease and oxide. These can be removed by filing or rubbing with sandpaper.

Fluxing
If you are using borax for flux, grind the flat end of the borax cone in a borax dish with a little water until the mixture resembles a thin cream. This can now be used as flux. Use a fine brush to paint it at 2mm depth around the join. Sufficient flux will then seep between the metal surfaces. Prepared fluxes are used directly from the bottle.

Applying the solder
First select the solder to be used for the job. If more than one soldering stage is to be carried out, make the first join with hard grade solder. Then use the medium, then the soft grade, which melt at successively lower temperatures. This ensures that the later joins can be made without melting earlier soldered work.

Cut the solder into small pieces. These pieces, called pallions, melt more quickly than large chunks and are easy to distribute evenly. With jeweler's shears, fringe the end of the solder into strips of about 1mm wide and 5mm long. With one finger against the end of the fringe, cut across the solder about 1mm from your finger. Pallions of solder should stay on your finger and they can then be dropped into a container ready for use. Pallions snipped without being held by your finger are liable to be lost.

When you are ready to apply the solder to the work, dip a fine brush into the flux. Then use the brush to pick up the pallions of solder and place them along the join. The pallions should touch the metal on both sides of the join. The amount of solder to use will be learnt by experience but, as a guide, begin by placing pallions at 3mm intervals.

Heating the work
Support the work on a suitable surface or stand. Hold the blow torch in one hand and a pair of steel tweezers in the other. This may feel awkward at first, but it is good work practice: it allows a quick response if something needs to be repositioned in the flame, and it

helps prevent the jeweler from accidentally touching the hot metal.

Gently move a soft flame across the work to be soldered. The water in the borax will evaporate, causing the borax to turn white and bubble; this is known as flowering. Continue heating gently. The borax and, with luck, the pallions of solder will re-settle along the join. If not, reposition them, using the tweezers, and carry on heating. An early indication that the solder is about to flow is the darkening in color of the borax. Soon after, the solder will melt and should run along the join. It will then show clearly as a bright silver line. Immediately this happens, remove the flame.

Solder flows when the temperature of the metal to be joined reaches the melting point of the solder. Heating only the solder may melt it, but it will not flow properly on the metal. Solder flows to the hottest point, so, to control the solder, encourage it along the join by moving the hottest part of the flame along the metal to the point where the solder is needed.

Do not heat small sections of metal directly. They become hot much more quickly than larger sections and may melt before the solder. Alternatively, the solder may flow on the smaller pieces of metal but not on the larger, cooler parts. To avoid these problems, heat the main body of the metal and allow it to conduct the heat through to the smaller sections.

Each time solder is reheated, it alloys with more of the surrounding metal. This change in composition causes the temperature at which the solder will re-melt to increase slightly. So, with care, several soldering operations may be carried out using the same grade of solder, without melting any of the joins made previously. However, when using this technique, borax should be applied along the earlier joins. Then, if the solder does happen to re-melt, it will tend to stay in place. If the solder will not flow, make sure that:

1 The metal is clean — free of oxide, grease and acid.
2 The borax and borax brush are clean.
3 The metal and solder are well boraxed.
4 The metal is maintained at a sufficiently high temperature.
5 There is sufficient solder.
6 The metal surfaces are touching.

SOLDERING BUTT JOINS
The butt join is probably the most common soldering join. To effect this type of join, the sections to be joined must be accurately fitted. In the hard soldering process, solder joins metal by alloying under heat with the adjacent metal. Solder should not be used to bridge gaps. If a gap is filled with solder, it is unlikely to remain filled for long. Further heating of the surrounding metal will probably cause the solder to alloy further. As a result, the solder is drawn out of the poorly fitted join, re-exposing the gap.

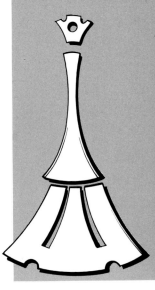

Cooling and cleaning

After soldering, allow the work to cool. Either leave it on the work surface or, to accelerate cooling, move it onto a small steel block. The work can be cooled much more quickly by dropping it in water, a technique called quenching. However, this is not generally recommended as the work may cool unevenly and become distorted.

To clean the work, simply leave it in pickle for about five minutes. If you are using alum solution, you will need to heat it gently. Place the solution in a small enamel, stainless steel or heat-resistant ceramic container and heat on a stove or Bunsen burner. Diluted sulfuric acid can be used when cold, but works more efficiently when warm. Again, put a small quantity of the acid in a heat- and acid-resistant container — using one with a lid will help to minimize fumes — and stand it on a tripod. Heat from beneath with the pilot light of a Bunsen burner; this gentle heat will be sufficient.

Use brass tweezers to move the work in or out of the acid. Steel reacts with pickle and will contaminate it. If steel tweezers are accidentally dipped in the acid, replace it with a fresh solution.

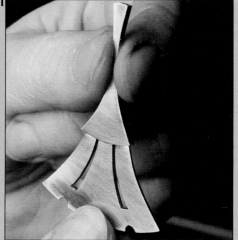

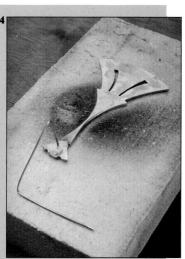

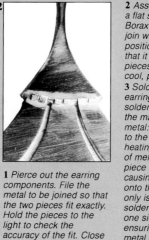

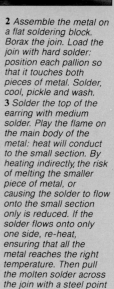

1 Pierce out the earring components. File the metal to be joined so that the two pieces fit exactly. Hold the pieces to the light to check the accuracy of the fit. Close any gaps before attempting to solder the pieces together.

2 Assemble the metal on a flat soldering block. Borax the join. Load the join with hard solder: position each pallion so that it touches both pieces of metal. Solder, cool, pickle and wash.
3 Solder the top of the earring with medium solder. Play the flame on the main body of the metal: heat will conduct to the small section. By heating indirectly, the risk of melting the smaller piece of metal, or causing the solder to flow onto the small section only is reduced. If the solder flows onto only one side, re-heat, ensuring that all the metal reaches the right temperature. Then pull the molten solder across the join with a steel point

(pointed steel tweezers will do).
4 Bend the wire for the post and position it on the earring. Borax the cleaned metal and load with easy solder. Again, heat the main body of the metal to reduce the risk of melting the fine wire. Cool and clean the piece. Then, cut the wire to leave a post about 12mm long. Construct or purchase a butterfly back. Alternatively, nylon backs are cheap and comfortable.

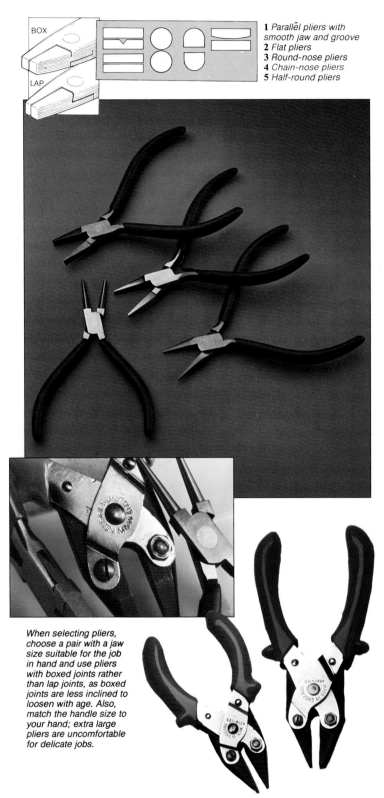

1 *Parallel pliers with smooth jaw and groove*
2 *Flat pliers*
3 *Round-nose pliers*
4 *Chain-nose pliers*
5 *Half-round pliers*

BOX

LAP

When selecting pliers, choose a pair with a jaw size suitable for the job in hand and use pliers with boxed joints rather than lap joints, as boxed joints are less inclined to loosen with age. Also, match the handle size to your hand; extra large pliers are uncomfortable for delicate jobs.

BENDING

Ideally, metal should be bent with the fingers, as this technique is the least damaging to the metal. But fingers are not always a suitable shape for the work or strong enough to bend the metal, so tools such as pliers and hammers are often necessary.

Pliers

Jewelers use pliers to grip, form and bend metal. Pliers are identified by the shape of the jaw and the type of joint at the pivot. Two main types of joint are used in ordinary pliers: the box joint and the lap joint. The box joint is preferable to the lap joint because even when this type of joint is worn, the jaws are less inclined to wobble.

Parallel pliers have a more complex pivoting mechanism than ordinary pliers, which makes the jaws open and shut with a parallel action. Such pliers are excellent for holding work securely without risk of it slipping from the jaws.

When selecting pliers, make sure that they fit comfortably in the hand, and match the size of jaws to the scale of the work being tackled. In all cases, the jaws should be smooth to minimize the marks made on metal.

Annealing

In most cases, metal must be softened to make it pliable. The process used to soften metal is called annealing. First, heat the metal until it is dull red in color. Then allow it to cool: either leave it on a steel block, or, when the red color has faded, quench it in cold water. Sudden quenching of hot metal in cold water may occasionally cause some distortion, however.

The metal becomes hard when subjected to mechanical working. This effect is called 'work hardening'. As soon as the metal becomes difficult to move, re-anneal it. Annealing will not damage the metal, but trying to bend work-hardened metal may cause it to crack or buckle.

Forming a cylindrical ring

To form a cylindrical ring, such as a wedding band, hold a strip of annealed metal in the fingers. Grip one end with the large, half-round pliers, and begin bending the metal — the half-round jaw should be on the inside of the curve. Slide the pliers along and bend the next few millimeters, and continue slid-

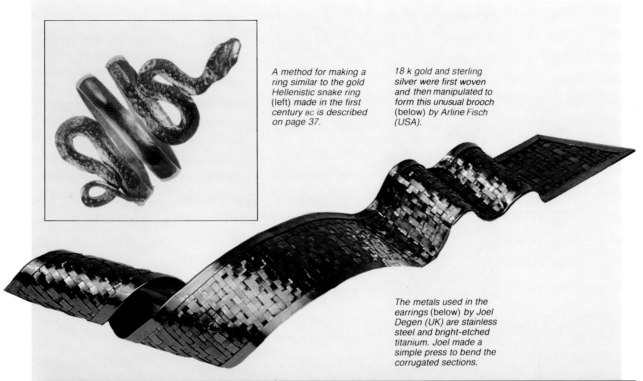

A method for making a ring similar to the gold Hellenistic snake ring (left) made in the first century BC is described on page 37.

18 k gold and sterling silver were first woven and then manipulated to form this unusual brooch (below) by Arline Fisch (USA).

The metals used in the earrings (below) by Joel Degen (UK) are stainless steel and bright-etched titanium. Joel made a simple press to bend the corrugated sections.

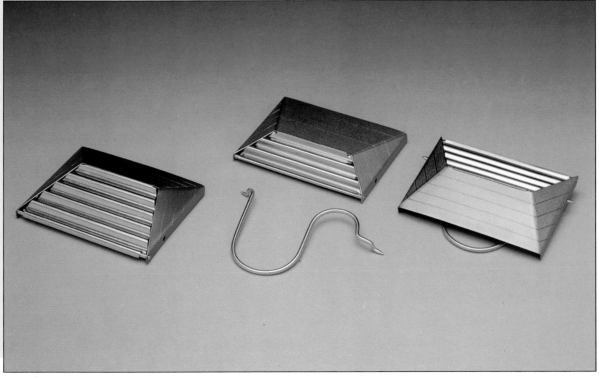

Making a cylindrical ring
1 Select a large pair of half-round pliers with a curved jaw that matches the curve of the proposed ring. Begin easing the metal around the curve of the jaw by turning the pliers and pulling the metal simultaneously. Re-anneal the metal as soon as it becomes springy or difficult to bend. Slide the pliers along the metal, curving small sections at a time. Continue bending until the metal overlaps and forms a complete loop. Saw through the double thickness of metal, then ease the two ends together. If the sawing is accurate, the ends will butt perfectly. Solder.

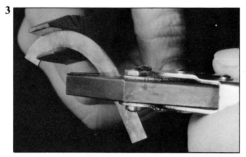

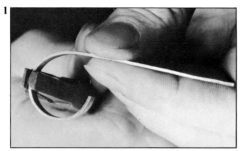

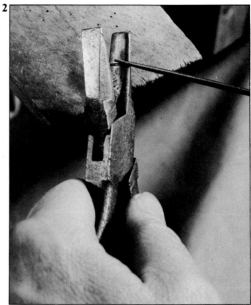

Making a flat ring
2 With a piercing saw, mark each jaw about 8mm from the tip and file a groove in each with a three-square needle file. Ensure that the grooves align and that each follows the shape of its jaw. File sharp edges.
3 Wedge the metal strip against the jaws of parallel pliers. Grip the strip in the grooves of the half-round pliers and pull the metal into the curve. This process requires frequent annealing: if the metal buckles, tap it flat with a wooden mallet.

Making a twist
4 Grip each end of the strip in flat-nose pliers and twist.

ing and bending a few millimeters at a time until the ring is circular. The amount of metal bent each time determines the curve of the ring. With practice, this becomes a quick, smooth action, and the resultant ring is well formed.

Forming a flat ring

Bending a strip of metal into a flat ring, like a washer, requires a pair of flat-nose parallel pliers and a pair of half-round pliers. To enable the half-round pliers to grip the metal firmly, file a groove in the curved jaw of the half-round pliers about 8mm from the tip of the jaw. First, mark the line with a piercing saw, then file a "V" shape with a three-square needle file. The "V" groove, about 1mm deep, should follow the curve of the jaw. This makes the pliers far more versatile.

Lightly support the annealed, flat strip of metal with the parallel pliers, about 3cm from one end of the strip. Swing this end away from the hand so that the metal pivots in the jaws. The back section of the metal should lock against the joint of the pliers. Now hold the pliers tightly. Locate the strip in the groove of the half-round pliers, with the half-round jaw closer to the parallel pliers. Grip the tip of the metal with the half-round pliers and slowly turn it toward the parallel pliers. Slide the half-round pliers along and turn the next section of metal. Anneal frequently to avoid tearing or buckling the metal.

Twisting metal

To twist a metal strip, hold each end in two pairs of flat-nose pliers and rotate them in opposite directions.

MAKING
A SNAKE RING

The numerous bends required to make a snake ring provide the opportunity to practice different types of bends with pliers of various shapes. Keep the metal well annealed to prevent tearing.

Tools and materials

Smooth, flat-jaw
  parallel pliers
Large half-round pliers
Round-nose pliers
Chain-nose pliers
Files
Heating equipment
Hammer, mallet and
  steel block for
  adjusting curves after
  bending
Ring mandrel for final
  shaping of ring
D-section wire: 20cm
  x 2.5mm x 1.5mm
  (any of the metals
  listed for earlier
  projects are suitable)
Hard solder

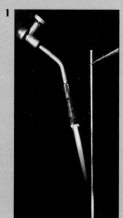

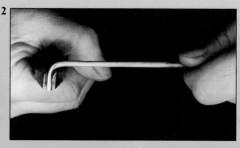

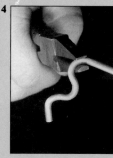

1 Hold the D-section strip of metal vertically in soldering tweezers and direct the flame down the metal. Move the red patch slowly down the strip to ensure even annealing.
2 Bend the first curve with grooved half-round pliers.
3 If the metal distorts, straighten it by tapping the edge with a metal hammer on a steel block.
4 Bend two more curves with half-round pliers.
5 If the curves buckle, tap them flat with a wooden mallet on a steel block.
6 Tighten the second and third curves with round-nose pliers by inserting the tips of the pliers in the curves and turning them.
7 Overlap the third curve by squeezing it with

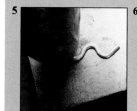

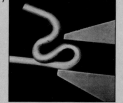

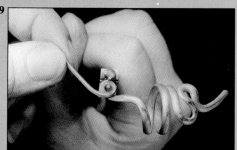

parallel pliers.
8 To wind up the body curves that form the ring shank, ease the metal into a spiral with large, half-round pliers.
9 Complete the tail curves with round-nose pliers.
10 If the ring is misshapen, tap it round with a wooden mallet on a ring mandrel.
11 File the head section. File away any unwanted marks left by the pliers. Then, solder the tail to the body of the ring. Either file with cut 4 files to produce a surface texture, or polish the ring (see page 42). To make the ring more like a Hellenic ring (see page 35), tap the surface with a dome-headed hammer.

HAMMERING

Various kinds of hammers and mallets are used to shape, stretch and decorate metal. In general, hammers have steel heads and will shape, stretch and mark metal. Wooden mallets shape metal and stretch it a little, but do not mark it if care is taken, and rawhide mallets shape metal and should neither mark nor stretch it. Horn hammers are occasionally used to shape metal without marking it: they have small heads and are therefore useful where a wooden or hide mallet is too big.

The metal may be beaten on a flat support, or on a shaped support called a former. In addition to supporting the metal, a former helps to shape it too. Formers are made of any firm material that will withstand hammer blows, and come in various shapes and sizes.

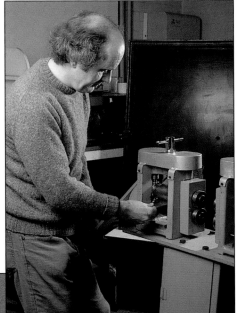

Hand rolling mills
Metal can be stretched, reduced in thickness, and decorated by using hand rolling mills. Although mills are unlikely to be the first purchase for the beginner, many jewelers will have access to this useful piece of machinery in colleges. The steel rolls can be flat for sheet metal, grooved for wire, or patterned for decorating strips. To use the mill, roll annealed metal through suitably adjusted rolls. Do not try to reduce the thickness of the metal too rapidly as it may tear. Metal shaped by hammering, like this silver bracelet (right) by Susan May, is said to be forged. The Tunisian hammered link chain (far right) is made of gold-plated brass.

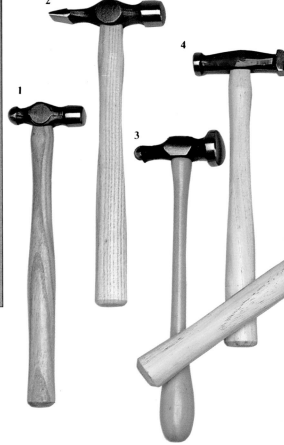

Three essential tools for working metal are: a steel bench anvil; a ring mandrel for stretching and shaping; and a steel block for flattening metal (above, from left to right).
1 *General purpose ball-pein hammer.*
2 *Warrington hammer.*
3 *Chasing hammer. The bulbous handle helps to achieve the smooth bounce needed for chasing.*
4 *Planishing hammer for smoothing metal.*
5 *Raising hammer for stretching metal.*
6 *Wooden bossing mallet.*
7 *Tinman's wooden mallet.*
8 *Rawhide mallet.*

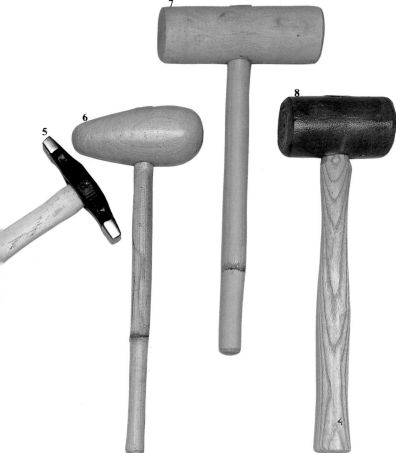

Hammers, mallets and formers

A 4oz/115g, ball-pein hammer is an extremely useful tool. Its head has one domed end and one flat, circular end, and is suitable for a wide variety of tasks. A 9oz/225g raising hammer has a rectangular-faced head and is a good weight for most jewelry-making purposes. (A raising hammer is a silversmith's tool for beating flat sheets of metal into three-dimensional forms.) Also useful are a 3.8cm rawhide mallet and a 5cm bossing mallet. A bossing mallet is a wooden mallet with a tapered head; both ends of the head are domed, and the larger end measures 5cm across.

The two most commonly used supports are a small, hardened tool-steel block (7.5cm × 7.5cm), and a ring mandrel. A ring mandrel is a round, tapered steel bar used as a former for shaping rings and other curved metalwork; the 8mm to 3.3cm size meets most requirements.

Shaping and stretching metal

Before attempting to shape metal by hammering, anneal it to make it soft. Then start hammering, maneuvering the metal as it changes shape to bring the next section into line for hammering. Hammering causes metal to become work-hardened, so, when hammering metal into shape, it is necessary

Hammering techniques

Hammering work hardens metal, so re-anneal as soon as the metal becomes difficult to move. A skillful technician will detect the need to re-anneal from the sound of the strike as well as the feel of it. Initially, the hammer thuds into the soft metal. As the metal becomes work hardened, the blows begin to ring as the metal springs against the steel block. In the following exercises, hammer the metal on a flat steel block.

1 To curve a metal strip, hammer along one side only, using either a flat-headed or domed hammer. The metal is stretched on that side, so that the strip curves away from the hammered side.
2 Widen a strip of metal by hammering with a raising hammer, keeping the rectangular head parallel to the strip.
3 Dish part of a strip of metal by hammering in concentric circles with a dome-shaped head. This

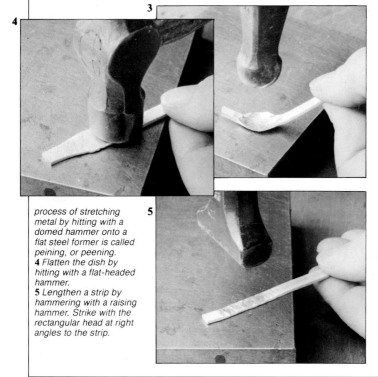

process of stretching metal by hitting with a domed hammer onto a flat steel former is called peining, or peening.
4 Flatten the dish by hitting with a flat-headed hammer.
5 Lengthen a strip by hammering with a raising hammer. Strike with the rectangular head at right angles to the strip.

to anneal the work frequently. Re-anneal the metal whenever it begins to spring back instead of changing shape. The kind of shape the metal takes is determined by the shape of both the hammer head and the support for the metal. For example, a round hammer head pushes metal evenly in all directions from the point of contact, and a rectangular-faced head generally pushes metal away from the longer edges of the head. To achieve maximum movement of the metal, support it on a steel former and strike it with a steel hammer.

To lengthen a strip of metal, beat across it with a rectangular-faced hammer head; to widen a strip, beat it with a rectangular head

MAKING A BANGLE

Tools and materials

Equipment for transferring patterns Piercing saw and blades Files Wooden or hide mallet Planishing hammer Former — a steel or wooden rod 5cm in diameter is suitable **Metal sheet:** 1mm thick and sufficient	for the pattern. Trace the pattern onto paper and check that the length and width are comfortable. If necessary, adjust the pattern before purchasing the metal.

This project describes how to make a bangle similar to the hammered gold bangles made in the Sinu region of Colombia around the 1500s. To make the pattern for the bangle, first decide on the width, length and type of end curves. As a guide, the width of the bangles illustrated is just over 8cm. Calculate the length by wrapping a strip of paper around your wrist: a gap of 3cm

will allow the bangle to be eased on and off. Sketch the end curves or use a compass.
1 Choose a steel or hardwood former that matches the curve of the proposed bangle. A slightly smaller diameter curve can be used instead, but a fuller curve is unsuitable. (A wood turner can make a hardwood former for you, or the leg of an old table may be suitable.)

aligned along it. In both cases, support the metal on a flat steel block.

If the center of a sheet of metal is hammered on a flat steel block, the surrounding metal restricts its lateral movement. As a result, the central area moves upward, so that a bulge appears. On the other hand, if the sheet is hammered near one edge, the metal will bulge sideways, resulting in a curved edge.

Any marks on the hammer head will be transferred to the metal. This effect is sometimes used deliberately as a way of texturing metal surfaces. A grooved hammer head, for example, forms raised lines on metal, and a domed head produces round dents.

On hammering, marks on the hammer head will transfer to the metal. This can be used to advantage when texturing metal. First, file a pattern of grooves on the hammer head. Then, supporting the annealed metal on a steel block, hammer the metal to texture it.

3 *The process of leveling the surface and hardening the metal is called planishing. Before starting, check that the head of the planishing hammer is unmarked and polished: the better the hammer, the better the finish obtained. Hold the bangle on the former and begin hitting with even blows and in straight lines. The bangle should be in contact with the former and cause the hammer blows to ring. A hollow sound indicates that the metal and former are not in proper contact. A well-planished surface has a dull polish.*

The pair of hammered gold bracelets (below) are from "The Gold of El Dorado" exhibition, held at the Royal Academy, London, in 1978. They come from the Sinu region of Colombia.

2 *Anneal the metal. Rest it on the former and begin by malleting one end over the former with a rawhide or wooden mallet. Next mallet over the other end. For a smooth curve, tap down about 1cm, slide the metal further across the former, and then tap down the next centimeter, and so on. Re-anneal before shaping the middle section of the bangle.*

Large machines
1 *Objects and polished steel shot are loaded into a barrel polisher and tumbled together for several hours. Many objects can be polished at a time, but the process is suitable only for objects without flat surfaces or fine protrusions: rough surfaces can also be smoothed using an abrasive. In this polisher, vibration of the barrel produces the tumbling action. Most barrel polishers have rotating hexagonal barrels.*
2 *The ultrasonic cleaning machine is useful for removing grease and dirt after polishing with a buff.*

3 *The double-spindle motor of the bench-mounted polishing machine is mounted in an extractor unit. The low hood of the unit helps to prevent flying dust and objects from hitting the eyes. When standing at the machine, only the front of the buff and the object being polished can be seen. Follow the convention of using tripoli on the left and rouge on the right.*
4 *Buffs for use with the flexible shaft drill.*
5 *Buffs for the bench-mounted polishing machine.*

FINISHING

Metal usually needs to be finished with a surface treatment. The metal may be given an attractive, highly polished finish. But sometimes, a mat surface is found to be more suitable or a textured finish may be preferred to add interest.

Polishing metal

A brilliant shine can be achieved both by hand and by machine, provided the work is thorough, and this takes time. In a commercial jewelry workshop, the polishing stages sometimes take as long to complete as the whole of the rest of the manufacturing process.

To polish metal, first remove file marks and other major surface blemishes, using an abrasive. Then polish the surface by rubbing with successively finer abrasives.

Preparatory abrasives

Use the finest grade of sandpaper — flour-grade sandpaper — to remove surface marks from the metal. Although this is the finest grade of sandpaper, it is usually the coarsest abrasive used on jewelry after filing. Depending on the shape of the metal, sandpaper is either folded into pads or wrapped around a buff stick — a long, slim piece of wood, shaped according to the job in hand.

Scotch stones are lightly abrasive. Lubricated with water, they remove difficult or inaccessible marks. Because the stones are soft they can be easily shaped to suit the job in hand. They are 10cm long with a square cross-section; they range in width from 3mm to 2.5cm.

Complete the preparatory stage using grade 2/0 emery polishing paper. Like sandpaper, this can be folded into pads, or wrapped around a buff stick.

Polishing compounds

A bright shine can usually be achieved using only two polishing stages. The coarse compound, tripoli luster, is a general purpose polish, and is used at the first stage.

Jeweler's rouge is the fine finishing polish used at the second stage. The extra superfine rouge block gives a good polish without excess grease. Rouge powder has a specific use and will be dealt with later, together with other specialist polishes.

Hand polishing tools

Variously shaped sticks with suede glued to them are the most useful hand tools for polishing. Keep separate sticks for tripoli and rouge.

Holes and narrow slots can be polished using polish-impregnated thread or a wooden cocktail stick coated with polish.

Machines for polishing

The flexible shaft drill is a suspended, variable speed, electric motor connected to a flexible shaft. At the other end of the shaft are a handle and a chuck. the best flexible shaft motors are controlled from a foot pedal. The small brushes and buffs that fit the chuck of a flexible shaft drill are excellent for polishing small-scale work, but are generally unsuitable for larger items.

A bench-mounted polishing motor can provide the power necessary for dealing

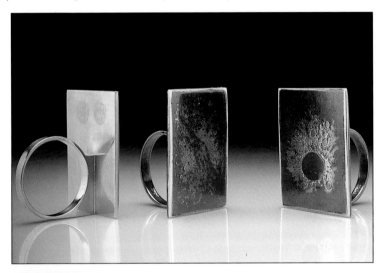

Dynamic effects can be achieved by the imaginative use of surface treatments. The possibilities are limitless and new finishes can be discovered by experiment. In the rings (below) by Siglinde Brennan, the dramatic surface craters are framed by a simple rectangle that rests across two fingers.

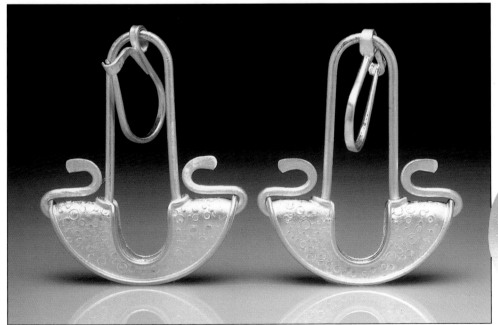

By using various surface treatments on one piece, the results can be both subtle and striking. The success of such contrasts is seen (left and below) in the work of Yehuda Tigat. The earrings (left) are made of 18 k gold and the brooch (below) is made of 18 k gold and set with opal and topaz.

with large areas. A pad called a polishing buff is fitted to the motor shaft. A motor running at between 2800 and 3000 rpm (revolutions per minute) produces the best polish on precious metals. The power of the motor ranges from $1/12$ hp (horse power) upward. A $1/4$ hp motor is a reasonable choice for the average home jeweler.

Make sure that the correct safety precautions are taken to protect the operator from the moving buffs. The supplier will advise on the right guard for the machine. Also, polishing produces vast quantities of dust, so it is worth obtaining an extractor fan.

Polishing machine accessories

An extensive range of accessories is available for polishing.

With flexible shaft drills, use felt and muslin buffs for tripoli and wool buffs for rouge. Choose shapes that suit the job in hand. Buffs for flexible shaft drills wear quickly, so it is wise to buy several at a time. To help with the preparatory stages, abrasive rubber wheels and points are also available for use with flexible shaft drills. A split spindle to hold small rectangles of sandpaper speeds up the work on areas like the inside of rings.

Of the many polishing attachments for bench-mounted machines, a 7.6cm unstitched, hard muslin buff for tripoli, and a 7.6cm canton flannel buff for rouge are sufficient for the beginner.

Felt buffs are used for lapping (polishing flat surfaces) but these are not recommended for the beginner as, without extreme care, excessive quantities of metal are polished away.

If the jewelry to be polished includes many deeply textured surfaces, a small, black bristle brush will be useful.

Felt cones for polishing the inside of rings are available. Choose one with a wooden centre — its rigidity makes it easier for the beginner to use.

Abrasive rubber wheels may be used on bench-mounted machines, but these must be used with great care since they abrade very rapidly. For this reason, they are not recommended for beginners.

Preparing for polishing

Remove all work marks from the metal with sandpaper. Where possible, use a buff stick. Fold small pads of sandpaper to erase marks from less accessible places. Rub deep

marks with a Scotch stone moistened with water. Frequently wipe away the residue with a tissue so that the gradual disappearance of the mark is carefully monitored. Otherwise, you may accidentally rub away too much metal.

To use small, abrasive rubber wheels and points, secure the shaft of the attachment in the correct size chuck (the gripping head of the drill) of the flexible shaft drill. Operate the drill with the foot pedal; this turns the motor on and off and also controls the speed. Increase the speed until the abrasive is working — it is not necessary to race the motor. Hold the work in one hand and the handle of the flexible drive shaft in the other. To help prevent slipping, rest both wrists on the edge of the bench. This allows just enough mobility to move the rotating abrasive gently across the surface of the metal.

Sandpaper threaded down a split spindle makes a very useful tool. You can purchase a split spindle, or make one by annealing and then sawing down the center of an old shaft. Slot a piece of sandpaper into the cut and wrap it around the shaft. Wrap the paper in

Principles of finishing
1 *Ensure the work is held firmly against the buff.*
2 *To polish inside slots and holes, hold polishing threads taut. Slide the article rapidly back and forth to avoid grooving.*
3 *For quick sandpapering, cut a rectangle of sandpaper about 2cm x 3cm.*
4 *Slot sandpaper into a split spindle secured in the flexible shaft drill. Rotate the spindle to bed down the sandpaper.*
5 *To polish chain, place it over a block of wood and hold the loose ends.*
6 *To make a buff stick, wrap the stick tightly in sandpaper. Hold the paper in place with binding wire or a thumbtack.*
7 *Prepare a buff by removing all loose fibers. Hold the tang end of an old file in the turning buff.*
8 *Clean off protruding fibers by setting light to them very briefly.*

the same direction as the rotation of the shaft so that it does not unwind when used.

Complete the preparatory stage with emery polishing paper, rubbing the whole surface with the paper on a buff stick or folded into a pad, as appropriate.

Initial polishing

To begin, use tripoli polishing compound. If polishing by hand, load the suede sticks with tripoli by rubbing the block of polish over the suede. Then buff the metal vigorously. Ensure that the buffing strokes follow the flow of the metal so that flat areas do not appear on curved surfaces.

If polishing with a flexible shaft drill, secure the buff shaft in the chuck. Load the buff with tripoli by pressing the rotating buff into the block of polish. Then ease the turning buff over the surface of the metal. Do not hesitate, as inconsistent movements may cause the buff to hollow out parts of the surface that should be flat. This may be imperceptible until the light catches the surface. Always aim for a flawless, professional finish.

If using a polishing machine, wind the dressed, hard muslin buff onto the threaded, tapered spindle. The buffs have exposed staples on one side. For safety, these should face the machine. Always fix the buff on the spindle in the same way. This ensures a good tight fit, and the outside fibers, which do the polishing, will then always bed down in the same direction.

Stand back from the buff and turn the machine on at the on/off switch. The buff should turn toward the operator. Articles being polished should touch the buff just below spindle level. If the work is held too high, it may start to shudder, and is liable to be thrown out from the buff. And articles held too low on the buff are liable to be pulled from the operator's hand.

First, load the rotating buff with tripoli by pushing the block of polish into it. Then firmly grip the item you wish to polish and present one surface of it to the buff. Never present a leading edge to the rotating buff as this will pull the article from your hand. Hold the article firmly against the turning buff, moving it so that all parts are evenly polished. When the first polishing has been completed, turn off the machine.

Special precautions must be taken when polishing chain (*see page 46*).

Polishing chain

Polishing loose chain is extremely dangerous since the chain can become caught in the buff and may pull your hand into the turning machine. To prevent this happening, wrap the chain over a block of wood and hold the loose ends behind it. Then polish the chain from the middle to the edge of the block. Turn the block around and polish the remainder of the surface. Move the next section of the chain onto the front of the block and polish in the same way.

Polishing in slots and holes

Where access is difficult, special polishing techniques must be adopted. For very small jobs, such as polishing fine decoration around stones, fix one end of a bunch of polishing threads to the bench and hold the free end. Apply polish to the threads. Take the item to be polished and slide it vigorously up and down against the threads; this technique is called threading. For larger jobs, such as polishing the inside of rings, strips of suede can be used in the same way.

Small, pointed sticks can be used to polish areas that other devices cannot reach. To apply polish, either rub the sticks by hand, or rotate them in a flexible shaft drill. Do not press hard as the sticks break easily.

Washing

After polishing with tripoli, wash the article thoroughly in detergent and water. Brush away stubborn grease with a mixture of 50 per cent cloudy ammonia and 50 per cent detergent. The item must be washed thoroughly as any remaining traces of coarse polish will prevent the fine polish used in the next stage from working properly.

1 Florentining *Lines cut by a multi-line engraving tool are close together and evenly spaced. To avoid a crooked line, cut small amounts of metal at a time.*

2 Dental-burr texturing *Experiment for the most suitable effect. This was achieved by scribbling with a rotating burr in a flexible shaft drill.*

3 Hand-graver texturing *Deep lines cut toward each other with a flat graver reflect light in opposite directions. This causes a shimmer when the ring is rotated.*

4 Hammer texturing *Metal resting on a steel former and struck by a domed hammer produces this dimpled effect.*

5 Melting surfaces *This reticulated surface is achieved by heating the metal until the surface begins to melt, and then removing the flame immediately. This surface is usually induced on the metal before the piece is constructed.*

6 Roll texturing *This effect was achieved by enclosing copper gauze between two sheets of annealed silver and passing the sandwich through a rolling mill.*

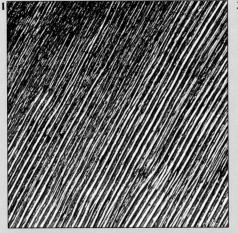

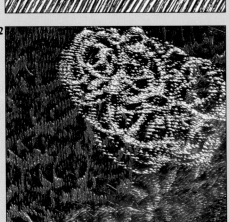
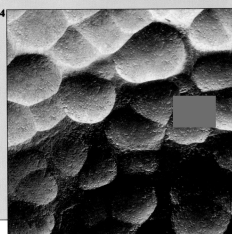

The final stages

Polish with rouge, using the technique described for polishing with tripoli. Take great care not to use the same buffs or buff sticks: traces of tripoli on the buff or buff stick to be used in this final stage will contaminate the rouge and prevent it from polishing as brightly as it should.

After the final polish, re-wash the article thoroughly in detergent and water, and then allow it to dry. Jewelers used to drop the article into boxwood sawdust to dry it. This prevented water marks from appearing on the surface of the metal.

Technical tips

Black stains sometimes show on the surface of silver when it is polished. These marks, known as fire stain, consist of black copper oxide, which is formed when copper on the surface of the silver oxidizes. The stain, which is only a few molecules thick, is easily removed by filing, and then rubbing with sandpaper and, finally, emery paper. Do not try to polish the stain away. Copper oxide is harder than silver so the buff will simply skate over the fire stain and gouge out the softer silver around it.

Do not try to polish out grooves or file marks in metal. The fibers of the polishing buff catch in the cavities and enlarge them. The effect is similar to that caused by trucks continually running over a pot hole in the road. Instead of smoothing the surface, they break up the edges of the hole, thus spreading the damage further.

Texturing metal

Textured or rough surfaces reflect less light than shiny surfaces and, as a result, they appear to recede. Consequently, when set beside a polished surface, a textured surface can appear as shadow, and highlight the adjacent polished area. Sometimes a surface is textured to resemble a natural substance, such as fur.

Texturing may be even or random, but the particular texture chosen must suit the design. In most cases, the jeweler will need to experiment to find the most appropriate finish.

Standard techniques for texturing metal include hammering, reticulating, cutting with a graver, and abrading with a grindstone or a burr in a flexible shaft drill.

For a hammered texture, either use an ordinary hammer head or file a pattern on the head of an old hammer. To transfer the pattern, hit the annealed metal with the hammer. The pattern will appear in reversed form on the metal; grooves on the hammer head will appear as ridges on the metal.

To reticulate a metal surface, heat it without flux until the whole surface begins to shimmer. Then remove the heat immediately; a moment's hesitation may cause the whole piece to melt. In the absence of flux on the metal, oxide formed during heating holds the surface intact just long enough for the desired effect to be achieved.

A graver is a steel cutting tool and is available in a variety of shapes. The type known as a multi-line shading or Florentining tool is most suitable for texturing. Buy a round handle for it and fit it in the same way as a file handle. The graver handle should fit com-

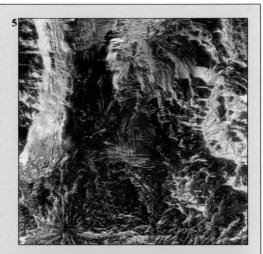

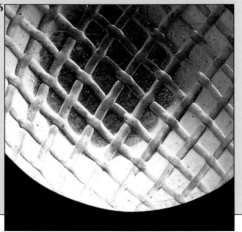

fortably in the palm of the hand, with the thumb and forefinger supporting the cutting tip. Experiment with the graver to obtain the desired texturing effect. Cutting is easier if small gouges, rather than long strokes, are made.

A grindstone or burr used in a flexible shaft drill can produce a wide range of textures. Old dental burrs can also be used. When they have become too blunt to use on they are still effective on most jewelry materials.

Mat finishing

A mat surface is appropriate when the color of the metal is more important than the surface shine. Prepare the metal in the same way as for polishing: successively reduce marks on the article by filing, sandpapering and emery papering. Then brush with a fiberglass brush or a brass brush in order to obtain the mat finish.

The best type of fiberglass brush for this purpose is in the form of a retractable pencil, since the bound type is inclined to unbind in use and release the fibers, which, being glass, are sharp and painful if they penetrate the skin.

Brass scratch brushes are always used in conjunction with detergent and water. Without this lubricant, brass might be deposited on the surface of the metal being brushed, leaving it yellow and dirty-looking. Brass brushes are available for hand use and for use in polishing machines and flexible shaft drills. Wear protective clothing and goggles when using the brush in a machine, as the lubricant will spray out.

Special satin-finishing brushes with rows of mobile steel wires are available for use with machines. They are graded fine, medium and thick. The fine grade brush is most suitable for the beginner. The thick grade brush cuts quite deeply and is useful for obtaining a textured bark effect. Goggles should be worn when using these brushes, as wires are sometimes released while the brush is rotating.

Burnishing metal

To burnish metal, rub a polished steel or agate tool firmly over it; a shiny finish is obtained. Burnishing is an effective method of polishing edges as this technique avoids unwanted rounding, which can occur when polishing with a buff.

MAKING A LEO PENDANT

Different finishing techniques are used on the five elements that make up this piece. The elements are joined by "rabbiting" — using chenier to rivet.

1 Trace, pierce out and file the five elements. Drill four as indicated. Saw three lengths of chenier of, say, 8mm, 7mm and 6mm — using different lengths enables you to thread one at a time. Solder the three lengths of chenier to the back of the first element in line with the drilled holes of the elements. Solder the other pendant fitting to element 5.

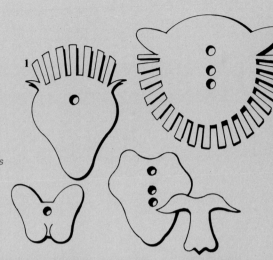

2 Remove marks from the flat surface with flour-grade sandpaper wrapped around a buff stick.
3 Rub a small pad of flour-grade sandpaper over the edges to remove file marks. Repeat steps 2 and 3 using emery paper.
4 Polish the first element with tripoli. Then wash in detergent, polish with jeweler's rouge and wash again.

5 *Sandpaper the surface and edges of element 2, then texture the flat surface with a dental burr in a flexible shaft drill. Use small circular movements to achieve the effect illustrated.*
6 *Burnish the edges by rubbing firmly. This will give a bright, shiny edge. The two holes in the second element coincide with the chenier on the first. Assemble the first two elements.*
7 *Fit a spacer ring over the third peice of chenier. Without this ring, later elements will wobble. Sandpaper the third element using sandpaper threaded through a split spindle and rotated in a flexible shaft drill. Polish by hand or machine and wash.*

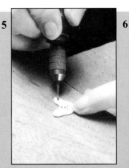

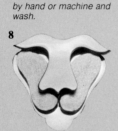

8 *Assemble the third element behind the others.*
9 *Texture the fourth element with a multi-line graver. Ensure that the lines follow the natural lines of the hair.*
10 *Polish the back with a felt buff on a flexible shaft drill: the tangle of the mane makes large buffs unsafe.*
11 *Assemble the fourth piece behind the other three.*

12 *Use tripoli on a wooden cocktail stick fixed in a flexible shaft drill to polish the mane.*
13 *Countersink the holes on the back of the fifth element with a burr. Assemble the fifth element behind the other four.*
14 *Saw off the chenier so that it protrudes no more than 0.5mm above the surface. Roll the point of a scriber in the hole of the chenier to spread it into the countersunk hole.*

Tools and materials

Equipment for transferring patterns	second polish
Piercing saw and blades	A flexible shaft motor and burr for machine
Drill and 1.5mm drill bit	texturing or files for
Files	hand texturing
Buff sticks with flour-grade paper and 400 grade emery paper	Oval steel burnisher for burnishing edges
Suede-covered buff sticks for hand polishing or a polishing motor with muslin and canton flannel buffs for machine polishing	Cocktail sticks or polishing threads for polishing less accessible sections
	Scriber for spreading chenier (tube) rivets
Tripoli polishing compound for the first polish	**Metal sheet:** 0.8mm to 1mm thick and sufficient for the patterns
Rouge polishing compound for the	3cm of chenier (tube), 1.5mm outside diameter
	Flour-grade sandpaper
	Grade 400 emery paper

ELEMENTS OF DESIGN

Designing involves a combination of skills: observing, recording, selecting, analyzing, and initiating and arranging visual information, all with a particular purpose in mind. The idea for the design may come from real or imaginary sources. The purpose may be to make an earring, or a ring; to try out an idea; to experiment with new materials; or to communicate information. In the industrial context, design also includes planning the mechanical aspects of a job, and organizing them into a logical sequence.

WHY DESIGN?

There may be occasions when it proves impossible to find precisely the ready-made article you require. This is a good time to begin designing. It is difficult to begin work without a plan. By determining the sequence of tasks in advance, possible errors can be anticipated and avoided. Occasionally, a random approach does produce a good result but, more frequently, a great deal of time and material is wasted.

A design often communicates thoughts or ideas. Perhaps a piece of jewelry is to carry a message or mark an occasion, such as an engagement or wedding ring; perhaps it is intended to declare certain views, for example a cross or a political badge; or perhaps the designer simply wants to draw attention to a pleasing image, such as a flower.

Whatever the motive for the design, the end result — the piece of jewelry — should have an appeal of its own, regardless of whether the chosen images or symbols are obvious or obscure.

INSTANT JEWELRY

Many readily available items can be easily converted into instant jewelry that is fashionable and fun. Making such jewelry does not always require special craft skills, but a good sense of design is essential. The ready-made items from which this jewelry is constructed must be selected carefully and used in a way that suits both the object and the way it will be worn. Skill in selecting materials is one of the first elements of design that must be mastered.

Items for use in the making of instant jewelry can be found almost anywhere — in all stationery, hardware and department stores, or even salvaged from the junk box. Ingenious and inventive searching can lead to novel and amusing jewelry.

Sticks and stirrers as sweater pins

Cocktail sticks and stirrers are available in a wide range of shapes, sizes and colors. They are usually plastic, but are sometimes made of glass, paper or wood. With ingenuity, almost any type can be adapted for use as jewelry. Shops specializing in decorative accessories for glassware and drinks usually offer a choice of attractive sticks and stirrers. Many department stores, stationery stores and liquor stores now sell them, too.

Cocktail sticks

Some small cocktail sticks are immediately usable as sweater pins; thread the stick section through the sweater. Wear them singly, or arranged in a pattern to suit the sweater.

Cocktail stirrers

As stirrers usually have a balled end, they must be modified before pinning them through a sweater. Cut off the ball end with a piercing saw. File the cut end of the stirrer to a gentle taper; the point should not be too

The cocktail sticks in the cocktail-stick sweater pins (above) by Susan Small (UK) are used to pin the patches of plastic in place. Patches can be changed to co-ordinate with different clothes. A rubber table mat has been used to make the necklace (above right). Red cord laced through drilled holes provides both decoration and a means of tying the necklace in place. To make the feather earring (right), glue the ends of several feathers into a section of plastic or metal tube. The tube prevents the ends of the feathers from splitting. Attach the ear fitting to the tube by drilling a hole in it, or, as has been done here, by gluing in a small "eye" through which the ear-wire is threaded.

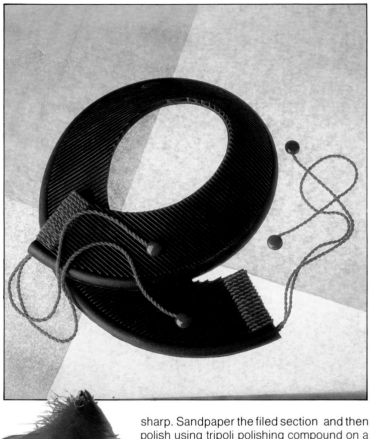

assorted sizes and colors. You may also find a suitable offcut of electric cable.

To strip the plastic insulation from the wire, first cut around the plastic with a sharp knife or razor blade. Be careful not to cut into the wire. You should now be able to pull the plastic from the wire by hand. If not, use wire cutters to ease the plastic from the wire. With most cables, only about two centimeters of plastic can be stripped at a time.

Glue the plastic tube around the base of the feather with any fabric glue. Then drill a small hole through the tip of the plastic and feather to take a ready-made ear fitting Select a type of ear fitting that will hold the feather in the way you want. For example, you may wish to wear it as a stud, or have it flat against the ear, or suspended and swinging freely. The section on ear fittings (*see page 106*) details the possibilities.

Thread the ear fitting through the hole in the plastic tube. For this fairly delicate operation, it may help to hold the plastic protector in chain-nose pliers. The earring is now ready to wear.

Rubber mats as neck pieces
Floppy rubber table mats can be used to make attractive collars. The rubber mats sold for floors and cars are generally too stiff to mold to the shape of the shoulders. Experiment with stiff paper to decide on the size and position of the hole. The hole might be central or offset; it might be big enough to fit over the head, or quite small, so that the collar lies snugly around the neck. If the hole is smaller than the head, cut a slot to enable the piece to be placed in position.

From the paper pattern, mark the position of the hole. Support the mat on a flat cutting board and cut out the hole with a scalpel or craft knife. Accurate cutting leaves an edge that requires no further treatment. A rough edge may need trimming with scissors.

For an access slot, simply cut a straight line from the neck hole toward the outer rim of the mat; it may not be necessary to cut all the way to the edge. The flexibility and weight of the rubber should keep the collar in place. If not, a shoe-lace tied through holes drilled near the inner edge will secure the collar and provide extra decoration.

Table mats as bangles
Small, flexible plastic table mats can be made into bangles simply by cutting a hole

sharp. Sandpaper the filed section and then polish using tripoli polishing compound on a suede-covered buff stick.

The sweater pin can be worn in a variety of ways: thread the stem of the stirrer through a loosely knitted sweater, through your hair, or through a button hole.

Adhesive signs as badges
Aluminum adhesive letters, numbers, arrows and other symbols sold by hardware stores are wearable as instant badges. The smaller types will stay fixed to clothing for several wearings. The large stickers are not suitable as their weight tends to make them fall off fairly quickly.

Feather earrings
Small, brightly colored feathers from a feather duster can be used to make attractive earrings. Since the base of a feather is usually rough and liable to split, it needs firstly to be protected and strengthened. A fine-bore plastic tube is ideal for this purpose and available from craft suppliers' in

for the wrist. If you cut out a round hole, the bangle will stand out from the arm when worn; bangles of this type look particularly attractive when worn in twos or threes. Alternatively, by making an elliptical-shaped cut instead of a round one, the bangle can be made to lie along the arm, or can be folded back to form a kind of cuff.

Before cutting the round hole, you must first determine the size that will comfortably fit your arm. The easiest way to do this is to experiment with different sized holes cut in a piece of stiff paper. When you have selected the appropriate size, use dividers to mark out the circle on the mat, either centrally or offset, as required.

Various tools can be used to cut out the hole. Scissors are suitable for some plastics, while others can be cut with a scalpel or craft knife; in some cases, it will be necessary to use a piercing saw. If the hole is accurately cut, no finishing will be necessary, but, if the hole is uneven or sharp, sandpaper around it, and then remove the sandpaper marks using a plastic polishing compound on cotton batting.

If an elliptical-shaped cut is wanted rather than a round one, you must first decide on its position and length. Experimenting with paper is again a good way to decide on the best position for the bangle and the most suitable size of hole. When this has been determined, mark the line to be cut, then drill a hole 2mm to 3mm in diameter at each end of the line; the holes will help to stop the material from tearing. Choose the most appropriate cutting tool for the material, and make the cut between the two holes. If necessary, sandpaper and polish to finish.

Rubber "O" rings as bangles
Many cars and household appliances contain rubber rings, either as part of the driving mechanism or as seals. Consequently, you will find that rings of various sizes are available from garages and domestic appliance stores. If you are looking for bangles, simply buy rings to fit your wrists. Larger rubber rings that are the right size for use as necklaces are available, but these tend to be rather stiff and do not lie comfortably over the shoulders.

Map pins and thumbtacks as studs
Wear a map pin as an ear stud; decorate a collar or a lapel with a single thumbtack;

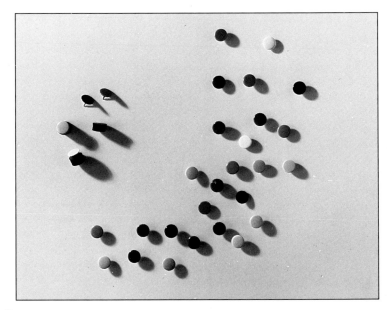

arrange pins in a variety of colors and shapes over the front of a sweater; or arrange studs in a line across the shoulder or along the sleeve. Jewelry of this kind can be arranged differently each time it is worn. Arrangement is another important design skill to be learned.

Map pins for ear studs
Map pins are more suitable than thumbtacks for use as ear studs, because the pin wire is longer and, therefore, easier to locate and secure in the pierced ear.

To make an ear stud, first remove the point of the map pin, using a pair of wire cutters. Avoid using jeweler's shears, as a hard steel pin may damage the edges.

With a barrette needle file, shape the cut end of the pin wire into a smooth dome that will not scratch the ear when pushed through it. Filing will leave a slightly rough surface, so sandpaper the end, first with flour-grade paper, and then with fine emery paper (grade 400 is ideal). Polish with tripoli on a piece of suede. Sometimes it is more convenient to stick the suede to a length of wood to make a buff stick, which is easier to manipulate.

Buy a nylon stud back to fit on the wire. A stud back is a small disk with a tapering hole through it. After pushing the stud wire through the pierced ear, push the stud back onto the wire to hold the stud in place.

Otto Künzli (Germany) made these thumbtack brooches, which are hel in place by small rubbe pads (above).

DESIGN DEVELOPMENT

Design involves planning the appearance of a piece and deciding the way in which it will be made. Each person works in an individual way, and the problem for a new jeweler is to find the approach to design that best suits his or her way of working. The following examples show how three jewelers tackled different design problems.

Sporty jewelry by Carolyn Sewell

In this case, the jeweler was asked to design

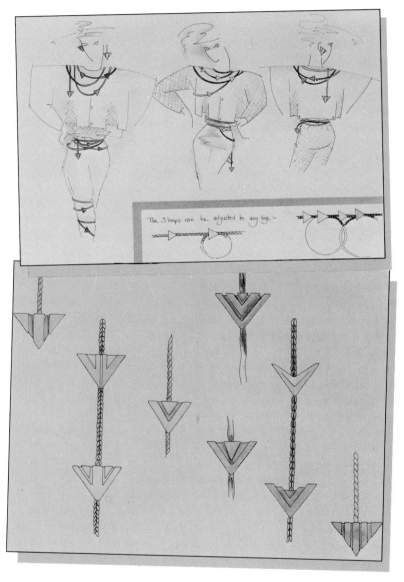

sporty look. The final piece had to be colorful, inexpensive, and easy to make in large quantities.

In order to understand the nature of the design problem, and because no idea suggested itself immediately, Carolyn began by listing words associated with movement and sport. Her next task was to find an image suggested by these words. However, this proved difficult and the jeweler decided to try a different approach. She investigated the process of stamping to see if it would lead to an idea. The stamping process is often used for the mass production of cheap jewelry.

Carolyn had used the process before, and had several experimental samples from a previous job. She sketched the earlier stamped shape again, and then tried several alternatives. One shape that seemed to convey the feeling of movement and activity that she was looking for was a triangle, for it suggested an arrow head.

Carolyn decided to make the jewelry suitable for casual wear and perhaps for sports players. Since the piece might have to stay in place during strenuous activity, conventional brooch fittings would not have been secure enough. The designer solved this problem by inventing a way of threading the triangular stamped units along a cord, which could be tied around the waist, arm, shoulders or leg, in a way that would be decorative, comfortable and secure.

The next consideration was the material. The piece had to be colorful, light and suitable for stamping. After research in the library, and specialist advice from the jewelry department of an art college, it became clear that the ideal metal was niobium. This metal is easily colored and very malleable, and is therefore easily shaped by hammering or stamping.

Once Carolyn had decided on the triangular shape, she needed to determine the details of the surface decoration and make any fine adjustments to the shape. The illustration (above) shows the alternatives she tried. Notice that she always included the cord in the drawing. The strong line that the cord makes through the triangle influences its appearance. If this line had been ignored in the development of the design, the chosen proportions of the triangle might not have been so appealing when the cord was attached. Carolyn then drew the piece as it might be worn. The mood of the drawing and the clothes of the wearers (top) are in line with the brief to design jewelry for the sporty look. Good drawing skills save an enormous amount of time. Without the ability to visualize the end result in this way, Carolyn would have had to make the piece up to see how it would look. She also included information about how the pieces might be adjusted. Technical details must be finalized at this stage, as they may dictate the order in which the piece is constructed.

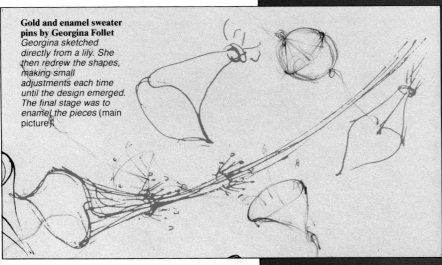

Gold and enamel sweater pins by Georgina Follet
Georgina sketched directly from a lily. She then redrew the shapes, making small adjustments each time until the design emerged. The final stage was to enamel the pieces (main picture).

Sweater pin by Georgina Follett

Georgina was asked to make a gold sweater pin to be worn on special occasions. She decided to base the design on the form of a flower, and found a variety of lily that suited the idea she had in mind.

She wanted to do more than simply reproduce the form of the lily in metal. She wanted the sweater pin to catch the delicate quality of the flower, but the pin had also to be easy to wear and suitable for construction in metal. When working in metal, the form an object takes is likely to be different from that appropriate to another material, such as wood. Metal is ideal if the designer wants a strong, thin-walled, hollow form.

With these points in mind, Georgina began sketching and re-sketching the lily, changing it a little each time. Eventually, she arrived at the shape she wanted. The drawings at this stage were not elaborate or perfect likenesses of the flower, they were simply quick notes to help clarify her ideas.

Once she had established the shape, the next problem was to decide how the pin should be worn. In this case, the shape of the pin suggested a long stem to locate it in the sweater, with a delicate chain and clasp to hold it in place. And so the work on paper was completed, and the stages of construction determined, but this was not the end of the designing process. Throughout the making of the piece, the jeweler remained alert to its changing appearance, continually making adjustments as necessary.

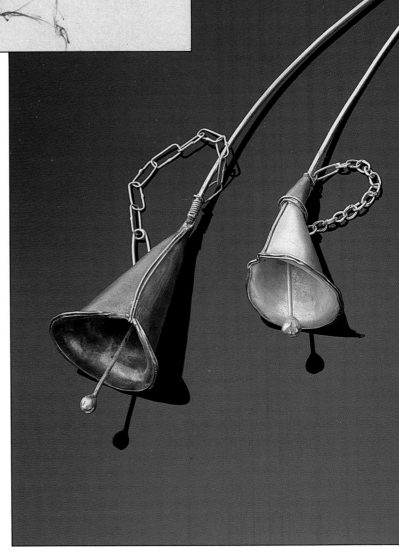

Paper jewelry by Christine Tomas

Christine had no particular commission to fill. Her aim was to evolve her own individual work approach. She had found that traditional techniques and metals did not suit her, yet she enjoyed the scale and decorative qualities of jewelry.

Two factors influenced the way Christine began — photography and fashion. She wanted, in some way, to involve both these elements in her jewelry work.

While in Paris, Christine had photographed the Eiffel Tower from various positions, and she felt that she might now use the photographs as the basis for a design. She began by selecting parts of the photographs that showed the patterns of girders. By superimposing these images, and then tracing the lines from the result, Christine developed a pattern that she liked.

At this stage, Christine did not know how best to develop the pattern into a piece of jewelry. After thinking about the problem for some time, she decided to cut up the drawing and arrange it as a necklace to see if the new association of lines suggested anything to her. Immediately, she realized that the pieces of patterned paper could themselves become the links of a necklace. She then worked on each link, adjusting the shape to suit the pattern on it.

The next problem was to find a way of treating the paper to make it more durable. She experimented with lacquers and plastic coatings and eventually found that thick, clear plastic adhesive sheeting provided the finish she wanted.

Joining the links with paper clips seemed an obvious extension of the paper theme, and it gave exactly the right degree of flexi-

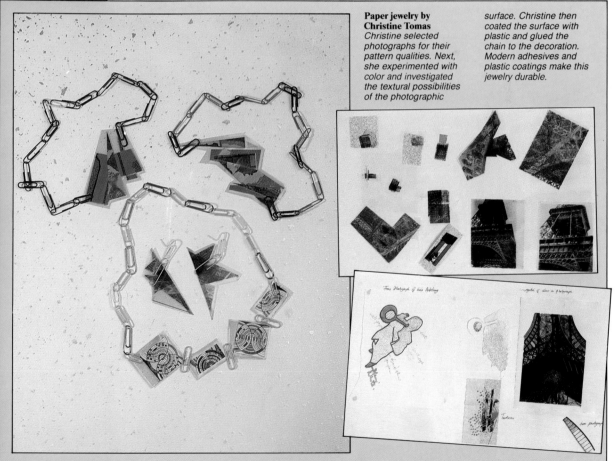

Paper jewelry by Christine Tomas
Christine selected photographs for their pattern qualities. Next, she experimented with color and investigated the textural possibilities of the photographic surface. Christine then coated the surface with plastic and glued the chain to the decoration. Modern adhesives and plastic coatings make this jewelry durable.

bility to the necklace. Modern adhesives bond strongly, so the paper clips were glued in place.

Christine thus discovered a way of working that suited her. She has continued developing this technique and is now making a variety of colorful, fashionable jewelry — all in paper.

STAGES IN DESIGN

The following five stages summarize a general approach to design:

1 Identify the problem.
2 Decide on a starting point for the design.
3 Research the idea.
4 Select relevant information.
5 Develop the design.
6 Select the materials and determine the techniques.
7 Finalize the design.

Identifying the problem is sometimes the hardest task of all but, unless this is done, a satisfactory result is unlikely. For instance, if you wish to make a ring, you must ask yourself who will it be for, and when, where and how often will it be worn? Or, if you would like to try casting, you must determine what shapes can or cannot be cast. If you want simply to make something, you must decide what you like or dislike. The answers to such questions will probably lead to a starting point.

The starting points for each of the three designs discussed above were all different: in the first case, the designer started with an object — a lily; Carolyn began with a process — stamping; and Christine began with a series of photographic images. Other possible starting points might be an emotion (for example, anger), or an idea (for example, mystery).

Be constantly alert to your surroundings. Whenever they occur, note (either mentally or in writing, by collecting pictures, by taking photographs, or by drawing) any ideas, images or combination of images that appeal. You will find that some images recur more frequently than others. Use these as a springboard for a design. Once you identify an interest, discover as much information as possible about the subject. Then, from the

Every designer develops ideas in an individual and unique way. In many cases, he or she begins with one image and alters it by stages so that gradually a totally new image evolves. In the development illustrated below, Bert Kitchen (UK) worked in a different way. He began with a page of lines and tones in which no shape was clearly defined. He did not predict the end result, but instead allowed the marks on the paper to suggest his next move. Gradually he defined a clear image from an amorphous background. This is not a quick process, nor is it one that can be carried out in a hurry on the back of a cigarette packet. It requires concentration and a constant alertness to the changing work.

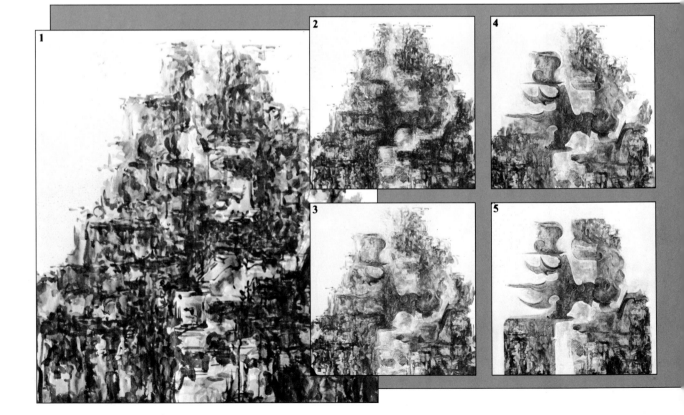

research material, select only important or only relevant items, so that the development of the design is purposeful. Do not try to use too much information or too many ideas in any one design; the ability to select is a particularly important skill for the designer to master.

Developing a design means changing it by degrees until it is right. It takes time and practice to be able to assess at what stage the design is finished.

When choosing materials, make sure that they suit the design and its purpose. The materials chosen will normally dictate the techniques used in construction.

Finally, consider carefully whether or not the design will work. For example, if it's a brooch, will it stay in place with the catch selected for it? Modify the design in order to overcome any anticipated problems. The design may now be finalized, but always be prepared to make further changes during construction if the need becomes apparent.

Sketches and scraps
Most designers keep files of information to refer to and draw from when designing. They collect and store this information in various ways, the most common method being to keep a sketch book and a scrap book. The sketch book is not a book of perfect drawings, but rather a collection of quick notes in words and sketches, and a convenient place to try out ideas. When a design problem is identified, refer to the sketch book first. The starting point for developing a design may already exist in note form.

The sketch book can be any size. Some designers prefer small pocket books with heavy art paper, while others work on A4-size layout pads with thin paper. A scrap book containing photographs, postcards and pictures cut from newspapers and magazines is another useful source of information. These pictures can be of anything; it may be the subject, the color or the lines that appeal.

The use of pictures or sketches might not be immediately obvious, but they do sometimes provide starting points for later design work, or help in identifying a particular area of interest.

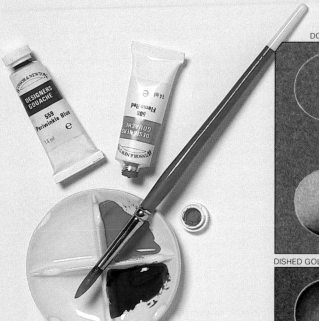

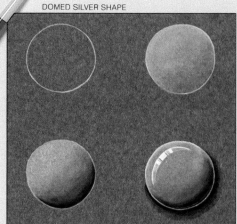

DOMED SILVER SHAPE

DISHED GOLD SHAPE

DESIGN PRESENTATION

Sketches made while developing designs are usually rough and serve merely as *aide-memoires*. An accurate illustration is sometimes needed to give a clear image of the design before the work commences. This is useful when other technicians are commissioned to work on a job; for it is essential that they fully understand the designer's intentions. If the jewelry is to be made for someone else, it is generally advisable to agree on the design details first, and often the only way of explaining what you have in mind is to draw or paint the jewelry exactly as it will appear when finished. Lastly, when a number of alternatives are to be discussed, it is more economic, in terms of both time and materials, to illustrate rather than construct each one.

How to illustrate

The illustrations are intended to convey information, rather than to be works of art in their own right. Many illustrative techniques convey the illusion of finished jewelry, but beginners usually adopt various well-established ways of representing their jewelry in a simple, stylized form. From this, jewelers develop distinctive illustrative styles as their design work progresses.

POLISHED SILVER SHEET

GOLD TEXTURED SHEET

SQUARE SILVER WIRE

GOLD POLISHED CYLINDER

ROUND GOLD WIRE

TITANIUM

ENAMEL

Illustrating metal objects
Illustrations of metal must convey the hardness of the material. Crisp, clear lines help; form is defined by line, light and shade. Remember always to outline the shape first. To achieve even washes of color, mix the paint with plenty of water, float the paint over the paper, and draw off excess water with a dry brush. Apply subsequent washes to build up tone if necessary. Allow paint to dry between applications.
Domed silver shape
Apply a thin wash of white, fading to the bottom right. Fade in a thin grey shadow line and paint a strong white crescent highlight.
Dished gold shape *Follow the instructions for a domed silver shape, using yellow and adding final white highlights.*
Polished silver sheet
Apply a thin white wash before painting the strong white flashes.
Gold textured sheet
Apply a thin wash in yellow ocher. Lightly brush the surface of the paper with a dry brush loaded with brilliant yellow. Apply shadows of dark brown.
Polished square silver
Follow the method for illustrating silver sheet.
Polished round gold wire
Fade a thin yellow wash down one side and a dark brown shadow line down the other. Add yellow and white highlights.
Gold polished cylinder
Follow the method for illustrating round gold wire.
Titanium *Apply a strong even wash of waterproof white ink. Next, apply washes of colors, blending them where they meet.*
Enamel *Apply a thin yellow wash to the whole shape. Then outline the enamel area and apply a wash of waterproof white ink. Add a stronger texture line of white ink to the enamel shapes and wash on the enamel color. Add dark brown shadows to the enamel and metal and paint white metal highlights.*

Illustrating stones

Here, what is needed is to convey the overall impression of a stone and even beginners can produce effective results with a little practice. It helps to use a dark background and a minimum of paint and always outline the shape first.

Diamonds *Cover the shape with a thin wash of white. Paint the fine facet lines — curved lines give the best effect. Block out highlights with strong white and paint in pale and bold white triangles to suggest reflections. Paint in the shadow.*

Coloured stones *Paint is easier but waterproof ink creates a livelier effect. Paint method: follow the method for painting diamonds, substituting a color wash for the first thin wash of white. Then, paint in a thin wash of white. Ink method: use white waterproof ink instead of white paint, using white gouache for the final highlights. Paint a second thin wash of color before adding highlights.*

Semi-transparent cabochon stones *Apply thin white gouache bottom right, fading in. Paint a round, white highlight top left and blend in "tails." Finally, suggest reflected light and paint in shadow.*

Opaque cabochon stones *Follow the method for semi-transparent stones, using thin black gouache bottom right. Add a thin white crescent above left. Highlight as shown.*

Cream pearls *Paint a shadow color bottom right and a cream highlight top left. Use a bright white gouache to highlight.*

Black pearls *Apply a mixed wash of black and green and highlight as shown.*

Opals *Outline in gouache, painting the shape with waterproof white ink. Add thin streaks and dots of linden green, marigold, and brilliant yellow. Paint a crescent with thin white gouache.*

DIAMONDS AND COLORED STONES: PAINT METHOD

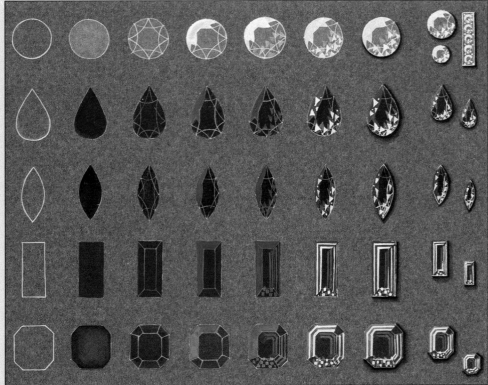

OPALS

COLORED STONES: INK METHOD

SEMI-TRANSPARENT CABOCHON STONES

CREAM PEARLS

OPAQUE CABOCHON STONES

BLACK PEARLS

Design equipment
1 *Drawing boards vary in size and material but the wooden board, the Formica-covered board and the adjustable board are the 3 most popular models.*
2 *T-squares are available in plastic or metal. Place the top of the 'T' over the side of the board and move the T-square up and down to draw parallel lines.*
3 *A compositor's typescale is graduated in different point sizes and used for measuring the width of a column of type.*
4 *No designer should be*

without a ruler and a scale ruler is useful for enlarging or reducing the scale.
5 *60° and 45° set squares are most commonly used.*
6 *Angles can be measured very precisely with this 180° plastic protractor.*
7 *An adjustable set square is more versatile than regular set squares.*
8 *Many degrees of curve can be drawn with a French curve.*
9 *The designer can draw circular shapes accurately and in perspective with a template.*

Tools and materials

Canson paper in the following shades: maroon, tobacco, dark grey, mid grey, black
Medium weight, high-quality tracing paper
Mounting board
Brushes: Winsor and Newton series 7 or series 16, nos. 1 and 2
Pencils: B for sketching, 5H for tracing and transferring designs
Staedtler plastic or rechargeable pencil eraser
Sharpener
Paint: Winsor and Newton designers' gouache: permanent white, brilliant yellow, yellow ocher, black, Van Dyke brown, linden green, marigold yellow, cerulean blue; Winsor and Newton artists' watercolors; alizarin crimson, cerulean blue, chrome deep, chrome orange, Hooker's green light, indigo, manganese blue, permanent blue, permanent magenta, Prussion blue, purple madder, Winsor green, Winsor violet, Payne's grey, sepia
Rotring waterproof ink
Drawing instruments
For cutting mounts: scalpel handle and 10A blades or mat cutting tool; heavy duty knife
Drawing board

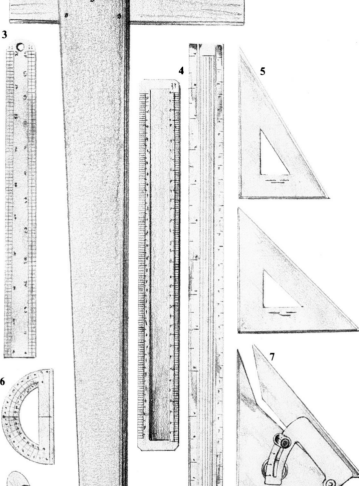

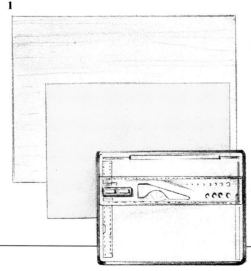

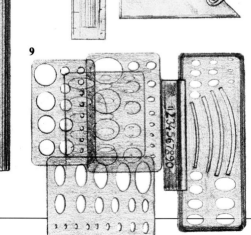

10 *This technical drawing set contains 2 sizes of spring bow compass, a small radius compass, dividers, ruling pens and extension bar.*
11 *The tubular nibs of drawing pens ensure that they write evenly.*
12 *A stylo-tip pen can be attached to a spring bow compass with the device shown.*
13 *The blade of a mat cutting tool is held in place at an angle and can be adjusted by a screw.*
14 *Used for fine cutting, surgical scalpels have interchangeable blades.*
15 *Use a trimming knife for heavy duty cutting.*

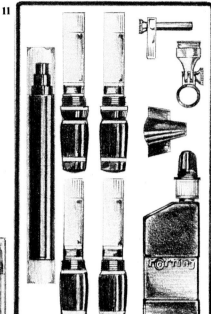

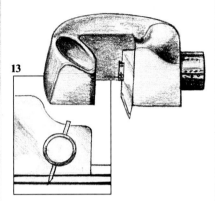

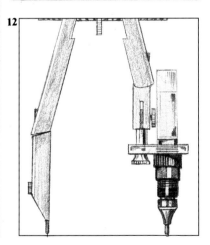

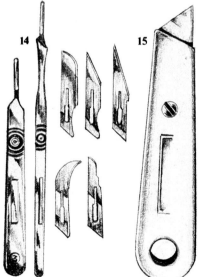

16 *Metal pencil sharpeners give pencils a sharp point.*
17 *A rechargeable clutch rubber will rub out ink.*
18 *For accurate drawing, keep your pencil sharpened.*
19 *A plastic eraser rubs out pencil marks and a folioplast removes ink lines.*

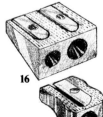

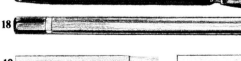

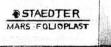

Presenting your design
First, draw out the plan of the piece (right). Then project lines from the plan to help draw an accurate side view. Trace the design onto tracing paper with a 5H pencil. Shade the back of the tracing paper with a B pencil. Transfer the design to canson paper and begin painting. Paint the metal first, then the stones. Finally, add the highlights and shadows. Once familiar with painting techniques, designers develop their own individual styles. The paintings by Sheelagh Burch (below left) and Carolyn Stephenson (below right) illustrate this point.

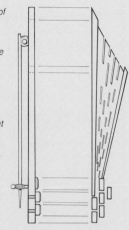

Drawing a ring in perspective
Begin by drawing the top view (plan) to scale, working to the correct finger size and stone sizes. Project lines from the top to determine exact positions of elements for the front view. Similarly, project lines sideways for accurate drawing of the side view. To establish where the front and side views should be drawn, place the point of the compass on the bottom right-hand corner of the top view and scribe an arc of suitable radius. Further arcs from this point provide a means of transferring heights from the front view to the side view. Information from all three views is needed to draw the perspective view accurately. The easiest way to draw a ring in perspective is to visualize it in a box. Transfer the perspective view to canson paper and paint the design.

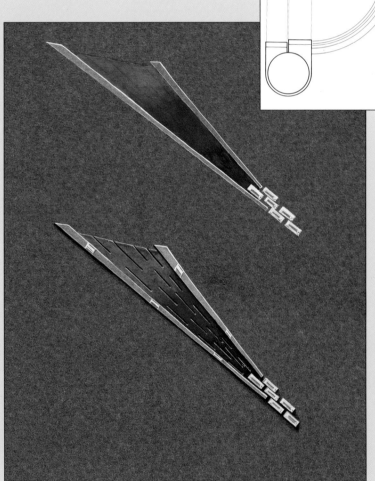

Mounting painted designs
1 *Choose the colors of mounting boards and slip or inset papers to complement the canson paper and painting colors.*
2 *Use cardboard L-shapes to determine a suitable size for the mount window. If a slip (inner mount) is to be included, two sets of L-shapes are helpful so that the width of the slip can be assessed at the same time. Measure the window sizes and mark these on the front of the mount.*
3 *To cut a bevel-edged window, use the mat cutting tool as shown. Alternatively, cut the window with a scalpel blade. Line up the mounting card on a cutting board. Use a T-square to ensure all right angles are accurate.*
4 *Line up the mounts with the painted design. Fix with glue or double-sided adhesive tape. Back with thick card for protection.*

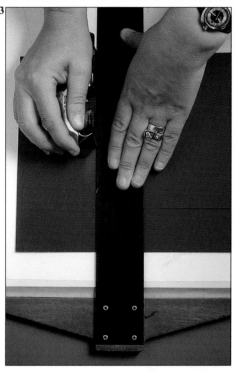

SPECIAL TECHNIQUES

A piece of jewelry is rarely constructed by using only one technique. A single piece might include a cast section, a carved part, precious stones and enameling work. Although each technique is described separately, new jewelry makers should experiment with combinations of techniques and materials.

TEXTILES

The tradition of wearing textile jewelry is well established. In a portrait by François Boucher, Madame de Pompadour (1721-1764) is wearing an elaborate ribbon necklace, and a portrait painted *circa* 1770 by A R Mengs shows Maria Louisa of Palma in a necklace of pink, ruffled material. In the late 1800s, ladies wore pendants suspended from ribbons and, in the early part of this century, Cartier combined diamonds with black velvet.

Jewelers today are using textiles more inventively than ever before. New techniques are being developed to suit the material and the design. There are no rules, and no established methods of working. Experiment with some of your own ideas, allowing the nature of the material — and its color, pattern, texture and thickness — to direct your ideas.

Cartier decorated this black velvet neckband (above) with an articulated leaf motif of gold, set with diamonds and pearls. This piece is in the Cartier collection in Paris. The braided choker in black silk (below left) is by Rachel Leach (UK). The characteristics of the braided silk tassels allow them to stay in position, either standing out from the body of the choker or lying flat.

The color, flexibility and surface qualities of textiles make them interesting materials for use in jewelry. In the portrait painted by François Boucher (right), Madame de Pompadour is wearing a necklace of ribbon that matches the ribbon decoration of her dress (Rothschild collection). If you make your own clothes, consider designing and making co-ordinated jewelry. Jayne Hierons used ruffled materials and cord in the top necklace (below left). On page 66 she demonstrates how this is made. In the bottom necklace she combined fabric with plastic beads constructed to reflect the adjacent material folds. The knitted necklace (below right) is by Jane Gower (UK).

MAKING A TEXTILE BEAD NECKLACE

Jayne Hierons used the natural folds of cloth to form the ruffled beads *(bottom)*. For full, rounded beads, the fabric pockets could be stuffed with cotton batting.

Tools and materials
Needle
Scissors
Safety pin
1m × 10cm soft material
0.5m heavy cord
Matching cotton

1 *For the pockets, draft a pattern to suit the chosen fabric. Link the pockets with a short, narrow passage. The beads will later be bound at the junctions. As a guide, for this silk, the bead-pockets are 5cm long by 4cm wide. The passage between the pockets is 1cm long by 1cm wide. Transfer the pattern to the fabric and stitch along the lines.*
2 *Cut away excess material between pockets.*
3 *Turn the stitched fabric inside-out with a safety pin. Thread the cord.*
4 *To bind between the beads, lay one end of the binding thread and a U-shaped wire along the cord. Bind over the thread and wire. Knot the ends of the thread and pull them beneath the binding with the wire.*

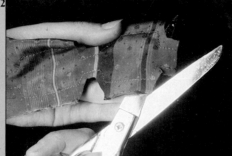

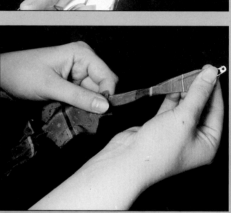

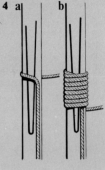

4 a | b

c | d

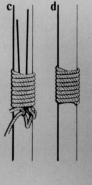

Textile techniques with wire

Most metals used by jewelers are available in both wire and sheet form. Of these, some can be made into extremely fine, flexible wire which, being easy to manipulate, is ideal for certain textile techniques, such as weaving, knitting, crocheting and plaiting.

Some wires soon become work-hardened; that is, they become harder due to the amount of bending that they undergo. As a result, they need frequent softening by annealing (*see below*). As fine wire is easily melted accidentally, avoid using such metals whenever possible. Instead, use wire that remains easy to manipulate without frequent annealing, such as gold of at least 14 karat, fine silver, Britannia silver, copper or aluminum. Once annealed initially, these all

remain flexible when in the form of fine wire (0.2mm to 0.5mm diameter). If you buy wire which has been annealed, and is of the required cross-section, no further annealing will be needed.

Reels of fine, annealed copper wire are sold by electrical stores, and reels of fine, anodized aluminum wire are sold by craft stores. Annealed precious metals can be purchased from bullion dealers.

Round and square wires are easily obtained in various sizes, but other shapes will usually have to be made from round or square wire by means of a technique called drawing; the same method is also used to reduce round or square wire. Before it is drawn, hard wire must be softened by annealing.

FRENCH KNITTING WITH WIRE

1 Hammer 4 headless nails into a small wooden cylinder like an old sewing thread spool. Wind the wire once around each nail.
2 Make a second loop around the first nail.
3 With a crochet hook, lift the bottom loop over the top one and drop it into the hole through the spool.
4 Continue nail by nail.

Drawing wire
To draw wire by hand, secure the draw plate in a vise (below). File a point on the wire and thread it through the hole. Pull the wire with draw tongs. Draw down heavier wire on a draw bench (right).

Annealing

To anneal wire, hold it vertically in steel tweezers and direct the flame down the wire. Do not move the flame across the wire as it is likely to produce uneven annealing and hence uneven wire. If the wire is long, coil it tightly and anneal the coil with a soft flame. One way to anneal fine, coiled wire is to submerge it in charcoal chips contained in a small steel tin, and then heat the tin until it is red. The wire inside will be annealed. If you overheat the tin and the wire is accidentally melted, it is sometimes possible to repair it by soldering.

Drawing

Drawing entails pulling wire through successively smaller holes in a steel plate called a draw plate. Its purpose is to gradually decrease the diameter of the wire. As the diameter of the wire is reduced, so its length increases. To make drawing easier, warm the wire and rub a block of beeswax along it. The wax will melt onto the warm wire and act as a lubricant. If the wire has just been annealed, the wax should be applied after allowing the wire to cool for a few minutes. Secure the draw plate in a vise, so that the plate is horizontal. It is always advisable to use jaw protectors to prevent any damage occurring to the draw plate.

File a taper of about 2cm at one end of the wire, so that it can be threaded through the holes in the draw plate. Locate the largest hole that the wire will not pass through easily. Thread the taper through the hole from the back (countersunk side), gripping the end with wire-drawing tongs. These have strong, serrated jaws for firm gripping, and a hook on one handle to prevent the hand from slipping. Standing with one foot in front of the other, and with your arms straight, lean back and draw the wire through the plate. Do not bend your arms, and let the weight of your body do the work. If your arms are bent, there is a risk of hitting yourself if the wire suddenly runs through the draw plate more rapidly than expected.

Continue drawing through progressively smaller holes until the required size is obtained. Anneal whenever drawing becomes difficult, which is usually after the wire has been through three or four holes. When the wire is of the required cross-section, anneal it once again before using it for textile-type pieces.

This effect (below) is achieved by French knitting with chain, using a bobbin, thread and hook. The chain is pulled through the hole in the bobbin. Some jewelers, prefer to use just metal thread and a small hook.

French knitting

French knitting is an old technique used for making a continuous tube from wool. To knit in this way with wire, drill a hole in a piece of wood, and hammer at least three nails without heads around the edge to protrude from the wood by no more than 5mm. The size of the hole determines the diameter of the finished knitting; the distance of the nails from the edge of the hole determines the length of the stitch; and the size and number of nails determine the closeness of the knitting. Experiment to find the combination you prefer.

To begin knitting, loop the wire once around each nail, then loop it around the first nail a second time. With a crochet hook, lift the bottom loop over the top one. Continue working round the nails in order, looping and lifting; the knitting will appear through the bottom of the hole. To even out a finished length of knitting, drill a slightly smaller hole

through another piece of wood and draw the whole knitted tube through it.

Crocheting

Crocheting is the process of pulling, twisting and drawing loops of thread through each other with a steel hook; the result is an open, lacy pattern. The size of the steel hook determines the openness of the stitch.

For those already skilled in crocheting, almost any pattern can be tackled with wire. For beginners, the step-by-step instructions show how to construct a simple piece using this technique (*see page 67*).

Other textile techniques with wire

Wire can also be twisted, braided, knitted, or woven. If you already have skills in any of these areas, experiment with the techniques in wire. The illustrations on this page show creative designs by some contemporary jewelers who specialize in wire work.

The braided wire necklace in silver (right) was designed by Simon Harrison and Ian Young. The knitted wire necklace (below) is by Ruth Robinson. The structure is so strong and flexible that the necklace can be tied like a scarf.

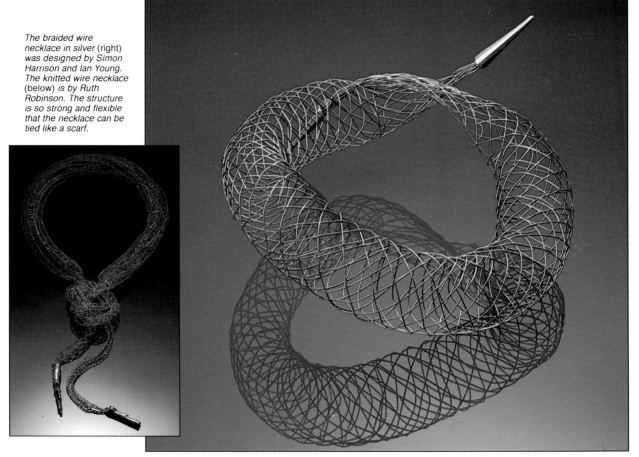

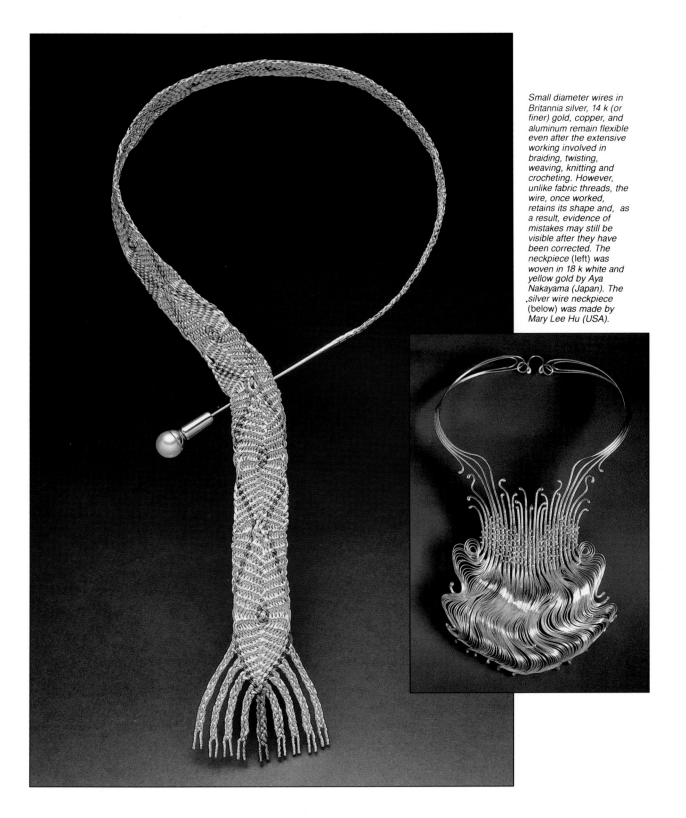

Small diameter wires in Britannia silver, 14 k (or finer) gold, copper, and aluminum remain flexible even after the extensive working involved in braiding, twisting, weaving, knitting and crocheting. However, unlike fabric threads, the wire, once worked, retains its shape and, as a result, evidence of mistakes may still be visible after they have been corrected. The neckpiece (left) was woven in 18 k white and yellow gold by Aya Nakayama (Japan). The silver wire neckpiece (below) was made by Mary Lee Hu (USA).

Many plastics are suitable for jewelry. When designing plastic jewelry, exploit the qualities of a particular kind of plastic. If you want to make colored jewelry, select *plastic that is easy to dye; if the jewelry needs to be flexible, select a plastic that can withstand frequent bending. In the bangles (below), Emmy Van Leersum (Holland), has* *laminated colored paper and PVC. While Rowena Park (UK) has exploited the pliability and colorability of nylon sheet to make the bracelet (bottom).*

PLASTICS

Plexiglass, nylon, polyester resin, and other plastics are firmly established as jewelers' materials. At first, plastics tended to be used to simulate other materials; for example, resin was used to imitate enamel. Now, however, jewelers are exploiting the characteristics of plastic to achieve completely new effects. For example, since plastic is colorful, light and strong, large, brightly colored items can be made from it. And the flexibility of plastic makes it ideal where the quality of movement is required, both for functional reasons — for bracelet joints and catches — and for decorative reasons — for fine, delicate streamers that waft in the wind.

Plastics are now so widely used in industry that they can be purchased in most areas. Furthermore, the piercing saw, files and buff sticks specified for metal also suit plastics. Size 1 piercing saw blades with offset teeth cut plastics easily. Coarser files are less likely to clog and are therefore more suitable for plastics than fine files.

MAKING A PLEXIGLASS NECKLACE

Plexiglass is light, so large pieces can be worn and are easy to work.
1 Decide on the number and sizes of disks to be used in the necklace. The disks shown here are 5cm across. Scribe the circles on plexiglass sheet. Saw out the disks. File away rough edges.
2 Buff the edges of the disks to remove file marks.
3 Experiment with the positions of the decorative spots, using adhesive colored paper dots. Mark the

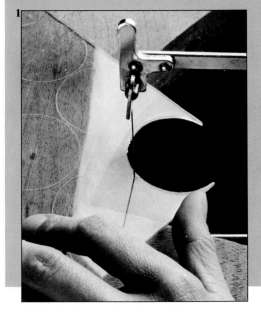

1

Plexiglass

One of the most common plastics used in jewelry is plexiglass. This rigid plastic can be clear or colored, opaque or transparent. It is available as sheet in thicknesses of 2mm, 3mm and 4mm. Most suppliers also stock a limited range of rods and tubes.

A solvent is used to join plexiglass. The join will show on transparent plexiglass unless it is clean and perfectly fitted, so start with opaque plexiglass.

Nylon

Nylon is a tough, strong and pliable plastic. It is available as sheet, "wire" (monofilament), rod or tube of almost any dimension likely to be required by jewelers. A scalpel blade will cut thin nylon, but thicker material needs to be sawn, or grooved and snapped. Cyanoacrylate glues stick nylon, but the join must be perfectly fitted for it to be strong. The main advantage of using nylon is that it can be colored with fabric dyes in a similar way to fabrics; the resulting colors are subtle.

Polyester resin

Polyester resin is a plastic sold in liquid form. The clear, thick liquid hardens when mixed with a hardening agent called a catalyst. Coloring agents can be added if required. Fumes from the liquid and airborne dust from filing or sawing the solid material are dangerous, so special work facilities and ventilation must be arranged. For this reason, polyester resin is no longer recommended for home use.

Other plastics

Polypropylene, PVC and acetate are, in many ways, similar to nylon. Polypropylene is more rigid than nylon, and may be more difficult to obtain. PVC (polyvinyl chloride) is more brittle than nylon. Many hardware stores stock PVC, and it may be worth obtaining some offcuts for experimentation. Acetate (cellulose acetate) will take strong colors if dyed. To dye acetate effectively, soak it in a solution of cold-water fabric dye dissolved in acetone.

positions of the threading holes with paper dots.
4 Mark the center of each paper dot by pressing with a scriber. Do not hammer the scriber as the plexiglass may crack. Drill through the paper into the plexiglass: for the threading holes, drill right through the plexiglass; for the decorative spots, create small hollows with smooth, round edges. Remove the paper dot.
5 Give the inside of the drilled hollows two coats of paint.
6 Pass the cord through the threading holes. The finished necklace is shown on page 72.

Tools and materials
Dividers
Piercing saw and size 1 saw blades
Buff stick with flour-grade sandpaper
Drill with 2mm and 5mm drill bits
Humbrol enamel paint
Sable hair paintbrush no. 1
Mineral spirits
Clear plexiglass sheet 2mm thick
1m of ribbon or cord

2

4

5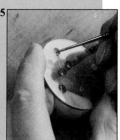

3

6

Jayne Hierons (UK) made these sporty pieces (right and below) from nylon threads. The idea for the pieces came from a bottle cleaning brush that had bristles held together by a central wire. Jayne experimented with ways of manipulating the threads to make them curly and thus more comfortable than spiky bristles.

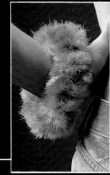

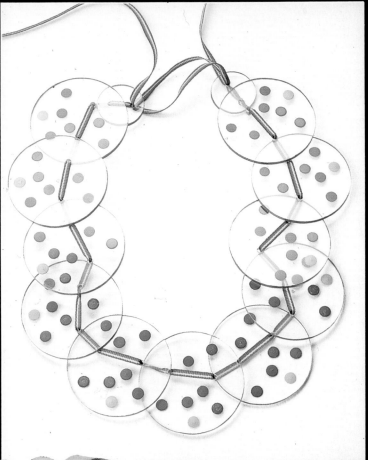

Instructions for making this plexiglass disk necklace (above) by Susan Fortune (UK) are given on pages 70-71. Susan developed the necklace to show just how much can be achieved with limited facilities and knowledge of a few basic techniques. She has included an ingenious slip-disk that allows the piece to be worn either short or long. The sponge rubber bangle (left) is by Lindsay Jordan (UK). Lindsay began experimenting with this material during her student days. Her graduation show in 1984 included a range of sponge rubber items.

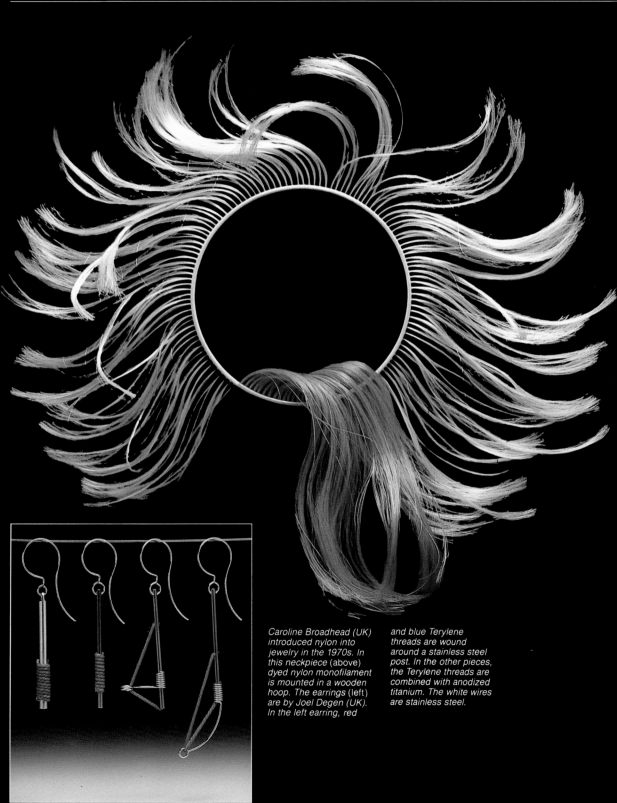

Caroline Broadhead (UK) introduced nylon into jewelry in the 1970s. In this neckpiece (above) dyed nylon monofilament is mounted in a wooden hoop. The earrings (left) are by Joel Degen (UK). In the left earring, red and blue Terylene threads are wound around a stainless steel post. In the other pieces, the Terylene threads are combined with anodized titanium. The white wires are stainless steel.

BEADS AND PEARLS

Strung beads are the oldest form of jewelry. The first beads were made of bone or shell and strung on flexible threads. Archaeologists believe that three necklaces of fish vertebrae found in a grave near Monaco may have been made as early as 25,000 BC. As technology developed, drilled stone and glass beads came to be used for necklaces, and some jewelers began threading beads on wire instead of thread, so that jewelry of different shapes could be created.

Contemporary jewelers string beads and pearls on both wire and thread. In some parts of the world, the art of decorative beading is highly developed. Some Africans thread small, colorful beads into lacy patterns, either for necklaces or for hair ornaments. Other African necklaces feature an enormous variety of beads, made from metal, plastic, glass, natural materials and found objects, such as coins.

In Europe, the art of stringing is concentrated in the pearl industry. However, a few jewelers are including beadwork in some of their new designs.

Beads and pearls are commonly strung on flexible threads but there are other ways to display their attractive shapes and colors. Try threading them on wire and then bending the wire into unusual shapes. Beads and pearls are available with holes drilled right through them, or with half-drilled holes. Mount half-drilled beads and pearls on posts (spikes of wire) and secure them, using pearl cement or another adhesive. Yuji Takahashi (Japan) won a Diamonds International Award with this brooch (below) in 1969. The pearls are mounted on a frame and set beside small, brilliant cut diamonds and larger, pear-shaped diamonds mounted in yellow gold.

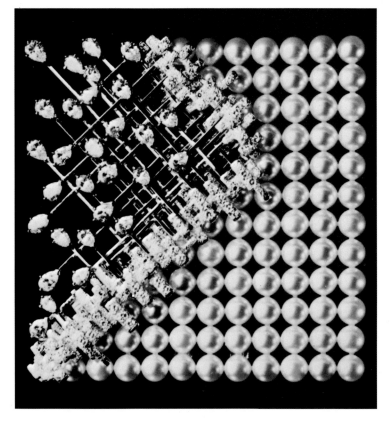

Grading and preparation

Before you begin stringing, pearls should be graded by size, and colored beads arranged in the required order. Otherwise mistakes, which may not be noticed until the string is complete, are easily made. Crease a piece of paper and place the beads or pearls in the groove. This will keep them in order prior to stringing.

The holes through pearls sometimes vary in diameter. This may result in a pearl being forced along the thread, causing either the pearl or thread to break. To avoid this problem, first enlarge a small hole with a broacher held in a pin vise. A broacher is a square, hard steel wire that tapers to a point. When twisted in a previously drilled hole, it cuts away the sides, enlarging the hole. The holes in some beads can be enlarged in a similar way, but others will be too hard for the steel to cut.

Principles of stringing

Beads and pearls can be threaded tightly together or separated by knots. Besides improving the appearance of the jewelry, the knots also provide security, flexibility and protection. If a knotted string of pearls breaks, only the pearls adjoining one knot will be lost. All the others will be held securely by the knots.

If the pearls are strung tightly together, so that the string is almost rigid, and if bending is then forced, either the string or the pearls will break. The spacing provided by the knots gives the string of pearls flexibility and prevents this from happening. The knots also prevent the pearlized surfaces from rubbing on each other.

Always string on a double thread, then, if there is a weakness in one thread, the second will provide a back-up. In knotted strings, the double thread also forms more attractive knots.

There are two main methods of knotting. In the first, every thread that runs through the pearls or beads is knotted between each bead. In the second, a core thread runs straight through all the beads, and a second thread is knotted around the core thread between each bead or pearl. The first technique is normally used for pearls. The second is suitable for beads separated by colored embroidery silk knots, large knots, or decorative knots, such as those used in macrame.

KNOTTING BEADS AND PEARLS

1 *Arrange the pearls or beads according to color and size, using a fold in a sheet of paper.*
2 *The pearl silk must be 6 times the desired length to allow for*

Tools and materials

Fine steel wire for threading needle
Scissors
Pearls or beads
Pearl silk to match hole size in the beads or pearls

Gimp (silver- or gold-colored)
Catch
Clear nail polish
Colored embroidery silk for colored knots, if required

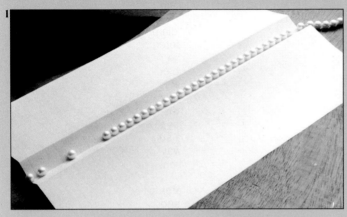

STRINGING BEADS WITH COLORED THREAD

Colored thread is more inclined to stretch than pearl silk and decorative knots in it tighten and separate, so core thread, usually of pearl silk, is used to keep the beads positioned. By using two or more colors for the threads, you can vary the colors of the knots: simply alternate the core and knotting threads.
1 *Measure off 1½ times*

the length of the beads for the core thread, and 3 times the length for the knotting thread. Slide some gimp, then the catch or ring, onto both threads and knot and secure. Hook the ring over a nail to keep the core thread taut and thread the first bead. Tie a decorative knot in the knotting thread.
2 *Pull the knot tight: tie a second knot if a single knot seems too small. Continue until all beads are knotted.*

doubling and knotting. Make a threader by bending a piece of fine steel wire in two and thread the silk through an 8mm length of gimp. Then thread the gimp through one half of the catch and tie the ends to the main string with a reef knot. Glue the loose ends to the main string with a tiny spot of clear nail polish. Allow the polish to dry and then begin threading.
3 *Slide the first pearl against the knotted gimp and tie a loose knot in the free length of thread.*
4 *Slide the knot tightly against the pearl with a needle held in a pin-vise.*
5 *Tighten the knot further, by pulling the threads away from each other. Secure the rest of the pearls. To finish, thread a further 8mm length of gimp onto the string and thread on the other half of the catch. Knot the thread around the main string, using a half-hitch knot. Dab nail polish on the thread and pass the end back through the last pearl.*

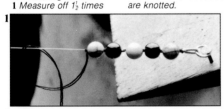

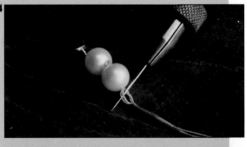

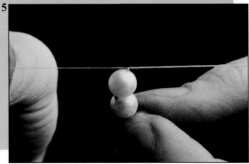

Needles and threads

Needles for threading beads and pearls are made from fine steel. If only one string is to be threaded, the jeweler can manage with size 32 binding wire, which is widely available. It is, however, more inclined to break than steel needle wire and, therefore, tiresome to use on long jobs.

Silk is by far the best thread for beads or pearls. Pearl-threading silk is strong, less inclined to stretch or rot than cotton, and allows knots to be slid tightly against each bead or pearl. Silk is available in a range of thicknesses: choose the thickest silk that can be threaded twice through the hole of the bead or pearl. Embroidery cotton is suitable for colored knots, but a silk thread should accompany it for strength. Nylon is unsuitable for knotting, as it tends to work loose, and cotton should be avoided as it is inclined to break during knotting.

To strengthen a necklace, beads and pearls can be threaded on chain or wire. Many nineteenth-century amber necklaces are strung on fine gold chains.

Catches and gimp

After the beads or pearls are strung, the ends of the thread are looped through catch fittings. The most vulnerable sections of strung beads are these end loops, which wear quickly as a result of the movement of the catches on the loops. To protect them, the loops are surrounded by a tight spiral of very fine wire, called gimp. Buy silver-colored or gold-colored gimp as required, and match it to the thickness of the thread. The size of the loop and, therefore, the length of the gimp depends on the hole allowed on the catch for attachment; the catch should not flop around on the loop. Catches can be either purchased with the beads or constructed by the jeweler. Refer to the section on catches and clips for appropriate fittings (*see page 104*).

Pearl stringers used to attach loose ends of thread to the main string with glue. However, many now use clear nail polish, which is probably best for the beginner, as the brush makes it easier to apply the right quantity to the right place.

Real and cultured pearls feel gritty on the teeth, unlike imitation pearls, which feel smooth. These small, rice-shaped pearls (below) are freshwater pearls from Lake Biwa, Japan.

In the necklace, earrings and ring (below), Jacqueline Mina (UK) has used baroque pearls threaded on 18 k gold wire.

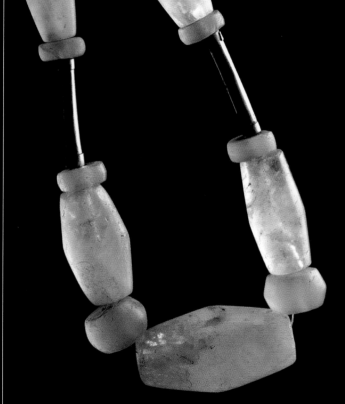

Beads are easy to work with and require little specialist equipment but outstanding pieces can be achieved only with careful design and imaginative selection. Annie Sherburne (UK) studied various bead-weaving techniques, then developed her own unique approach: this choker (above left) has a lacy, beaded edge and a long, flexible back pendant. In the Chinese head ornament (above), the coral beads are threaded on wire and butterfly wing is used to provide the blue. Beads are a very old form of jewelry; these beads (left) are pre-Colombian.

MOUNTING AND SETTING STONES

Mounting and setting are the techniques used for fixing stones in items of jewelry. Mounting refers to the construction of the metal parts of a piece of jewelry, including the supports for the stones. The supports are called settings, mounts or collets. Setting is the technique of easing metal over the stones to hold them in place.

A stone is kept in place by the adjacent metal, which prevents both sideways and up-and-down movement. The type of stone and the desired finish dictate the style of the setting, but, whatever the setting, there must be enough metal of adequate strength to secure the stone. For instance if only three

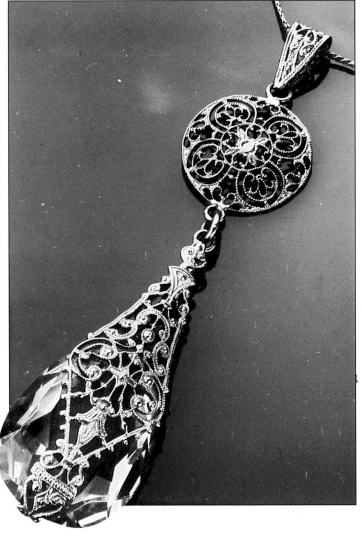

Types of setting
The items on these pages give an idea of the range of settings available, from the simple stringing of especially drilled stones (left) *to the large faceted stone in the drop pendant* (below left). *The cameo* (below right) *is literally framed by its ornate rub-over setting whereas the central emerald in the classic necklace* (below) *is set in a plain rub-over setting that is surrounded by pavé-set diamonds.*

prongs are used on a setting, they should be stronger than if six or more prongs are included. Similarly, because of the differing strengths of precious metals, a silver collet should be thicker than a 14 k gold one, while platinum can be surprisingly fine.

In fine jewelry, glue is not used because it is rarely as secure as conventional setting and it also tends to dull the stone, making it less attractive. Glue will not normally withstand the changes of temperature and the amount of wear-and-tear to which jewelry is usually subjected. For instance, the wearer of a ring may move from beside a hot fire to icy conditions outside, then return inside and rinse his or her hands in detergent. Stones secured properly by metal will

remain in place throughout such treatment; glued stones are less likely to do so.

Settings are normally described by the way the stone is held: in rub-over settings, the metal is pushed over the edges of the stones to hold them in place; prong settings have a number of small metal "prongs" that grip the stones; and, in spectacle-glass settings, a metal wire holds the stone around its perimeter.

In the jewelry trade, mounting and setting are separate and specialist tasks, and both take time for the beginner to master. The small pieces of metal used in these processes are initially difficult to handle, but the task soon becomes easier as the jeweler adjusts to small-scale work.

SPHERICAL STONES

Spherical stones are usually drilled and strung as beads, or mounted on posts as ear studs but the jewelry traditions of other countries or past eras may suggest a different approach. In the Mexican necklace *(below)*, the turquoise beads are set in lines in a simple, but secure and decorative, setting. The scallops of metal pushed between the beads are in keeping with the crimped edge of the scroll work on the links *(right)*. The amethysts are set in square, rub-over settings. When setting spherical stones, it is difficult to prevent movement. So you may prefer to devise a setting technique that allows the stones to move.

Making a bead earring

1 Line up the beads on plasticine. Measure the length of the line and the width and height of the beads. Cut a strip of silver 0.5mm thick and equal in width to the height of the beads. Open dividers to 1mm more than the width of the beads. Open a second pair of dividers to 1mm more than the length of the line of beads — the extra 1mm is to allow clearance. Mark off the lengths along the strips — short, long, short, long. Make 90° grooves along the marks with a square needle file until a faint line shows on the back of the metal. This will ensure sharp corners.
2 Bend up the setting and solder all four corners. Drill a hole in each end for threading the bead wire.
3 Solder a small ring on a length of wire, then thread all the beads on the wire.
4 Thread the wire through the holes in the setting. Bend over the bottom end of the wire to prevent the beads from falling off. To set the stones, first ease the metal between the stones with round-nose pliers; work from both sides so that the beads are set centrally. Warm setter's cement on the end of a cement stick, support the work in the cement, and allow the cement to set (see page 99). Push the metal around the beads with a pusher; use a rocking action to push the metal against a bead. Then rock the pusher over the top edge of the metal to push it firmly onto the bead. Work all the way around all the beads. Gradually the metal will be pushed firmly against them. Chip away the setter's cement with a spitstick and remove the piece. Turn it over and repeat the setting process on the other side before removing the work from the cement. Dissolve any excess cement in wood alcohol. Wash thoroughly. Sandpaper away setting marks and polish.

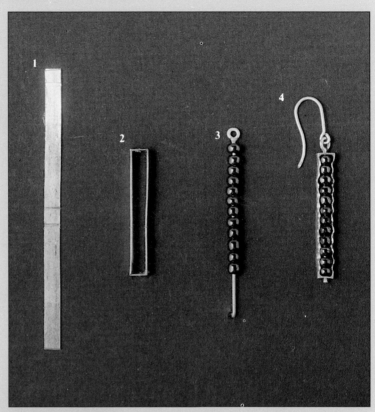

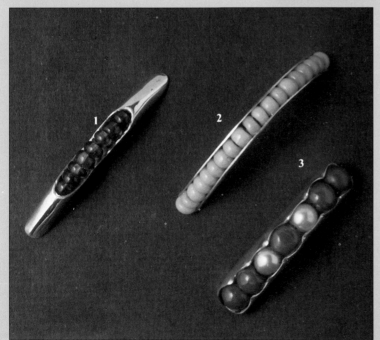

Other setting variations

1 A section of metal is filed from chenier to reveal decorative beads around the inside. The beads are threaded to keep them in place.
2 In this variation, the gap in the chenier is left wide enough for the beads to be seen but not so wide that they fall out.

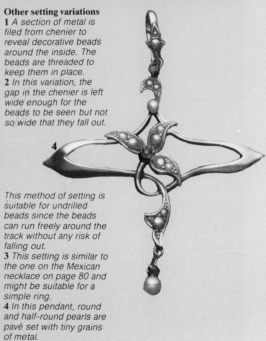

This method of setting is suitable for undrilled beads since the beads can run freely around the track without any risk of falling out.
3 This setting is similar to the one on the Mexican necklace on page 80 and might be suitable for a simple ring.
4 In this pendant, round and half-round pearls are pavé set with tiny grains of metal.

WIRE COLLETS FOR ROUND AND OVAL STONES

Wire collets are suitable for faceted stones but less appropriate for flat-backed stones, such as cabochon cuts, because they display the back of the stone. Diamonds are internally reflective, which means that most of the light coming in through the front of a diamond is refracted (bent) as it enters the stone, and then reflected off the back facets through the front of the stone: this is why diamonds sparkle so much. Consequently, the back of the collet for a brilliant cut diamond does not need light access. However, colored faceted stones do not have this property and are therefore enhanced by using a wire collet to allow light to enter the back of the stone.

TRIANGULAR-WIRE COLLET

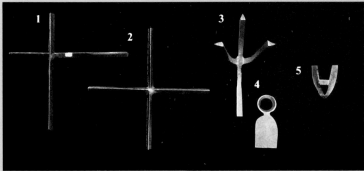

4-WIRE COLLET

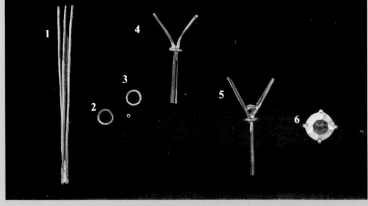

Triangular-wire collet

For a 6mm stone use triangular wire measuring 1.5mm from the base of the triangle to the tip. For the support, use sheet metal 0.7mm thick or a ring of 0.5mm round wire.
1 To make triangular wire, draw round or rectangular wire through a triangular draw plate. Cut off two lengths of wire and notch each in the middle so that they slot into each other when laid in a cross formation.
2 Solder the wires where they cross.
3 Saw the support from sheet metal or construct a support ring so that the support fits just below the girdle of the stone.
4 Bend up the triangular wires to fit the support and solder in the support.
5 Taper the wires towards the base of the collet for a more pleasing shape.
6 Solder the collet to the piece and set the stone; follow the instructions for prong setting on page 84.

4-wire collet

For a 6mm stone, use round wire 0.6mm in diameter for the prongs and 0.4mm for the rings.
1 Arrange four wires in a square formation. It is best to solder these at the tips to preserve the formation.
2 Make a ring to fit tightly over the four wires. Solder it at the point where it touches each wire.
3 Ease the wires apart so that they follow the base lines of the stone. Solder a second ring inside the separated wires to hold them at the correct angle: the ring should rest about halfway between the culet (bottom tip of the stone) and the girdle (outside edge of the stone).
4 Cut the prongs to length and set the stone, follow the instructions for prong setting on page 84.

X-wire collet

For a stone 8mm in diameter, use 0.8mm round wire.

1 *Make the support ring so that when the stone rests in it none of the metal can be seen from above.*

2 *Make a second, smaller ring. This should rest around the inside edge of the first ring.*

3 *Bend an X-wire.*

4 *File grooves in a cross on the end of a steel rod. Use it to punch the centre of the X-wire, so that both arms are pushed into the same plane for soldering.*

5 *Position the large ring over the 'X' and solder the four touching points.*

6 *Invert the piece and solder the small ring to the other side of the 'X': the X-wire is now sandwiched between the two rings.*

7 *Cut off the section of wire that links the two pairs of prongs. Make a small saw nick in the prong wires at the point* where they meet the large ring. This is to ensure that bending is tight and accurate. Bend the prongs upright and squeeze them tight against the ring with chain-nose pliers. Solder the upright prongs to the ring. If possible, use only hard solder up to this stage.

8 *Solder the collet to the piece of jewelry and then saw out the center cross. It is best to leave this until last to reduce the risk of prongs moving when the collet is soldered to the work.*

9 *Set the stone, following the instructions for prong setting on page 84.*
The wire collets in the brooch (above right) are joined by a series of tiny balls. Wires soldered to the back of the wire collet arrangement pass through holes in the baguette section and are riveted or bent over to hold the two elements in place.

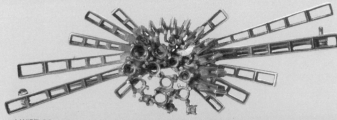

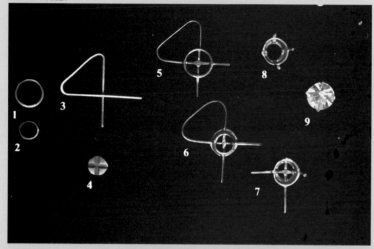

X-WIRE COLLET

Simple sawn setting

Cut prongs from sheet metal. The metal should not be too thin or the prongs will be too weak. The metal for this ring is 1.4mm thick.

1 *Since the whole collet is cut from sheet metal, the sheet must be shaped to allow for the depth of the stone before the collet is cut. Open out a hole with a sloping side, so that the girdle of the stone rests just over the top edge of the hole. This must be done accurately: if too much metal is removed at this stage, there will be insufficient left to push over the stone.*

2 *Mark out all prongs accurately. Each prong should be at least 1mm wide at the top. Saw straight down from the hole on either side of the prong. Then saw out the scallop, sloping the blade while sawing the curve. File away rough marks and make the depths of all scallops equal.*

3 *To set the stone, cut a nick in the end of each prong with a saw* or a spitstick. Ease the metal above the nick upright with a pusher. The stone should drop between the uprights and sit on the parts of each prong below the nicks.

4 *Push the uprights onto the metal as for prong setting (see page 84). Shape the prongs and clean and polish the ring.* Diamonds are set in sawn collets in the Victorian rings (below). Note that at the junction between the stones, one prong supports two stones; the prong is made broader at the top.

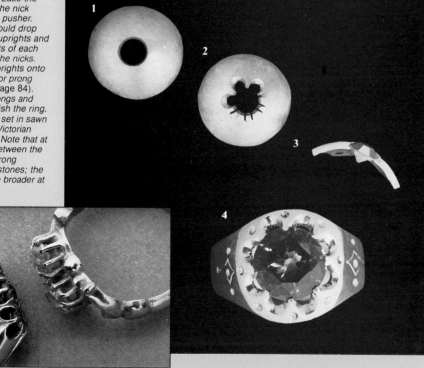

PRONG SETTINGS

The same principles of prong setting apply whether the prongs are made of wire or sawn from sheet metal. The collet is made so that the stone rests halfway across the top of each prong. Setting involves lowering the stone into the collet and making fine adjustments to ensure that the stone is level, then pushing the prongs over the stone. First reduce the thickness of the prongs so that the stone will drop into the collet. If a diamond or other hard stone is being set, small notches can be filed or cut with a flat scorper at the same level in each prong and the stone clicked into place. This method is unsuitable for soft stones, however, as the pressure needed to push them into the notches may chip the girdles. Alternatively, thin the inside of the prong just below the top by cutting away metal by hand with a bullstick, or with a ball burr in a flexible shaft drill. Next, fit the stone.

1 Adjust the thickness of the prongs, if necessary, to ensure that the stone is level.
2 Push prongs upright with a pusher: position the pusher against the prong and just above the girdle of the stone. Since the prong is thinner next to the girdle, the metal should bend there. (If the prong has not been thinned enough, it will bend along its whole length.) The stone should now be secure.
3 Push the prong down onto the stone with the rocking action of the pusher. Place the pusher against the prong and rock it down onto the stone until there is no gap between the stone and the prong.
4 Finally, shape the tops of the prongs with a file or a flat scorper. The most usual prong shapes are thumb nail (D-shaped), spear head (triangular), and pico (round).

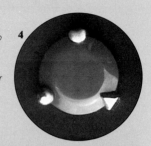

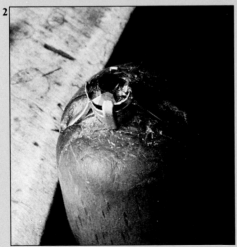

Setting a prong collet
1 Secure the ring in setter's cement. The ring shown here is supported by setter's cement in a ring clamp. Reduce the thickness of the prongs just below the tops with either a bullstick or a ball burr as shown.
2 Hold the stone in place with your thumb nail and, with your other hand, use a pusher to push the prongs against the stone to hold it in place. Then push the prongs firmly onto the stone.

3 Shape the top of the prongs and, finally, polish the piece.

Joel Degen (UK) has devised a way of securing stones in prong settings by using miniature screws or rivets to hold the prongs in place on the ring (above). Experiment with variations of your own.

MARQUISE STONES

Marquise stones are boat-shaped, with a point at each end and are usually faceted like brilliant cut stones. They should be set in collets that protect their fragile points. As with other collets, the height must allow clearance for the base of the stones. Pear-shaped stones have a point at one end and a curve at the other. Collets suitable for marquise stones can easily be adapted for pear-shaped stones. The emeralds in the earrings *(right)* by Robin Kyte are surrounded by marquise stones.

This brooch (below) includes triangular-wire marquise collets and round collets; it shows the heights of the prongs prior to setting. The next stage is to polish the piece. Usually the piece is sent to a professional polisher.

ROUND-WIRE COLLET

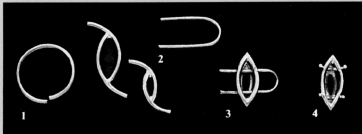

TRIANGULAR-WIRE COLLET

SHEET-METAL COLLET

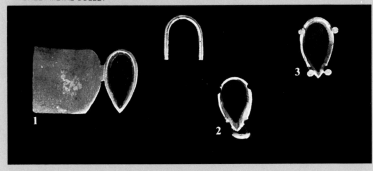

Round-wire collet
For a stone 6mm long, use 0.6mm round wire.
1 *Wind the wire on a round former. Cut off lengths of the wire rings formed and solder them into two marquise shapes, one smaller than the other.*
2 *File up the ends. Bend a U-wire and solder it across the larger marquise shape. Solder the smaller marquise shape to the other side. Cut off the curve of the U-wire.*
3 *Make saw nicks in the prong wires beside the larger marquise shape. Bend up prongs and push against the support; solder in place.*
4 *Solder the collet to the work. Set the stone as for prong setting (page 84).*

Triangular-wire collet
For a stone 6mm long, use triangular wire 1.5mm from base to top, and sheet metal 1mm thick.
1 *Cut off a length of wire and bend into a U-shape. Cut 5mm-long grooves in the ends of the prongs.*
2 *Saw the stone support from the sheet metal. Slope the cuts. Solder in place.*
3 *Taper the triangular wire at the base of the collet. Set the stone: saw a thin wedge of metal from the corner of each collet and ease over the stone.*

Sheet-metal collet
For a 6mm-long stone, use sheet metal 1.4mm thick and wire 0.5mm round.
1 *Saw the stone support from the sheet metal. File the outside upright.*
2 *File notches in the sides.*
3 *Spring the U-wire into the two notches and solder all prongs. Remove the top of the U-wire. Set stone as for prong setting (page 84).*

Collet from a marquise-shaped tube
For a 6mm-long stone, use sheet metal 0.8mm thick.
1 *Cut two strips of metal 8mm wide. Swage to fit the girdle of the stone. File the edges. Solder the join. Saw off a 5mm length of tube.*
2 *Cut out the prongs. File. Saw two slots parallel with the base.*
3 *Wedge two pieces of metal in the ends of the slots and solder. Solder the collet to the work. Set the stone as for the triangular-wire collet.*

RUB-OVER COLLETS FOR FACETED OR CABOCHON STONES

Cabochon stones have flat backs and smooth, curved tops and may be transparent or opaque. Collets for cabochon stones usually hide the back and edge of the stone, so rub-over collets are suitable. Sometimes designers prefer to frame a faceted stone in metal, rather than have it surrounded by a series of points.

Making chenier (tube) for chenier collets

1 The wall of the collet should be thick enough to provide both a bearer (supporting ledge) and metal to rub over the stone: for a 6mm stone, use metal 1mm thick. To calculate the width of the strip needed, multiply the diameter of the stone by 3½. So, for a stone 6mm in diameter, prepare a strip 21mm wide. File the edges of the strip to ensure that they are straight and parallel. Cut a point on one end of the strip.

2 Make the strip U-shaped by swaging it in a swage block (see page 160).

3 With a hammer, gently tap the edges until they almost meet. Warm the metal, coat the outside with beeswax, then draw the rounded strip down through successively smaller holes in a round draw plate until the chenier is the right size for the stone — that is, the girdle of the stone rests halfway across the wall of the collet. Solder the join.

Making a chenier collet

1 Prepare the tube.
2 Check that the girdle rests halfway across the collet wall.
3 Cut the bearer with a ball stick.
4 Hold the stone in place with a thumb nail and push the metal over at three or four points around the stone. Push the remainder of the metal over the stone.
5 File off the setting marks. Use a spitstick or flat scorper to trim carefully around the edge. Shape the set edge of the collet.

Wall heights for cabochon stones
The collet for a cabochon must be made to suit the height and curvature of the stone. If the collet wall is too deep, too much of the stone will be covered after setting. If the collet wall is not deep enough, the stone will fall out. Shallow curves need low collets; high curves need high collets.

Setting cabochon stones
1 *Ensure that the wall height is sufficient to hold the stone.*
2 *File the outside of the collet wall to a taper.*
3 *Push the metal down onto the stone in the same way as for chenier collets. Bright cut the top edge of the collet with a flat scorper to provide a reflective edge around the stone, or file the edge down and blend it into the collet. There should still be sufficient metal remaining to hold the stone securely.*

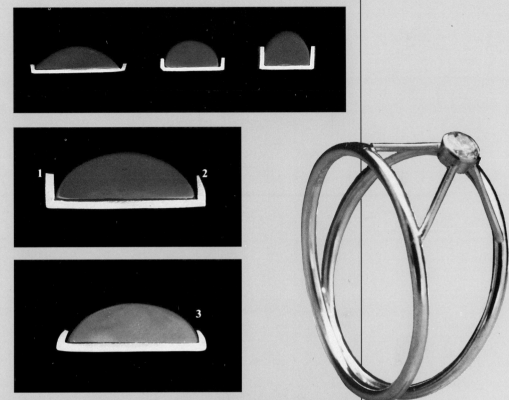

The pear-shaped and oval cabochon rubies (left) are set in 18 k gold rub-over collets. A decorative oval wire surrounds the rub-over collets. The diamond in this gold ring (above) by Graham Fuller (UK) is set in a rub-over collet. The collet is raised from the finger on four wire supports.

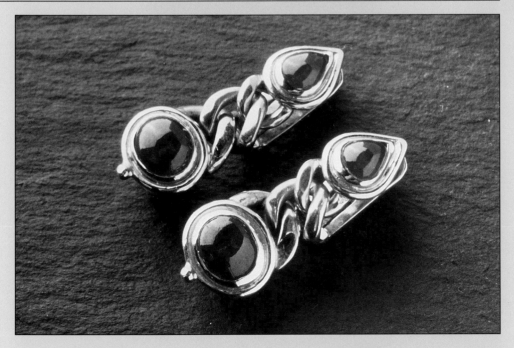

MAKING A RUB-OVER COLLET WITH A TWIST WIRE DECORATION

1 Saw a strip of metal the correct width for the height of the stone: the thickness of the metal can be as much as 0.8mm. Bend the strip to fit the stone exactly, checking the fit frequently.

2 Solder the strip and recheck the fit of the stone. It is often easier to judge the accuracy of the collet from the back.

3 Check that the wall height allows sufficient metal to hold the stone securely when the piece is finished.

4 If the collet is left as it is, the stone will fall out of the back. So make an oval ring from 0.5mm square wire to fit exactly

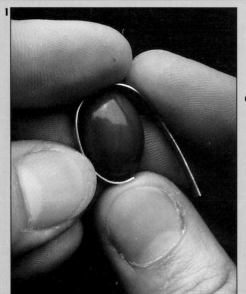

inside the collet. Solder it in place using as little solder as possible. If solder is flooded around the wire edge, the stone will not rest firmly on its ledge.

5 To make the twist wire decoration, clamp two pieces of evenly annealed wire in a vise at one end and in a twist drill at the other. Turn the handle of the twist drill to twist the wire. Keep winding until the required twist is achieved.

6 Make the oval twist wire to fit the outside of the collet. Ensure that there is still access to the setting edge of the collet. If the edge is obstructed, it cannot be pushed over

the stone. Sandpaper the outside of the collet, then solder the twist in place.

7 Solder on the pendant loop. Make sure that the chain or cord chosen will pass through the loop, otherwise a second ring, called a jump ring, will be needed.

8 Secure the collet in setter's cement on a cement stick. Push the cement over the twist to hold the collet in place. When the cement is set, support the stone with the thumb nail and push over the four points as shown.

9 By this stage, the stone should be secure and firm. Working systematically around the stone, push over the remaining metal. Next, clean up the set edge with a spitstick and chip away the cement to remove the set piece. Clean off the cement with wood alcohol. This can damage some soft stones, so test it on the back of the stone first. Sandpaper and polish the piece and thread it on suitable cord.

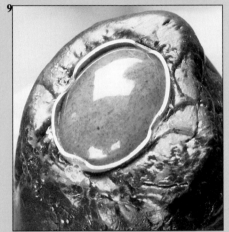

The frosted cabochon stones in rub-over settings (above) are by Selina Preece for Sphinx. If a heavy or chunky edge is required, it is often easier to back-set the stone. Make the front decoration so that the stone will not pass through. Then solder a small collet or low prongs to the back. Push the stone in from behind and push the metal over the back of the stone. The uncut diamonds (left) are held in rub-over settings with a filed prong decoration. This is a very old style of setting, the origin of which is uncertain, but it is possible that the style developed from pinching metal around the stone rather than pushing it over, to take up the slack. Notice that the bottom collets are themselves set in sawn prong collets.

SQUARE AND RECTANGULAR FACETED STONES

Square and rectangular faceted stones are cut either with sharp corners or with cut-off corners. The cut with pointed corners is called an emerald cut while the stone with cut-off corners is known as a trap cut. The collet must provide support and protection in the corners.

Sawn collet for an emerald cut stone

1 To draft the pattern for the collet, first measure the short and long sides of the stone at the girdle. Transfer the short length to a sheet of paper. Decide on the slope of the sides and the height of the collet and draw an end view. Repeat for the long side. Align the short and long sides as shown. Transfer the pattern to metal 1mm thick and cut it out. File a 90° groove along the corners with a square needle file.
2 Bend up the collet and solder the corners.
3 Mark the positions of the prongs, stone and base support. Pierce out the collet. file the stone support bars to a knife edge to make the collet appear lighter.
4 If required, solder on a shank. To set sharp-cornered stones, cut a tiny wedge of metal away from the top corner of each prong. Ease the metal onto the stone from each side of the corner. This is a very delicate operation.

Collet for a large trap cut stone

1 Cut a strip of metal 3mm wide and 1mm thick. With three separate pairs of dividers, measure the length at the girdle of the short side, the cut-off corner, and the long side. Transfer these measurements to the strip of metal, making nicks as shown. Do not cut to the top of the metal. The size of the nick determines the slope of the collet: the wider the nick, the more sloping the collet wall.
2 Bend the strip as shown. File a 60° groove along each cut with a three-square needle file.
3 Carefully bend up the collet and solder each corner.
4 Cut the prongs from metal 1.5mm thick. File a notch in the prong to fit tightly over the cut-off

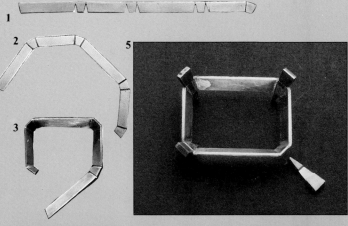

corner of the collet. Adjust the notch so that all prongs slope evenly.
5 Solder the prongs in place. Ideally, the prongs should fit tightly. If they do not, hold them with a twist of binding wire for soldering.
6 To support the collet, saw a base with sloping sides from sheet metal 1.4mm thick.
7 If the stone is for a pendant, solder the four points of the collet prongs to the centers of the cut-off corners of the flat support. If it is for a ring, curve the support to follow the shape of the ring before soldering the collet in place. Set the stone as for prong setting (see page 84).

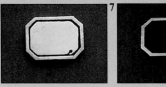

**Non-faceted square
and rectangular stones**
These stones (right) *are
often cut with straight
sides and only a small
bevel at the top edge
over which to push the
metal. If no bevel exists,
the alternatives are to
cover some of the top of
the stone with metal or to
use adhesives. Friction
alone will not hold the
stone because metal and
stone expand and
contract at different rates.
For instance, the stone
might stay in place on a
cold day but fall out on a
hot day.*

**Rub-over collet for a
square stone**
1 *From a strip of metal
1mm thick and as high as
the stone, score (groove)
and bend up a collet to fit
the stone.*
2 *Solder the collet to a
flat base, or solder a
ledge inside, as for the
oval stone collet (see
page 82).*
3 *File away excess metal
and sandpaper the
outside of the collet.*
4 *Drop the stone in the
collet. Ensure that the top
of the collet is level with
the top of the stone.
Begin pushing the metal
along the sides over the
stone. Leave the corners
until last. Push the metal
either side of each
corner, continually
moving closer to the
corner until a small
wedge of metal protrudes
at the corner. File this
away, then push the
metal firmly at each side
of the corner — pushing
onto the top of the corner
may break it off. To finish
the setting, file a bevel
along the set edge.*

*The variously shaped
stones in the antique
brooch* (above) *are held
in place by prongs cut
from the walls of rub-over
settings. In the antique
ring* (left) *the prongs
holding the trap cut stone
have a filed groove to
give an impression of
delicacy.*

GRAIN SETTING

Grain setting involves securing stones with tiny grains raised up from the surface of the metal. It is a style of setting that is frequently used with other types of setting, as in the diamond and sapphire ring *(below)*, which includes grain setting with rub-over setting.

Mounting lines of stones
This unset ring (below), shows the spacing of stone holes needed to allow sufficient metal for raising the grains between the stones. The back view shows how the metal is pierced to allow light behind the central coloured stone and also to allow access for cleaning.

Raising grains
It takes control and a steady hand to raise a grain without cutting it away altogether. This is a technique worth practicing before working on a piece of jewelry. The part of the grain that holds the stone in place is a small bulge of metal, hidden beneath the visible shiny grain. It requires skill to maneuver this bulge over the edge of the stone. To position the stone correctly for raising grains over its edge, it must be dropped below the surface of the metal. Begin by drilling a hole where the stone is to go. Then open the hole with a piercing saw or a burr. The hole should have sloping sides and allow the girdle of the stone to rest on the edge of the hole. Turn the piece over and open out the back hole to allow light and cleaning access to the backs of the stones. Back holes are cut at a more

acute angle than the front holes and are usually round, square, or in a pattern resembling a rope twist. At the front of the work, use the outside curve of a bullstick to cut the bearer (ledge) in the wall of the hole. If you are right-handed, cut in an anti-clockwise direction. With setter's wax, lift the stone and position it in the hole; it should rest on the ledge with about 0.5mm of metal above the girdle. The stone must not wobble but should rest firmly on the bearer and tightly against the wall of the opening. Adjust the bearer until the stone fits correctly. To raise a grain, dig a half-round scorper into the metal about 1mm from the edge of the hole and push downward. A

bulge of metal should be pushed ahead of the scorper and over the edge of the stone. Do not push forward: this is likely to cut out the grain completely. Next, put the scorper back into the cut just made and turn it to the left. Then return the scorper to the original cut and turn it to the right. This cuts free the back of the grain so that the grain can be shaped into a tiny ball. Only the top decorative section is cut. The bulge holding the stone in place is firmly attached to the main body of metal. To make the top of the grain smooth and shiny, take a grain tool matched to the size of the grain and roll it on top of the point of metal.

Lines of stones
Stones are often grain set in straight lines, as in the diamond and sapphire stickpin (below), or in curved lines. Usually the aim is to position the stones so that their girdles almost touch. The size of the stones and the tightness of the arrangement determine the number of grains that can be raised between stones. Four standard patterns of grains are shown here (right).

1 *This is the most secure pattern of grains. The stones are adjusted in the metal so that their girdles are almost touching and there is no metal between the stones at that point. Four grains are raised over each stone to hold it in place. Then a grain is raised each side of the adjacent girdles so that it holds both stones. The grains form a pattern of threes in each triangle of metal.*
2 *If the stones are*

positioned farther apart, a large grain is raised in the blank area of metal between them. The grains form a pattern of five grains between

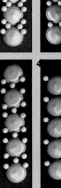

the stones.
3 *If very tiny stones are set in a line, there is little room for grains. So only two grains are raised between adjacent stones, each grain holding both stones.*
4 *Some antique pieces have only a pair of grains to hold each stone. This does not make a very secure setting.*

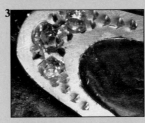

Pavé mounting and setting

The unset brooch (right) shows the arrangement and spacing of holes when an area is to be covered in stones. Each hole has been opened to fit a particular stone. Notice the sloping sides of the holes — these are opened with a piercing saw or a burr in a flexible shaft drill. The back holes are also opened to allow access for light and cleaning. To set these stones, three grains must be raised in each triangle of metal between them.

Thread cutting

After the grains have been raised, all unnecessary metal is chipped away with a spitstick, leaving the grains separate. To finish off the edge of the line or area of setting, a beveled edge called a thread is cut with a flat scorper; the back of the scorper is kept polished so that the cut is bright and shiny. Cutting the beveled edge is called thread cutting. The metal lines between the areas of stones on the thread cut leaf (below) are also thread cut.

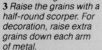

GRAIN SETTING A PIERCED PENDANT

1 Pierce out the pendant shape. Mark the positions for the stones, drill holes in the center of each stone position, then open out the holes with a piercing saw or a burr. Fix the piece in setter's cement.

2 With a bullstick, cut the bearer for each stone. Adjust the bearer until the stones can drop far enough into the holes for the grains to be raised over their edges.

3 Raise the grains with a half-round scorper. For decoration, raise extra grains down each arm of metal.

4 Chip away excess metal with a spitstick and cut the thread with a flat scorper. Run a milligrain wheel along the knife edge of the thread.

5 Ball the grains with a grain tool.

6 The finished pendant is set with diamonds, a central peridot, and a suspended amethyst.

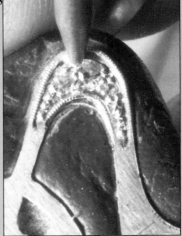

BAGUETTE STONES

The word 'baguette' describes the cut of the stone *(far right)*. Baguettes are always rectangular and usually small: a common size is 4mm x 2mm. Like the garnets and spinels *(right)*, they are also usually transparent. Baguettes can be mounted singly or in blocks. They are normally chosen for geometric shapes and straight lines, or to add blocks of color or some sparkle to a piece. "Calibres" are baguettes cut to curves. When setting a baguette stone, make sure that the metal holds the stone firmly. The setting must prevent horizontal movement, so the stone will not wobble, and vertical movement, so the stone will not fall out.

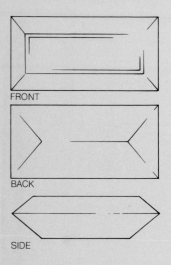

FRONT

BACK

SIDE

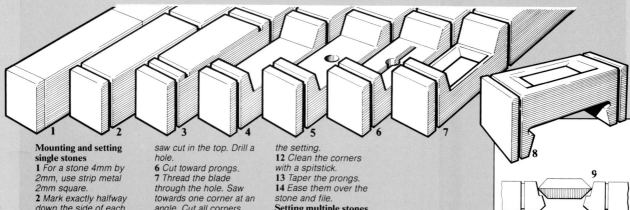

Mounting and setting single stones
1 For a stone 4mm by 2mm, use strip metal 2mm square.
2 Mark exactly halfway down the side of each strip. The length required is 4mm for the stone and 1mm for each prong, a total of 6mm.
3 Mark four 6mm lengths with dividers.
4 Deepen with a saw.
5 Mark 1mm over each

saw cut in the top. Drill a hole.
6 Cut toward prongs.
7 Thread the blade through the hole. Saw towards one corner at an angle. Cut all corners, then remove the rest of the metal by using a saw blade like a file.
8 Turn over and open the back hole.
9, 10, 11 Reduce the prongs with a ball stick so the stone drops into

the setting.
12 Clean the corners with a spitstick.
13 Taper the prongs.
14 Ease them over the stone and file.

Setting multiple stones
Support the piece in setter's cement. With a continuous surround, set the stones as for the single stone setting, or tuck the stone under the wire and set the prong (see page 84).

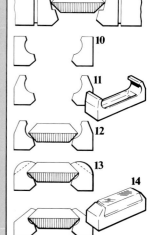

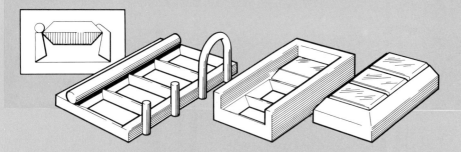

Ring with baguette shoulders

1 *After sawing out a collet, as for the emerald cut stone, saw out the baguette settings from 1.4mm sheet metal. Then make up the finger bezel (shaped support for the bottom of the collets). Solder the sawn collet in the centre. Solder solid end supports made from 1mm-thick metal under the outside edge of each of the two smallest shoulder collets. Solder the shoulders against the sawn collet, as shown.*
2 *Solder square support wires under each corner of the remaining shoulder baguettes. Solder on the shank and file up the outside of the ring.*
3 *Saw out the finger bezel in line with the shoulder collets.*

1

2

3

*The choker is made of silver and the flexible pendant is set with garnets (left). The design was derived from drawings of the distribution of foliage down the trunk of a tree. The arrangement and distribution of the foliage and its effect on the line of the trunk were the important factors in the development of the design. Baguettes were chosen for the piece because they emphasized the pattern quality of the design, rather than the leaf qualities of the tree.
The brooch (below) is made from gold. The top bar is set with diamonds and the falling stones are rubies. The designer was working with the effects of disrupted lines and this piece was one of a series of brooches based on the same theme. The linear quality of the baguettes emphasizes the theme of the design. This geometric style and approach to design is characteristic of work made in the 1970s.*

MAKING A SET OF BAGUETTE RINGS

Each ring contains a single baguette. The rings can be worn singly or in groups.

1 *Cut all the settings required from a single length of metal. Open out the settings using the saw blade as a file.*

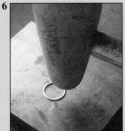

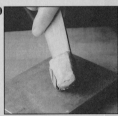

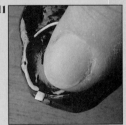

2 *Pick up the stone with some plasticine or setter's wax and check that the stone fits. Saw off the individual settings.*
3 *Wind up the shanks around a round former.*
4 *Slide the shanks to the end of the former and saw them off one at a time.*
5 *Solder the ring, then tap it round on a ring mandrel.*
6 *Tap the ring flat on a steel block.*
7 *Saw through the join in the shank. Ease the ends apart and line up one end with a setting. Solder with easy solder.*
8 *Position the other end of the setting and shank. Solder the join with medium solder.*
9 *To prepare for setting, warm setter's cement in a soft flame.*
10 *Shape the soft cement by rolling it on a steel block.*
11 *Place the ring in the soft cement. With a wet finger, push the soft cement around the ring and under the setting.*
12 *After 5 minutes, when the cement has hardened, prepare the setting as directed and push over the claws. File and shape the setting. Chip the ring from the cement. Remove traces of cement with wood alcohol and polish the ring.*

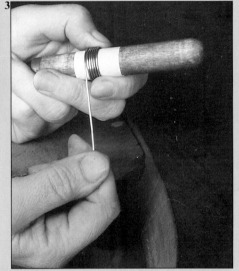

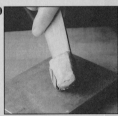

Styles of setting

The main purpose of a setting is to hold the stones in place on a piece of jewelry and, usually, the decorative qualities of the piece are an integral part of its construction. Sometimes, however, it is the style of setting that is the feature.

Gypsy setting

Gypsy-set stones are surrounded by a tight edge of metal, resulting in a very secure and long-lasting setting. Only stones on curved surfaces can be gypsy set, as the setting marks cannot be easily removed from a flat surface without making a shallow depression. The ring shown was cast in cuttlefish; the shape of the ring was carved directly into both halves of the cuttlefish mould.

Roman setting

The Roman setting was traditionally used for seal rings. It has a channel around the outside of the stone that makes the seal appear framed when the ring is pushed into sealing wax. This setting also provides a way of setting a stone into sheet metal without using prongs.

Spectacle-glass setting

This collet provides a tiny frame around the outside of a stone. It is suitable for double cabochon stones and is the type of setting commonly used to hold moonstones. Once the stone is in place, the collet can be closed with a small jump ring.

Illusion setting

Illusion settings enhance the appearance of small stones, making them seem bigger. By cutting facets on the illusion plate with a flat scorper or a square graver, the metal will catch and reflect light, adding to the sparkle of the stone.

Tension setting

Tension setting involves stones being held in place by the tension of the metal. In these luxurious examples, diamonds are held by platinum tension rings designed by Niessing.

GYPSY SETTING

SPECTACLE-GLASS SETTING

ROMAN SETTING

ILLUSION SETTING

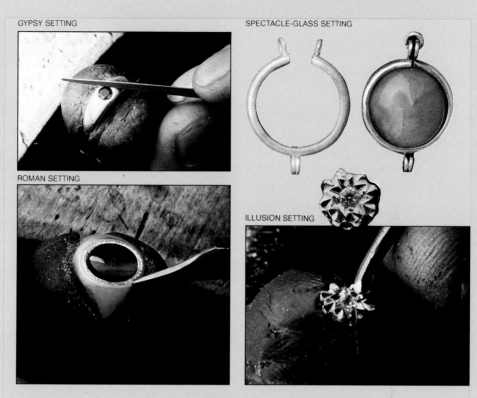

TENSION SETTING

Stones for jewellery
In this table (below), some of the more easily obtainable stones are listed under their most common color category. The hardness of the stones is given as this often determines the way in which they are mounted and set: soft stones are best mounted in a protective setting,

whereas hard stones can be exposed. The hardness of a stone is indicated by its position on Mohs' scale of hardness, which gives comparative hardnesses rather than absolute values. Thus you can see which stones are likely to be accidentally damaged by filing. The file hardness is 6.5.

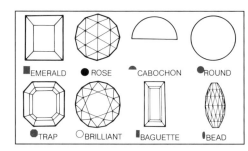

COLOR	STONE	TRANSPARENCY	HARDNESS	USUAL CUT
White	Cubic zirconia	clear	6	
	Diamond	clear	10	
	Moonstone	translucent	6	
	Pearl	pearlized	2.5 — 3.5	
	Rock crystal (Quartz)	clear	7	
	Spinel	clear	8	
	Zircon	clear	7.5	
Red	Cornelian	translucent	7	
	Garnet	transparent	6.5 — 7.5	
	Ruby (Corundum)	transparent	9	
Pink	Coral	opaque	3.5	
	Rhodochrosite	opaque	4	
	Rhodonite	opaque	5 — 6	
	Rose quartz	translucent	7	
	Tourmaline	transparent	7 — 7.5	
Purple	Amethyst (Quartz)	transparent	7	
Blue	Aquamarine	transparent	7.5 — 8	
	Fluospar (Blue John)	opaque	4	
	Lapis lazuli	opaque	6	
	Sapphire (Corundum)	transparent	9	
	Turquoise	opaque	6	
Green	Alexandrite	transparent	8.5	
	Aventurine (Quartz)	opaque	7	
	Emerald (Beryl)	transparent	7.5 — 8	
	Jade	translucent	6.5 — 7	
	Malachite	opaque	3.5	
	Nephrite	translucent	6 — 6.5	
	Peridot	transparent	6.5 — 7	
	Tourmaline	transparent	7 — 7.5	
Yellow	Amber	opaque	2 — 2.5	
	Chrysoberyl	transparent	8.5	
	Citrine (Quartz)	transparent	7	
	Jasper (Quartz)	opaque	7	
	Tiger's eye (Quartz)	opaque	7	
	Topaz	transparent	8	
Brown	Agate (Quartz)	opaque	7	
	Smoky quartz	transparent	7	
Black	Haematite	opaque	5.5 — 6	
	Jet	opaque	3.5	
	Onyx (Quartz)	opaque	7	
Grey	Agate (Quartz)	opaque	7	
	Labradorite	opaque	6.5	
	Marcasite (pyrites)	opaque	6 — 6.5	
Multi-colored	Bloodstone	opaque	7	
	Opal	translucent	5 — 6.5	

Tools and materials for mounting and setting stones

Setter's cement and cement stick *The best means of support is a cement stick, a wooden handle with the top covered with setter's cement. The cement is made from shellac and plaster of Paris.*

Setter's block *For a flat piece, secure in setter's cement on a setter's block.*

Ring clamp *Hold the piece in a ring clamp while you work on the mount.*

Scorpers *The gravers used for carving metal are also used for setting stones. The sizes given in brackets are the ones most likely to be used for both carving and setting.*

Bullstick — 17, (19), 21 A bullstick is a scorper used for cutting a bearer (ledge) on which the stone rests.

Half-round — 2, 4, (6) A half-round scorper is used for raising grains of metal in pavé setting.

Flat — 10, (14), 18 A flat scorper is used for cutting a thread — the bright, decorative edge around some stones.

Spitstick — 6, (10), 14 A spitstick is used for cleaning away excess metal, usually after grain setting.

Pusher *A pusher is used to push metal over a stone. It is made of copper or soft steel to reduce the risk of damaging stones.*

Grain tools *Rolling the correct size grain tool on the top of raised grains smooths and rounds them.*

Grain tool sharpener *A grain tool sharpener consists of a line of ball-ended, hard steel cones, each corresponding in size to one of the grain tools.*

Milligrain wheel *A milligrain wheel is a small, decorated wheel that leaves a trail of tiny balls when rolled along a sharp edge of metal.*

Setter's wax *Setters use wax to enable them to pick up small stones easily.*

SETTER'S CEMENT

MILLIGRAIN WHEEL

SETTER'S WAX

GRAIN TOOL
SHARPENER

SETTER'S BLOCK

PUSHERS

CEMENT STICK

SET OF GRAIN TOOLS
AND HANDLE

SCORPERS

CEMENT STICK

RING CLAMP

Filed safety catch
1 *File a groove in 3mm square wire, leaving a cube.*
2 *Round off the corners of the cube and drill a hole 1.2mm in diameter.*
3 *Draw down chenier with a wall thickness of 0.4mm to fit through the hole.*
4 *Solder on a thumb piece.*
5 *Saw the slot and solder the hook to the brooch. Ease the catch open. Insert the chenier and push the metal back to grip it. Move the thumb piece to the back. Saw the gap for the pin. The general rule is: thumb piece back — catch open; thumb piece forward — catch closed.*

CATCHES AND CLIPS

Catches and clips are the devices that keep jewelry in place. Many are now mass produced, and the general term describing these and other manufactured components for jewelry is "findings." Bullion dealers and tool suppliers sell a variety of findings. However, standard fittings are not always appropriate, and individual catches or clips sometimes need to be made by hand. Once the mechanical principles of a catch are understood, it is easy to adapt its operation and appearance to suit any piece.

Joints, pins and catches for brooches

There are many types of brooch joints, pins and catches, but they are usually attached to the brooch in a standard way. With the brooch face down on the bench and the top farthest away from you, the hinged joint is positioned on the right, and the catch on the left with its opening facing the bottom of the brooch. This arrangement is a result of the now outmoded fashion for wearing a brooch on the left shoulder. It was found easier to attach the brooch with the pin pointing outward; the catch opening faced downward so that the weight of the brooch kept the pin in the catch. Brooches are now worn anywhere on the clothing, but the conventional arrangement of fittings has survived and it is useful to know this if older brooches are to be renovated or repaired.

The joint is held together with a rivet. The rivet is inserted from the top so that it is less likely to fall out if it becomes loose. The joint, pin and catch should be attached to the upper part of the brooch; if they are too low, the brooch will tend to droop forward when it is being worn.

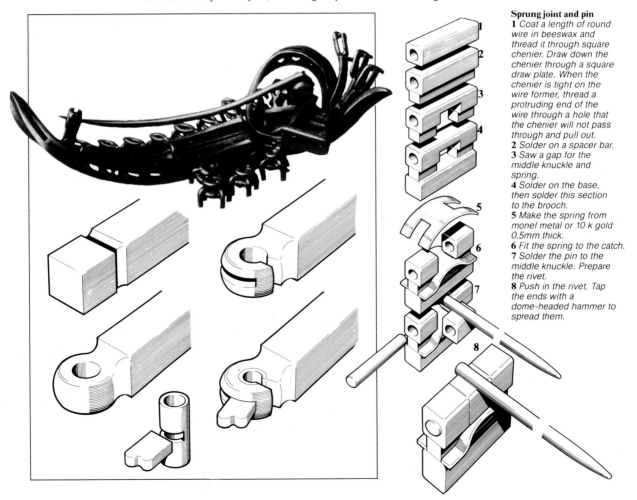

Sprung joint and pin
1 *Coat a length of round wire in beeswax and thread it through square chenier. Draw down the chenier through a square draw plate. When the chenier is tight on the wire former, thread a protruding end of the wire through a hole that the chenier will not pass through and pull out.*
2 *Solder on a spacer bar.*
3 *Saw a gap for the middle knuckle and spring.*
4 *Solder on the base, then solder this section to the brooch.*
5 *Make the spring from monel metal or 10 k gold 0.5mm thick.*
6 *Fit the spring to the catch.*
7 *Solder the pin to the middle knuckle. Prepare the rivet.*
8 *Push in the rivet. Tap the ends with a dome-headed hammer to spread them.*

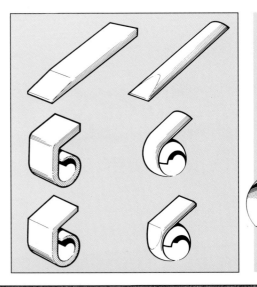

Simple catch

Bend a piece of rectangular or D-section wire into the shape shown (left). The tight curl should prevent the pin from falling out. File the base flat so that the catch can stand by itself, ready for soldering onto a brooch.

D-wire safety catch

1 Bend a catch in D-section wire.
2 Saw a slot for the thumb piece. Solder the hook to the brooch.
3 Fit the chenier through the catch hook.
4 Solder the thumb piece to the chenier.
5 Ease open the catch to insert the chenier. With the thumb piece at the back, saw out the gap in the chenier. Move the thumb piece to the front to close the catch.

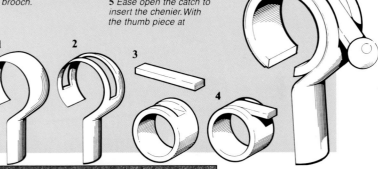

This antique brooch (left) has a simple catch: the pin is held in the top of the catch by the spring action of the pin against the joint. Note the decorative tapering of the chenier in the hinge. The safety chain is attached to the main body of the brooch by a small jump ring, and the chain is held to the clothing by a safety pin, bent from a single length of wire.

X-wire safety catch

1 *Solder a simple catch to the brooch.*
2 *Solder a length of chenier 3mm to 4mm from the catch.*
3 *Blow a hard flame directly onto the boraxed tip of a length of wire to melt a small ball on the tip. Thread the wire through the chenier.*
4 *Melt a ball on the other end of the wire and bend the wire ends into an X-shape.*
5 *Adjust the X-wire so that when the pin is in the catch the pin is pushed to the top by the spring of the X-wire. The spring also keeps the X-wire in place.*

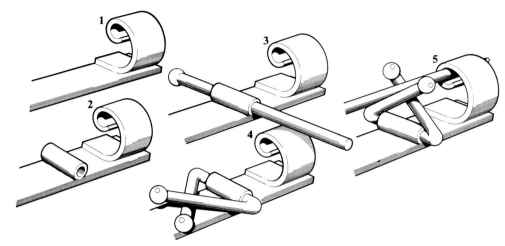

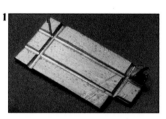

Double-pin spring clip

1 *Score a sheet of metal.*
2 *Bend up and solder the box. With a round needle file, groove the ends of the box to take the chenier; this is called "gapping."*
3 *Saw a gap in the chenier along the join. Solder in the chenier.*
4 *Saw out the bridge and solder the box to the brooch.*
5 *Make a spring from monel metal or 10 k gold 0.5mm thick. The length of the spring when flat should be no longer than the inside of the box.*
6 *Cut a length of chenier to fit the gap. Solder the double pin to one side and the spring operating wire to the other.*
7 *Clear out the holes with a broach to make a slightly tapered hole. File a taper on a rivet wire and push the rivet firmly into place. Saw off the rivet, leaving no more than 0.5mm at each end. Spread each end of the rivet.*

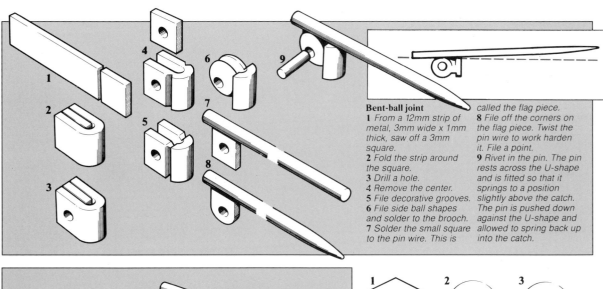

Bent-ball joint
1 From a 12mm strip of metal, 3mm wide x 1mm thick, saw off a 3mm square.
2 Fold the strip around the square.
3 Drill a hole.
4 Remove the center.
5 File decorative grooves.
6 File side ball shapes and solder to the brooch.
7 Solder the small square to the pin wire. This is called the flag piece.
8 File off the corners on the flag piece. Twist the pin wire to work harden it. File a point.
9 Rivet in the pin. The pin rests across the U-shape and is fitted so that it springs to a position slightly above the catch. The pin is pushed down against the U-shape and allowed to spring back up into the catch.

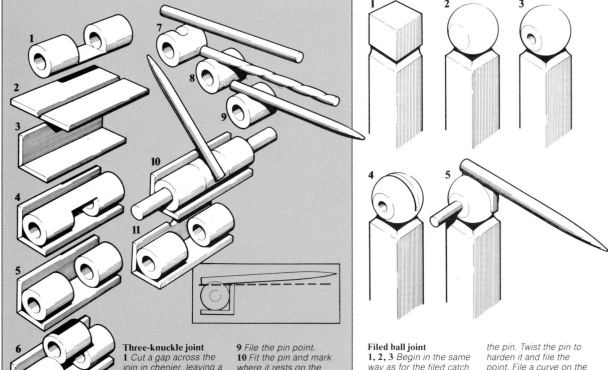

Three-knuckle joint
1 Cut a gap across the join in chenier, leaving a bridge.
2 File a 90° groove.
3 Bend and solder.
4 Solder in the chenier.
5 Saw out the bridge; solder to the brooch.
6 Fit the center knuckle.
7 Groove the knuckle.
8 Solder the pin and twist to harden it.
9 File the pin point.
10 Fit the pin and mark where it rests on the front plate.
11 File a groove until the height of the pin is just above the catch. Push the pin against the front plate and spring it up into the catch.

Filed ball joint
1, 2, 3 Begin in the same way as for the filed catch on page 100: the filed ball joint and catch are a matched pair.
4 Cut a slot straight across the top and extending to below the drilled hole. Solder to the brooch.
5 Solder a flag piece to the pin. Twist the pin to harden it and file the point. File a curve on the back of the flag piece only. Leave the front square — this forms a stop for the pin to spring against. Insert the flag piece in the slot and drill a hole. Clear the hole with a broach and rivet in the pin.

Catches for necklaces

Snaps, safety catches, or hooks and eyes are all suitable for joining necklaces. With a hook and eye catch, the weight of the necklace should keep the catch closed.

Since very few women now have maids to dress them, the intricate catches used on some old necklaces are no longer popular. Such catches were never intended to be opened and closed without assistance.

Snaps for bangles and bracelets

The snap for a wrist decoration must be particularly strong and often the bangle or bracelet will include a safety catch and safety chain. The "gravity" hooks and eyes used on necklaces are unsuitable as the movement of the arm would soon dislodge the hook. The skill in making snaps for bracelets and bangles lies in the jeweler's ability to integrate the snap mechanism into the design of the piece.

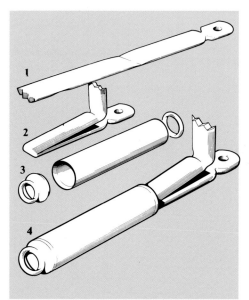

Barrel snap
1 Mark the middle of a length of D-wire, 3cm x 2.5mm, with a saw.
2 Form a shallow V-shape at the saw cut to facilitate bending the metal. File a groove for the catch ring and drill a hole in the end of the D-wire. Continue the groove over the top part of the wire and bend up the thumb piece.
3 Draw down chenier for the barrel. Allow 0.5mm to 1mm clearance around the double D-wire. Make a ring of 1mm round wire that fits tightly around the double D-wire and solder to one end of the barrel. Solder another ring to the other end to attach to the necklace.
4 Push the snap home; it should click. Adjust the depth of the grooves if the snap is not positive.

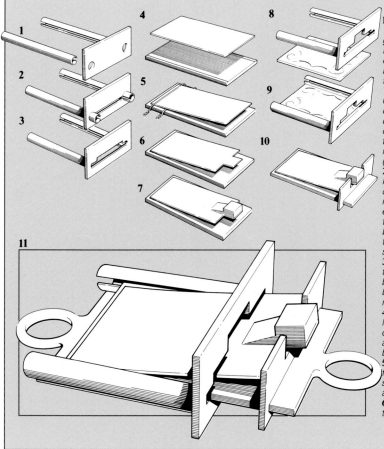

Runner snap
1 With a spitstick or graver, cut along the join in chenier so that the edge of the lower snap blade will be able to run freely along the groove. The lower blade can be 0.8mm thick and the other measurements depend on the dimensions of the rest of the piece. Drill two holes in a plate 1mm thick (called the face plate).
2 Cut two suitable lengths from the grooved chenier and solder them in the holes with the ends protruding through the face plate. Saw a slot between the two holes so that the lower blade just slides through.
3 From metal 0.6mm thick, make the upper blade so that it fits between the two chenier runners.
4 Solder the upper and lower blades together at one end. Hold the blades at an angle with a twist of binding wire.
5 Enlarge the slot in the face plate to take the two snap blades when they are pushed together.
6 Cut back the front of the upper blade where

the thumb piece will be fitted.
7 Shape the thumb piece and solder it in place.
8 Enlarge the slot in the face plate to accommodate the thumb piece: the snap should now work. The upper blade should spring up behind the two corners of the face plate either side of the gap for the thumb piece. If this does not happen, increase the height of the slot for the thumb piece.
9 Solder a decorated base plate beneath the runners. This protects the runners and keeps them in place.
10 To stop the snap blades sliding too far, solder a stop plate onto the bottom blade.
11 This snap mechanism is rarely used on its own; it is usually concealed behind decoration or inside a hollow. This is the type of mechanism found in better quality jewelry: it has a positive action and should run smoothly for the life of the piece. The runners prevent wobble in the blade and this reduces the risk of wear.

1
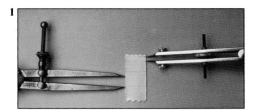

2

3

4

5

Box snap
1 *Set two pairs of dividers, one to the width and the other to the height of the box. Mark the width and the height twice side by side on the metal.*
2 *File 90° grooves along the marks with a square needle file to make a line on the back of the metal.*
3 *Break off the excess metal at each end.*
4 *Fold up the box and solder all corners. Solder square wire across the top to keep the snap shut.*
5 *Solder on the end plate and attachment loops.*
6 *Taper mill a strip of metal to a thickness of 0.6mm at one end and 0.8mm at the other.*
7 *Mark the middle of the strip and file a shallow groove. Then bend the strip in half. Saw the shoulders for the thumb*

piece and fold it over. Drill the holes.
8 *Push the snap home and adjust the gap in the top square wire until the snap operates positively.*

6

7

8

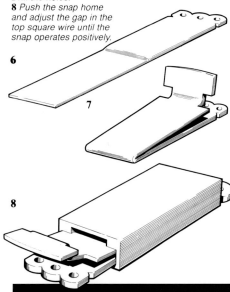

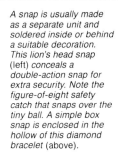

A snap is usually made as a separate unit and soldered inside or behind a suitable decoration. This lion's head snap (left) conceals a double-action snap for extra security. Note the figure-of-eight safety catch that snaps over the tiny ball. A simple box snap is enclosed in the hollow of this diamond bracelet (above).

Fittings for cuff links

The guideline for these fittings is to make sure to allow easy insertion and removal of the link from the cuff. A chain joining the front and back of the cuff link should be long enough to enable the two parts to lie flat beside each other when the cuff link is on the bench. The chain usually comprises five links to ensure adequate flexibility and sufficient strength. A cuff link swivel fitting should be designed to allow for complete straightening so that it may pass easily through the cuff hole.

Ring guards

People with large finger-joints frequently have trouble wearing rings. If the ring is big enough to fit over the finger-joint, it is often too loose on the finger. As a result, the ring tends to slip around, so that the decoration or stone is no longer displayed. The ring may also feel uncomfortable when it is too loose for the finger. To counter this problem, make a small spring clip that allows the ring to slide over the finger-joint but then springs against the finger to hold the ring still. Alternatively, reshape the band (shank) that encircles the finger to prevent easy slippage, or solder locating lugs to the shank. Locating lugs are small balls, usually three, hidden inside the ring shank to help prevent movement.

Ear fittings

Earrings are attached by a post through a pierced hole in the ear, a clip or clamp gripping the ear or even a hook over the ear. As in the case of brooches, the earring will face downward instead of forward if the fittings are positioned too low. Correctly positioned clips or posts will ensure that the design is properly displayed and that the earring is comfortable to wear.

Ring guards
The spring clip helps secure a ring made big enough to fit over a large finger joint (below). The three balls (bottom) prevent a ring with a large stone from swivelling on the finger.

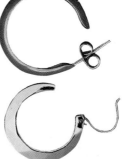

Spring back for a cuff link
There are many different shapes of spring back but the principle for making all of them is similar. A square wire is sandwiched against a spring so that it is stable only when the spring is pushing directly against a side of the square wire. These cuff link findings (right) are usually sold with the box containing the spring unfitted. Do not fit the box until the support has been soldered to the decoration, as heat will destroy the spring. Rivet the box in place when all filing and sandpapering is completed.

Swivel back for a cuff link
Saw out the hole in the support bar. Then thread the back attachment through the hole and solder it in place on the back of the cuff link (right).

Chain back for a cuff link
Note the positions of the rings on the back of the cuff link (right). This orientation of the rings helps to keep the cuff link in the correct position on the cuff.

Butterfly spring clips for posts
*1 To make the spring clip that holds the post in place, first cut a boat shape from sheet metal: it should be about 18mm long and 0.5mm thick.
2 Dome the centre of the shape and drill a hole. The dome helps to guide the post into the hole.
3 Roll up the ends with round-nose pliers.
4 The scrolls should spring against the post.*

Findings for earrings
A large number of commercially produced findings are available in both silver and various standards of gold. It is clear from the shapes shown how each can be made. Most jewelers prefer to purchase findings rather than spend time making them. However, if you need a non-standard finding, you will have to make it yourself.

1

2

3

4

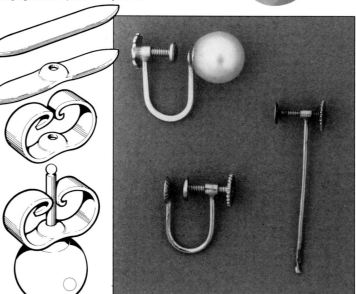

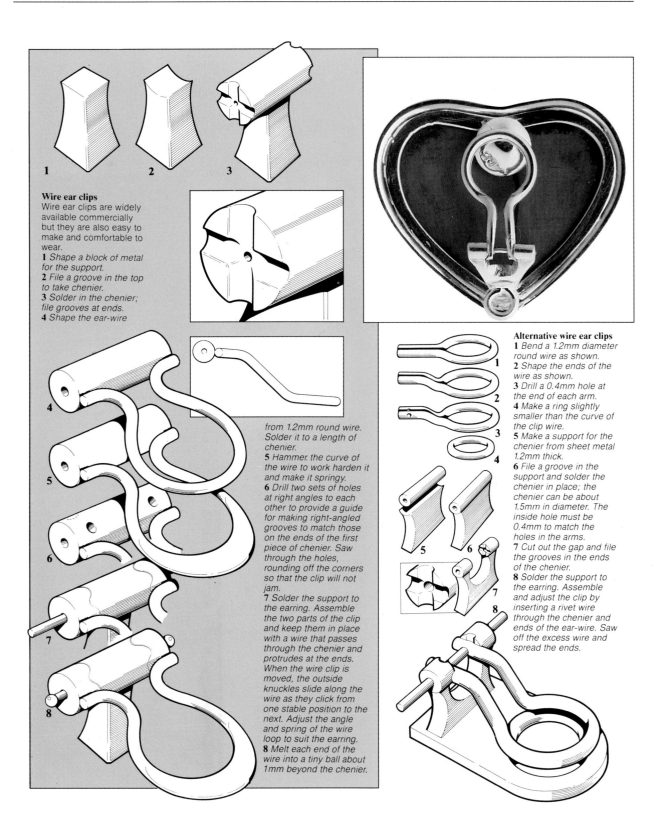

Wire ear clips

Wire ear clips are widely available commercially but they are also easy to make and comfortable to wear.
1 Shape a block of metal for the support.
2 File a groove in the top to take chenier.
3 Solder in the chenier; file grooves at ends.
4 Shape the ear-wire from 1.2mm round wire. Solder it to a length of chenier.
5 Hammer the curve of the wire to work harden it and make it springy.
6 Drill two sets of holes at right angles to each other to provide a guide for making right-angled grooves to match those on the ends of the first piece of chenier. Saw through the holes, rounding off the corners so that the clip will not jam.
7 Solder the support to the earring. Assemble the two parts of the clip and keep them in place with a wire that passes through the chenier and protrudes at the ends. When the wire clip is moved, the outside knuckles slide along the wire as they click from one stable position to the next. Adjust the angle and spring of the wire loop to suit the earring.
8 Melt each end of the wire into a tiny ball about 1mm beyond the chenier.

Alternative wire ear clips
1 Bend a 1.2mm diameter round wire as shown.
2 Shape the ends of the wire as shown.
3 Drill a 0.4mm hole at the end of each arm.
4 Make a ring slightly smaller than the curve of the clip wire.
5 Make a support for the chenier from sheet metal 1.2mm thick.
6 File a groove in the support and solder the chenier in place; the chenier can be about 1.5mm in diameter. The inside hole must be 0.4mm to match the holes in the arms.
7 Cut out the gap and file the grooves in the ends of the chenier.
8 Solder the support to the earring. Assemble and adjust the clip by inserting a rivet wire through the chenier and ends of the ear-wire. Saw off the excess wire and spread the ends.

ENAMELING

Enamel is a form of glass, and enameling is the process of fusing it to metal under heat. In jewelry, the technique is used for decorative purposes. The colors of enamel can be vivid or pastel, the surface shiny or mat, the glass opaque or transparent.

The oldest surviving examples of enamel are from the Mycenaean period, dating from 1400 BC. In this work, blue glass is fused into depressions in gold ornaments. Some earlier Egyptian jewelry has the appearance of enamel work, achieved by cutting the glass to shape and gluing it into strip metal frames.

During the period 1100 BC to 800 BC, enamel was used mainly to decorate lower quality pieces. The high quality jewelry of the aristocracy was inlaid with stones, usually garnets. But the art of enameling continued, developing in a variety of ways. Thus, whereas early Mycenaean jewelers enameled punched depressions in metal, the Celts enameled flat recessed areas cut into the metal surface, a process now known as champlevé enameling *(see page 112)*.

In Western Europe, as garnet became more scarce, enamel was frequently used to fill the cloisons (enclosures) that previously would have held stones. This technique, called cloisonné enamelling *(see page 115)*, advanced rapidly at this time. Its development coincided with an improvement in the status of enamel and, by *circa* AD 800, enamel was regarded as a desirable form of decoration even in high quality pieces.

In the 1200s, the technique called basse-taille *(see page 112)* evolved from the champlevé process. Instead of a flat recess, engraved and carved depressions were filled with transparent enamel. The enamel appeared lighter in shallow areas than deep areas, thus producing a shaded image.

In Paris during the 1300s, a new technique evolved from cloisonné enameling. The base plate was left off the work so that the cloisons filled with enamel resembled stained glass. This technique became known as plique-a-jour enameling *(see page 115)*.

During the 1400s in Limoges, some jewelers became highly skilled at painted enamel work. By the 1500s, a particular painting process called grisaille had been developed. This technique involves firing successive layers of white enamel onto dark

The range of colors and finishes obtainable in enameling is so large that most jewelers find it easy to develop an individual style. Experiment with colors, transparent and opaque enamels, and mat and glazed finishes to establish your own unique approach.
1 Earrings by Alison Richards.
2 In this necklace catch, Sarah Letts has combined enamel with diamonds.
3 Champlevé enamel pendant by Setsu Sato.
4 This flower ornament by Deborah Idiens is approximately 15cm long and stands in a miniature vase. It is one of Deborah's early experiments with enameling. New enamelers can achieve good results if their work is clean and accurate and the enameler is careful with all firings.
5 Pins by Siglinde Brennan.
6 Painted enamel by Jeanette Blake.

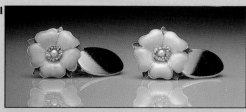

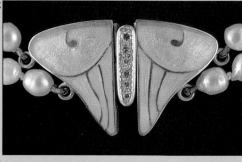

5

6

enamel; a tonal picture is built up as each layer merges into the background with each successive firing.

Basic enameling techniques

Metal is enameled by depositing on it a thin layer of enamel powder and then firing the piece in a kiln until the enamel melts and fuses with the metal. Fine (22 k) gold (916 parts per 1000), 18 k gold (750), fine silver (999) and Britannia silver (958) are most suited to enameling. Sterling silver (925) and copper can also be used, although it is inclined to affect some colors. To prevent this occurring, use a transparent enamel called flux for the first firing. Gilding metal and brass, although occasionally used by specialists, are not recommended for use by beginners. These metals can be fired only a few times, which makes them unsuitable for some enameling techniques, and there is also a high risk of the enamel becoming contaminated.

As enamel and metal contract at different rates on cooling, the metal may distort if it is not thick enough, or the enamel may crack and spring off. To begin with, it is wise to use metal at least 1.5mm thick. As your enameling skills improve, reduce the thickness of the metal and try counter enameling — the technique of enameling the back of the article as well as the front. On cooling, the forces exerted on the metal by the enamel on the front are counteracted by similar forces on the back, and the risk of the metal becoming distorted is greatly reduced. The shape of the metal may reduce its tendency to distort: a domed shape is less likely to distort than a flat one.

Articles joined with ordinary solder cannot then be enameled: the solder will melt before the enamel reaches the required temperature, and the solder will contaminate the enamel, causing discoloration. You should use special enameling solder, which has a high melting temperature, for any joining prior to enameling. However, even this will melt during enameling unless great care is taken, so it is better to begin by designing pieces that do not require soldering. One way of avoiding the problem is to set enameled pieces in jewelry as if they were stones.

Before the enameling process is carried out, the metal must be thoroughly cleaned and sufficient enamel prepared for use.

Cleaning the metal

Enamel may become discolored or flake off if applied to dirty metal. So eliminate all traces of grease, oxide or other contamination: anneal the metal either in the kiln or with a blow torch to de-grease it; pickle the metal to remove oxide and, under running water, brush away all traces of pickle with a glass brush. Information on annealing and pickling is given on pages 31, 33 and 34. Once the metal is clean, do not touch the area to be enameled with your fingers; handle the metal with tweezers or a palette knife to avoid damaging your skin.

Preparing the enamel

Enamel is purchased in powder form or, occasionally, in glassy nuggets. Prepare only enough enamel for the work in hand as it deteriorates unless kept absolutely air-free, and may give unpredictable color changes when fired.

If you purchase the enamel in nugget form, sandwich the nuggets between sheets of paper and hammer them until they are the size of granulated sugar grains. Then grind smaller in the same way as powdered enamel (see below).

To prepare powdered enamel, grind it underwater with a pestle and mortar until all grains are like fine sand; this should take about one minute. Besides breaking down any larger grains, this process also frees contaminants from the surface of the enamel particles. Pour off the water carefully, leaving the enamel in the mortar. Then remove all traces of dirt by rinsing the enamel with clean water; swill the water and enamel around in the mortar, allow the enamel to settle for a few seconds, and then carefully pour off the water. At this stage, the water will be cloudy. Continue rinsing the enamel until the water is clear. This could take 10 to 12 rinses.

Empty the washed enamel onto a clean ceramic painting palette or a saucer, leaving a layer of water on the enamel. Cover it immediately with a sheet of paper to prevent contamination by dust or other airborne particles. Dry the enamel near the warm kiln or under a lamp when it is needed.

Applying the enamel

There are two main ways of applying enamel to metal: dusting and wet-laying. Dusting with dry enamel powder is suitable for large areas requiring a single color. Wet-laying with damp enamel powder is appropriate for most other styles of enameling.

Before dusting, spray the area to be enameled with a weak solution of gum tragacanth; drugstores sell small plastic spray bottles suitable for applying the solution. If the spray clogs, the solution needs further dilution. When spraying is completed, place the powdered enamel in a fine sieve, such as a tea strainer, and gently tap the sieve over the metal. Place a clean sheet of paper under the metal to catch stray powder.

To prevent the powder building up around the edges or adhering to the back of the work, lay the piece on a steel trivet or washer so that all the edges are clear of the paper. Work from the edges to the center of the metal until a thin layer of powder has been deposited evenly over the whole surface. Tip off any loose powder, but check that the whole surface remains evenly covered. Unevenly distributed enamel may retract during firing to expose bare metal.

To wet-lay enamel, transfer the enamel powder to a ceramic painting palette and moisten it with distilled water. Then load the powder onto the metal, spreading the grains evenly and thinly over the surface with a quill. A quill is better than a pen or sable-haired brush as it will not contaminate the enamel. Moreover, the end can be shaped as required, using a scalpel. For most purposes, a pen-nib shape will be suitable.

The enamel is not wet enough if it sticks to the quill, and too wet if it falls off in lumps. Tap the edge of the metal with your finger to encourage the enamel to settle and any air bubbles to rise. Then carefully draw off the surface water by touching the edge of the enamel with the corner of a paper tissue.

Firing equipment

After applying the enamel to the metal, the work is ready to be transferred to the kiln. First place it on a support, so that it will not stick to the base of the kiln during firing. Various specialized stainless steel trivets and racks are available for supporting enameling work, but a piece of steel mesh is suitable for most purposes.

A firing fork is used to handle the support for the work when it is moved to or from the kiln. The fork has a long handle and two prongs and, for stability, the mesh firing

One of the most important conditions for successful enameling is cleanliness. Accurate and repeatable results are easier to achieve if the work area is orderly and the enamels clearly identified and stored in airtight containers. A clear view of the work being fired is essential, so, ideally, the position of the kiln should allow the enameler to watch the work without the discomfort of stooping or stretching.

Always test enamel colours before firing them on the jewelry. To minimize the risks of color variation, use the same supplier once you have decided on the colors that suit your work.

Tools and materials

Kiln
Mesh supports
Kiln fork
Mortar and pestle
Sable brush or quill for
  loading enamel
Glass brush
Dilute sulfuric acid for
  cleaning
Pumice or
  carborundum stone
Painter's ceramic palette
  dishes for washed
  enamel
Powder enamel

Champleve project:
  carving tools
  piercing saw and
  blades
  files
  cleaning and
  polishing equipment
  silver, gold or copper
  sheet 4cm x 4cm x
  1.5mm

Plique-à-jour project:
  small pliers
  soldering equipment
  wire cutters
  or
  piercing saw and
  blades
  gold wire 0.5mm
  round (each petal
  requires
  approximately 1cm)
  hard gold solder

support should be bent to fit closely, but not tightly, over the prongs.

The kiln consists of a chamber heated by gas or electricity. The chamber size required depends on the scale of the work undertaken. High quality enameling work requires a kiln that reaches a temperature of about 1832°F so that the enameling process can be carried out rapidly. It is useful to have a pyrometer to measure the temperature of the kiln if advanced work is to be tackled.

Most kilns used in small workshops allow air to circulate underneath to reduce the possibility of overheating the work-bench, but it is still a good idea to stand the kiln on a heat-proof board. It is also useful to have a steel sheet or block on which to place the work after it has been removed from the kiln.

Firing the enamel

Take a palette knife, and carefully transfer the enamel-loaded metal to the firing support. Make sure that there is no stray enamel around the edges or on the back of the piece. Then, using the firing fork, place the support and piece near the warm kiln to dry off any moisture. If any water is allowed to remain, it will boil during firing, and the steam will lift the enamel.

After drying, put the work and support in the hot kiln, using the firing fork. Watch the enamel carefully. It will darken, then begin to reticulate, and within a minute the surface will become pitted like orange peel. Remove the work immediately. Place on a steel plate or block and allow to cool.

Next, remove the metal oxide: hold the piece under running water and scratch off the oxide with a glass brush. If the oxide cannot be removed, pickle the piece and wash it again. Re-load the piece with a thin layer of enamel and fire as before, until it has reached the "orange peel" stage. Cool, and wash again; pickle only if necessary.

Load a third thin layer of enamel. This time, fire the piece beyond the "orange peel" stage until the enamel is seen to level out and the surface becomes glazed. The shiny finish obtained in this way is described as fire-glazed. Finally, cool, pickle and wash the piece.

Alternative finishes

To achieve a flatter and more evenly glazed finish, abrade the enamel surface with a pumice stone lubricated with plenty of water; this process is called stoning. Scrub the work under running water with a glass brush, and rinse in distilled water. Dry the piece, then re-fire. Cool, pickle and clean the piece, and then polish it with fine pumice powder and water mixed to the consistency of thin cream; toothpaste can also be used. This can be done by hand, with a suede or felt buff stick, or by a polishing machine, using a felt buff at the relatively slow speed of 900-1200rpm. A mat surface is achieved by abrading, using a Scotch stone. However, once this has been done, the enamel should not be re-fired, as it is impossible to clean all the residue from the surface of the enamel, and re-firing may result in discoloration. A mat surface is not suitable for transparent enamels as it destroys the transparent qualities.

Styles of enameling

Six of the main enameling techniques are described in detail below. They are champlevé and basse-taille, cloisonné and plique-à-jour, Limoges and grisaille.

Champlevé and basse-taille

In both champlevé and basse-taille enameling, the enamel fills depressions in the metal surface. In champlevé, however, the base of the depression is flat, and the cell filled with any color, whereas in basse-taille the base is decorated with a low relief design, and the cell filled only with transparent colors, resulting in a subtle shaded effect. The depressions can be etched, carved, stamped, chased, or made by soldering a pierced sheet to a flat base. They should not be more than 0.5mm deep; thick enamel is always liable to crack.

If a pierced sheet is to be soldered to a flat base, the metal should be soldered only with enameling-grade solder. Work cleanly and accurately, using the minimum of solder; excess solder is liable to discolor the enamel. Borax the back of the pierced sheet. Distribute pallions of enameling solder

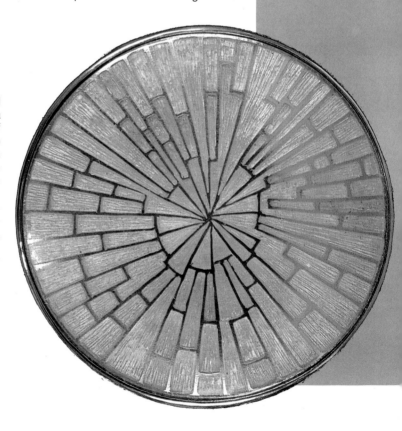

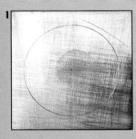

1 *Scribe a circle. Engrave the outline with a half-round graver. Carve circle to a depth of no more than 0.5mm with a flat graver.*

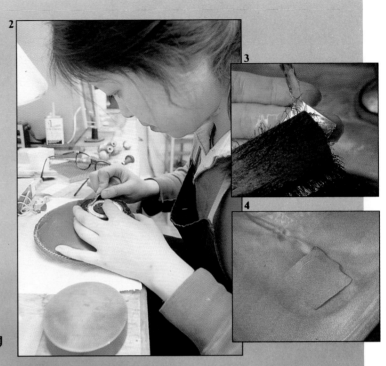

2 *Check that the depth is even by pushing plasticine into the depression. To prevent the enamel from cracking, spread the hole with a spitstick to make a smooth curve. Texture the base.*

3 *Scrub the piece thoroughly with detergent. Wash in running water.*

4 *To clean and key the surface, swiftly dip the piece in a solution of 3 parts concentrated nitric acid to 1 part water. Before mixing acid, read the warning on page 31.*

5 *Grind the enamel under water.*

6 *Swirl clean water over the enamel. Allow the enamel to settle. Pour the cloudy water off carefully, leaving the enamel in the bowl. Rewash until the water is completely clear after swirling.*

7 *Lay a thin coat of wet enamel grains in the carved circle.*

8 *Touch the edge of the enamel with a tissue to draw off excess water.*

9 *Place the piece on a gauze support. Carry it to the kiln with a firing fork. With the door of the kiln open, hold the piece outside the kiln to dry off the enamel. Wait until it stops steaming. Place the gauze and the work in the kiln. Remove the fork and close the door. Watch through the view hole: the enamel will darken, then begin to glaze over. Remove it immediately. The surface should be dimpled like orange peel.*

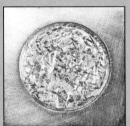

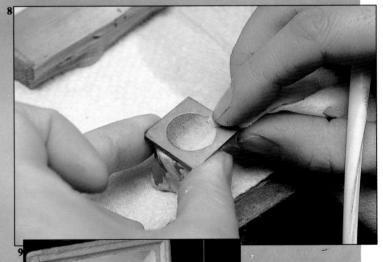

10 *If nitric acid was not used to etch away the surface copper, black oxide may have formed. Scrub it away with a glass brush and wash under running water.*
11 *Reload with a second thin layer of enamel.*
12 *Refire to 'orange peel'.*
13 *If necessary, reclean with the glass brush and running water.*

14 *Reload with enamel.*
15 *Refire for the third time; allow the enamel to pass the orange peel stage. Watch the work carefully through the view hole. The enamel should soon glow red and appear smooth and shiny. As soon as the surface glazes, remove the work. Stand it on an adjacent steel plate to cool. Do not cool too rapidly as the enamel may crack.*
16 *When the piece is completely cool, clean it in dilute sulfuric acid pickle (1 part acid to 10 parts water). Then wash it thoroughly under running water.*

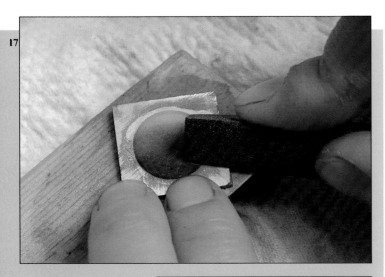

every 4mm to 5mm across the whole surface. Then heat the pierced sheet until the solder begins to melt; remove the heat before the solder starts to flow. Borax the backing sheet and secure it with binding wire or cotter, or split, pins behind the pre-soldered pierced sheet. Reheat the surface until the solder flows. Make sure that the bright line of flowing solder runs around all the edges, so that no gaps remain.

After creating the depression, you may need to finish off the edges with a carving tool. Ideally, the sides of the cell should be curved: sharp corners are liable to create points of tension and may cause the enamel to crack. For basse-taille, the distance between the high and low points need not be more than 0.2mm. Very deep areas simply appear dark and the subtleties of the base decoration are lost. A useful way to check the evenness of the base for champleve, or the definition of the low relief for basse-taille, is to push a lump of plasticine into the cell. The shaped plasticine is easier to judge than metal. Wet-lay the enamel into the depressions in three successive thin layers, as explained earlier (*see page 112*).

Both styles of enameling look better if they are abraded or stoned , fired and polished in such a way that the surfaces of the metal and enamel are level. Fire glazing is inclined to leave a slight hollow in the enamel, but this suits some designs.

17 Many styles of enamel look better if the enamel and metal surfaces are even. To achieve this, rub the surface with a carborundum stone or a pumice stone, which can be purchased from a drugstore. Pumice takes longer, but washes out more easily.

18 Scrub under running water with a glass brush to remove all traces of abrasive residue. Any stone left in the surface of the enamel will cause defects. Refire the piece until the mat enamel surface glazes over.

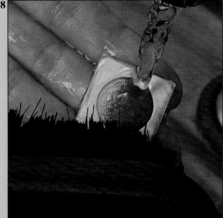

19 Polish the enamel with a little fine pumice powder mixed with water to the consistency of thick cream. Load a felt pad with the slurry and rub the piece on the pad. Alternatively, polish the piece on a slowly rotating felt lap buff.
Drill small holes in the corners of the piece and attach a cord or chain.

Cloisonné and plique-à-jour

For both these techniques, small, wire "fences" are used to enclose colored areas of enamel. Cloisonné work has a metal back behind the enamel, while plique-à-jour pieces are open-backed. In plique-à-jour work, transparent enamels give the appearance of stained glass. In modern plique-à-jour work, pierced sheet is sometimes used instead of wires.

Cloisonné wires The wires used in cloisonné work may be made of copper, silver, or gold. They should be 0.2mm to 0.3mm thick, and 1.5mm to 1.8mm deep. Round wire 0.4mm in diameter can be rolled down to approximately these dimensions.

Cloisonné wire must be annealed before use as, otherwise, it tends to move when fired for enameling. Avoid the danger of melting the thin wire during annealing by first coiling it or binding it in bundles. Then, place

the wire in a steel tin, cover with charcoal chips, and heat with a blow torch or in the kiln. When the tin becomes red hot on the outside, remove from the heat and allow to cool. The wire will now be annealed and should be pickled and washed.

The wires in cloisonné work stand on edge to form the cloisons, or cells. Cut the wires with jeweler's shears or side cutters, and bend them with appropriately shaped pliers to fit the lines in the design. Unsupported straight wires will not stand alone, so ensure that each wire either bends, or is held in place by wires supporting it at each side. When preparing the wires, it helps to cover a sheet of clear acetate with double-sided sticky tape and lay it over the design. You can then temporarily stick the wires down to check their shape.

Cloisonné enameling Enameling flux is a clear, transparent enamel. It is used in cloisonné work to secure the wires to the base plate. Prepare the flux and metal, and then fire one thin layer of flux over the metal base. Brush with a glass brush to remove oxide and then wash it. Dip the bottom edges of the cloisonné wires into a weak solution of

Cloisonné enamel can be recognized by the fine metal lines that surround each patch of colour. It is a technique often seen in Chinese enamel work, such as the Chinese cloisonné enamel pendant (right). The cloisonné pieces (above and left) are by Phil Barnes (UK).

gum tragacanth, and position them one by one on the fluxed base plate. Dry off the gum, then fire the plate and wires until the flux just adheres to the base of the wires. You will see it start to creep up the wires. Cool, pickle and wash the piece.

Working from the middle to the edge, successively wet-lay and fire three thin, even layers of enamel. The cells do not have to be filled to the top, and protruding wires can be stoned.

The finishing of cloisonné enamel depends on the effect required. Protruding cloisons and concave enamel areas are characteristic of work from Russia and Scandinavia. In other areas, wires and enamel are usually stoned to an even, flat surface, fired and then polished.

Plique-à-jour enclosures For plique-à-jour enameling, the cells for the enamel must be joined in advance, so construct the design in wire or pierce it from sheet. If using wire, solder only with enameling-grade solder. This is a particularly skilled task as the thin wires are liable to melt at the high temperature needed to melt the solder. For this reason, beginners are advised to pierce

1 Bend up each petal.
2 Use tweezers or very fine round-nose pliers to avoid marking the metal.
3 Solder the ends of each individual petal.
4 Solder units together *with enameling or hard solder. Experienced enamelers usually fire with easy solder, but it is not advisable for beginners. Use as little solder as possible as*

MAKING A PLIQUE-A-JOUR EAR STUD

The secret of successful plique-à-jour enameling is to ensure that the enamel is very thin and that it is held in place securely. The thin, round wires used in this project ensure that thin enamel is all that is necessary and the round cross-section acts as a keying device. Georgina Follett (UK) specializes in plique-à-jour work. The delicate, transparent shapes *(above)* are strong, despite their fragile appearance.

1

2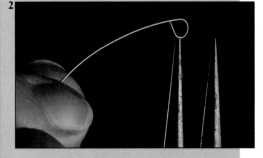

3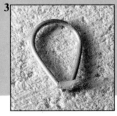

designs in sheet metal for their first attempts at plique-à-jour work.

Plique-à-jour enamel adheres best in holes without sharp corners and of less than 5mm diameter. Again, thin enamel is less likely to crack than thick, so, whether using wire or sheet, limit the thickness to 0.5mm.

Plique-à-jour enameling Transparent enamels are most suitable for plique-à-jour work. To effect a high quality transparency, grind lump enamel into particles about 0.3mm in diameter (similar to fine sand in size) before use.

The enamel can be fired with or without a backing sheet. If firing without a backing sheet, prepare mesh trays or special stainless steel firing supports to suspend the piece either vertically or horizontally. All areas to be enameled should be clear of obstruction. Suspend wet enamel into each cell and fire the piece immediately. The firing of wet enamel does not lift the enamel because the steam escapes from each side of the cell. Clean and wash the piece. Refill any cells that remain too thin, or have pulled back from the metal, and re-fire, making sure to vary the approach to prevent the flow from being all in one direction. The piece can then be stoned, fired and polished if required.

Various materials are used as backing sheets for plique-à-jour enameling. The most suitable material for beginners is platinum foil, because it suits all designs and is easy to use: thick platinum foil is expensive, but much easier to peel from the piece after firing. Cut the foil to extend all around the piece to be enameled, and stick the foil to the back of the metal with weak gum tragacanth solution. Then wet-lay and fire three thin layers of enamel as in conventional cloisonné work. The first layers must be fired until the surface looks like granulated sugar, and until the cells are full. Glaze once filled. After the third firing, peel the platinum foil from the back, and stone, fire and polish the piece.

Limoges and grisaille

Limoges is a general term used to refer to painted enamel work, and grisaille is the particular skill of monochrome painting. In both cases, a picture is painted directly onto an enamel background with special painting enamels.

Preparing painting enamels First place the painting enamel on a ground glass sheet and grind with a flat-based ground glass rod; other grinding implements may contaminate

In jewelry, the technique of enamel painting is usually used for pictorial images but, in this enameled buckle (right), the painting technique has been used to decorate the surface with a pattern of flowers. When painting with enamels, begin with the strongest color: if light colors are used first, they tend to fade into the background with successive firings. Painters often find this approach difficult to adopt and you may prefer to start by painting patterns which are not dependent on precise tonal relationships.

excess may spoil the enamel. The piece should not be filed after soldering.
5 Solder all units together. Solder a small loop or eye on the back and a ball on the front. All soldering must be completed before enameling.

4

7
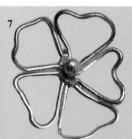

6,7 Carefully shape the petals with pliers.
8 Pack the petals with prepared wet enamel for the first firing. Suspend the piece by its back loop from a wire across a piece of gauze and put the piece straight into the kiln. Remove it as soon as the enamel crystallizes.

5

6
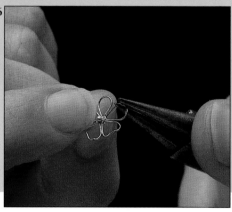

8
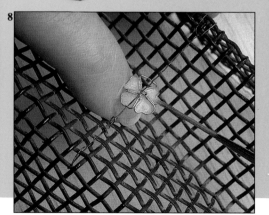

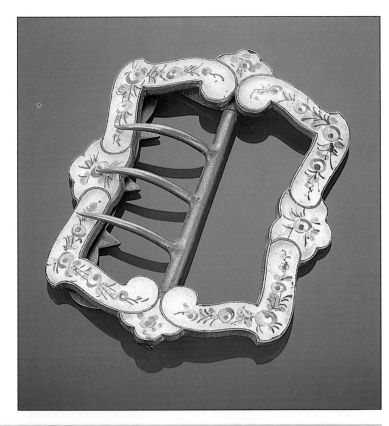

the enamel. Grind a small amount of the enamel powder with the supplier's painting medium until the mixture is smooth and creamy and no grains of enamel remain. With a palette knife, transfer the cream to a ceramic painting palette and cover until required. It is necessary, however, to prepare fresh enamels each day as they deteriorate soon after mixing, and may give poor colors; some colors, notably reds, deteriorate much more quickly than others.

Limoges enameling Miniature painting in enamel is a refinement of the original Limoges style. Enamel the background with three thin layers of white enamel, stone the surface flat, wash and then re-fire. Then, either take a brush and draw the design directly onto the white background with one of the strongest colors chosen for the painting, or trace and transfer the outline with a tracing material. In both cases, the outlines will fade during firing.

Choose a sable hair brush of a size that suits the scale of the painting and the subject matter. Begin painting the background with thin, even coats of enamel. Dry, and fire the enamel until it glazes. Then, remove it immediately and cool the metal. Clean the oxide from the edges with a glass brush.

Continue to build up the picture, firing as necessary to set the painted areas. Overpainting tends to dull colors, so plan the painting carefully and finish with the foreground subject and the sharpest details. Do not be discouraged if the result is less than perfect. It takes time to understand the reactions of different colors and to discover the best enameling technique to suit your style of painting.

Grisaille enameling Fire the background with three thin layers of black or transparent dark blue enamel, abrade the surface and re-fire. Then prepare white grisaille enamel paint with the supplier's painting medium. Apply the paint with a sable hair brush: well-thinned paint will fade into the background, while thicker paint will remain as defined lines. Begin by creating the shadows and shaded areas and gradually build up the design, firing to set the paint as necessary. Finish the piece by painting with highlights. Between firings do not clean the piece in acid, but stone the metal edges to ensure that no oxide.contaminates the enamel.

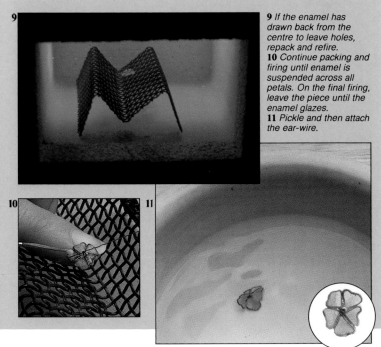

9 *If the enamel has drawn back from the centre to leave holes, repack and refire.*
10 *Continue packing and firing until enamel is suspended across all petals. On the final firing, leave the piece until the enamel glazes.*
11 *Pickle and then attach the ear-wire.*

COLORING METALS

The traditional way of introducing color into jewelry is to include stones or enamel in the piece, or to align metals of different natural colors side by side; for example, yellow gold beside white gold. Jewelers have also used chemicals to color metals; for example, it has been found that silver can easily be darkened using a sulfur compound. But what has attracted the greatest attention, from both the wearers and makers of jewelry, has been the impressive range of colors that can be produced on some of the refractory metals and on aluminum.

The refractory metals

Niobium, tantalum, titanium and zirconium all belong to the group of high-melting-point materials known as refractory metals. Jewelers in Britain pioneered experimental work in coloring these metals during the 1960s. The colors seen result from a coating of oxide over the surface of the metal. The metal appears colored because the oxide coating, which is transparent, causes interference in the light rays reflected from the metal. A similar effect can be seen in the rainbow colors on soap bubbles or floating oil on water.

The illusion of color perceived by the eye is determined by the thickness of the oxide layer, and researchers have investigated methods of controlling the oxide thickness in order to predetermine the color obtained. Possible colors range through yellow, golden-brown, purple, maroon, blue, green and grey, and remain permanent, provided that the oxide film remains unbroken; scratching the surface changes the color.

Because different surfaces reflect light in different ways, the surface finish of the metal also affects the color: a polished surface and a mat surface both anodized at the same voltage will appear to be different in color. The surface finishing of refractory metals follows the same procedure as the finishing of other metals used in jewelry. Experiment to find the most suitable surface for the coloring effect intended, making test pieces to color at first.

With regard to titanium, the most intense colors are produced on an etched surface. The chemicals for etching titanium are too dangerous to use at home, so purchase the titanium already etched.

Titanium
This easily colored metal is difficult to shape, so tends to be used in flat form. Since it cannot be soldered, jewelers set it in frames, in a similar way to stones, or rivet pieces together. The titanium jewelry (below and bottom) *is by Brian Eburah (UK).*

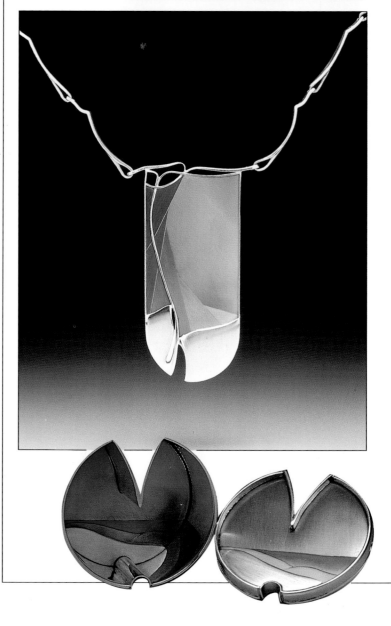

Niobium

In the three brooches (above left), *Alan Craxford (UK) used colors to highlight the engraved lines. The work (right) of Clarissa Mitchell (UK) shows the control jewelers now have when coloring niobium by anodizing, and the niobium pendant (below) by Pauline Gainsbury (UK) reveals the rich colors you can achieve with niobium. In the brooch (bottom), Kathy Morrell (UK) has used silver with niobium.*

Black Silver

The carved, blackened silver brooch (above far right), by Alan Craxford (UK), like those above left, is from his series of "Mandala" brooches. Daphne Krinos (UK) has combined blackened silver with 18 k gold and moonstones (far right).

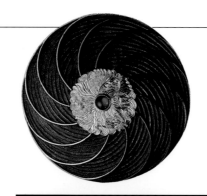

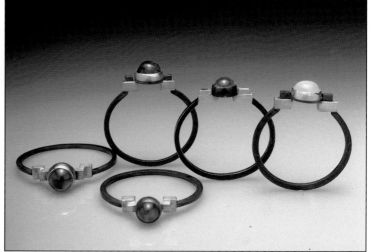

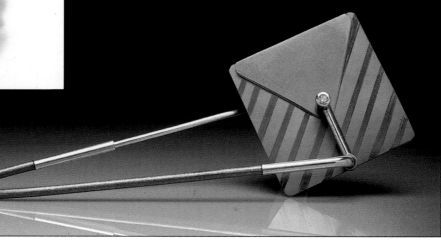

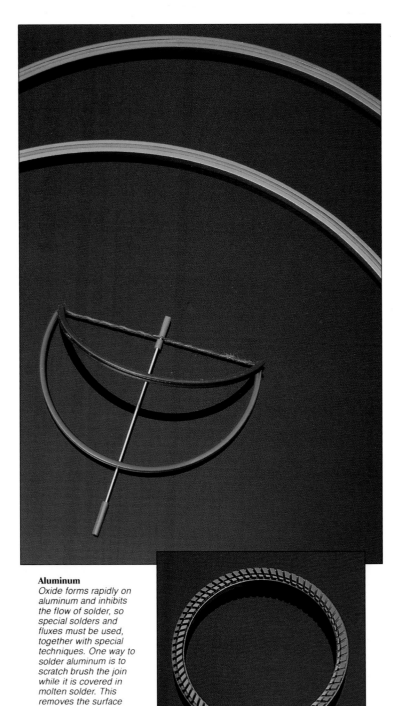

Aluminum
Oxide forms rapidly on aluminum and inhibits the flow of solder, so special solders and fluxes must be used, together with special techniques. One way to solder aluminum is to scratch brush the join while it is covered in molten solder. This removes the surface oxide and allows the solder to join the metal. The anodized aluminum neckpiece and brooches (right and above) are by Eric Spiller (UK).

Coloring by heating

Heating titanium in a kiln or with a blow torch causes oxidation and, hence, coloration. But it is difficult to control the amount of heat supplied, so producing just the right thickness of oxide in order to obtain a particular color is no easy task. However, some jewelers have become quite skilled in this technique, which has the advantage of requiring no specialist equipment. Beware of overheating titanium, as this produces murky colors.

Niobium, tantalum and zirconium are not successfully colored by heating and should be colored by anodizing.

Coloring by anodizing

The most successful process for the controlled deposit of oxide on refractory metals is anodizing. Anodizing is an electrochemical process: a direct current flows from the anode to the cathode through a conducting solution, known as the electrolyte. A solution of 10 per cent ammonium sulfate gives good results, but other solutions can be substituted.

The piece to be colored is attached to the anode and either immersed in the solution, or brushed with it. If the immersion technique is used, the most suitable cathode to use is platinized titanium mesh. If you intend brushing the solution, the cathode is the metal part of the paintbrush. Immersion of the piece produces even colors, and the brush technique is most suitable for patchy coloring or painted effects.

The voltage used determines the thickness of the oxide deposit and hence the apparent color obtained. Once the oxide has reached the thickness commensurate with the voltage being used, it stabilizes at that thickness. When using this process to obtain more than one color, begin with colors produced by subjecting the metal to the highest voltage, masking out other areas. Then, reduce the voltage and re-anodize the metal to obtain the color commensurate with the second highest voltage, and so on. High voltage colors are not affected by the application of lower voltages.

Different refractory metals color differently at the same voltage, so combining metals may lead to unusual or highly interesting effects.

Coloring controls
The project on pages 124 and 125 demonstrates the anodizing process. For greater control over the distribution of colors, try the following:
1 Begin with high voltage colors. Cover other areas with stopping-out varnish — nail polish is commonly used and works well. Remove some of the varnish (acetone removes nail polish), lower the voltage and induce the next color. Higher voltage colors are unaffected by exposure at lower voltages.
2 Stop-out with clear adhesive plastic sheet. Cut through the plastic for the first color and remove progressively more plastic for the next color.
3 To achieve a fading of color, gradually withdraw the piece while altering the voltage. WARNING: This technique is dangerous unless rubber gloves are worn.

2

1

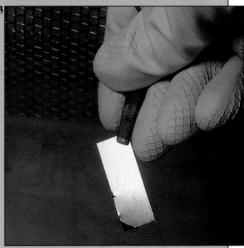

3

SAFETY IN ANODIZING

The equipment and chemicals used for anodizing are dangerous. Under no circumstances should this process be attempted at home unless a clean, dry work area is available. There should be no access to the anodizing facilities for children or animals. Several jewelers who have specialized in this work will anodize on commission, so send work out for coloring if you are unable to set up equipment safely at home.

Coloring aluminum

Aluminum is colored by a combination of anodizing and dyeing. The anodizing produces a porous film of oxide, which is then impregnated with dye and sealed.

The chemicals and equipment are not suitable for home use, but aluminum is anodized for use in industry and many of the anodizing firms will color pieces for jewelers. Each firm has its own dyes, so the shades of color may vary.

Blackening silver

Silver is colored black by using liver of sulfer (potassium sulfide). This is purchased in lump form, and deteriorates rapidly when exposed to light and air, so

The colored aluminum fashion jewelry (below) is by Cliff Grove and Judith Leggett.

remove one lump for use and re-seal the container immediately. There are three methods of using this chemical — as fumes, as a solution with hot water, or mixed with cold water.

The resulting black is soft and easily scratched, so its use is usually confined to the deeper hollows in a piece, which are protected from normal wear. Liver of sulfur produces a more even density on a mat surface than a polished one.

Fume method

Find a tin with a push-fit lid, and punch several small (3mm diameter) holes in the lid. Place a lump of liver of sulfur in the bottom of the tin, and suspend the silver inside on a piece of string. Then, warm the base of the tin. The fumes will color the silver, yellow, then brown, and finally, black. Although the yellows are attractive, they are not permanent and will eventually darken.

Hot water method

Dip a nylon paintbrush in hot water and load the brush with liver of sulfur, in the same way as loading a brush from a block of watercolor paint. Then paint on the cold silver in the places to be darkened. Use only nylon brushes as the chemical attacks natural hair brushes, causing them to fall apart and deposit hairs on the jewelry.

Cold water method

Grind the lump of liver of sulfur to powder, and mix this with a little water. Paint the solution onto the silver with a nylon brush, then warm the metal until it darkens.

COLORING NIOBIUM

A test strip showing possible colors can also be used as an earring.
1 Wash the piece with detergent and water. Clean further with acetone on a cotton bud.
2 With the power off, connect the anode (positive) insulated lead to the test strip with an alligator clip and connect the cathode (negative) insulated lead to the platinized titanium mesh. With the power still off, connect the plugs. Place the cathode and anode in the tank of electrolyte: do not allow the clips to touch the electrolyte.
3 Wear rubber gloves. Turn on the power and slowly increase the voltage. Produce the highest voltage color on the tip of the test piece — the color is produced in about 30 seconds. Then slowly reduce the voltage to zero.
4 Remove and check the strip. Rinse it in distilled water and dry it.
5 Repeat the process, immersing the strip further, and coloring at a lower voltage; the first color is not affected.
6,7,8 Continue until the whole strip is colored.

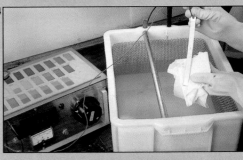

Anodizing equipment
A variable voltage power unit, insulated leads, a cathode, a plastic or glass tank for the electrolyte, and cleaning solutions comprise the basic anodizing equipment (right). *To begin work, use a cathode of platinized titanium mesh, and a 10 per cent solution of ammonium sulfate for the electrolyte. The chart* (below right) *shows the colors obtained on titanium, niobium, and tantalum when anodized at various voltages. Always keep the work area clean and dry and take note of the safety warning on page 123. Wear rubber gloves without holes while working.*

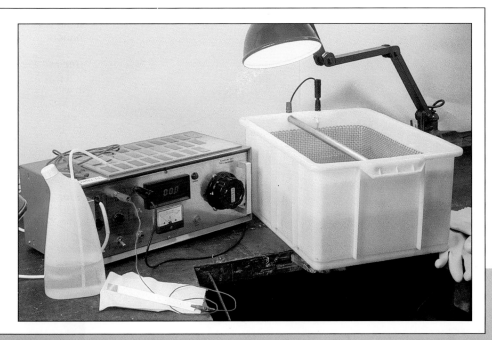

6

8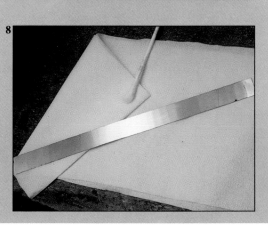

Volts	Titanium	Niobium	Tantalum
5			
10			
15			
20			
25			
30			
35			
40			
45			
50			
55			
60			
65			
70			
75			
80			
85			
90			
95			
100			

Volts	Niobium	Tantalum
105		
110		
115		
120		
125		
130		
135		
140		
145		
150		
155		
160		
165		
170		

STAMPING

Stamping is the technique of decorating or shaping metal by striking it with a tool called a punch. By the second century BC, jewelers were transferring multiple identical decorations to soften metal by repeatedly hammering it with a punch. The ancient Egyptians used bronze punches, and the Greeks probably used punches of wood or horn as early as the sixth century BC.

Stamped pieces can be either impression stamped or embossed. In impression stamping, the punching shows clearly on only one side of the work, while embossed metal shows the design on one side in relief, or cameo, and on the other side as a hollow, or intaglio.

Impression stamping

The most common example of impression stamping is hallmarking. The metal to be stamped is supported on a hard metal surface so that, when punched, the impression is clearly visible on one side, and only a small pressure mark shows on the other side. Impression stamping is also used for surface decoration.

Tools for impression stamping

For impression stamping, the jeweler needs a punch, a resisting surface and a hammer. Punches bearing letters, numbers or decoration can be purchased, and specially designed punches can be made from tool steel or brass.

The metal to be impressed must be supported on a hard surface, such as a steel block; if the surface is not hard enough, the result will be a dent, rather than a clear impression.

Use a heavy hammer for stamping — a 1lb/450g, broad, flat-faced head is recommended. And a wooden mallet is useful for flattening metal after stamping.

Making impression punches

Small punches are generally easier to use than large ones, so begin by taking a metal rod and making a punch no more than 5mm square. If possible, use tool steel; if this is not available, brass can be used for punches intended for limited stamping of well-annealed metal. Brass punches wear fairly quickly but can easily be reshaped.

Saw off a length of tool steel or brass rod and anneal it. A suitable length is about

On this Navajo Indian belt buckle (below), the edge decoration was made by impression stamping. The hallmark is probably the most commonly seen impression stamp (bottom). An important guarantee of quality to purchasers of precious metal objects, a hallmark gives information about the maker of a piece, the standard and type of precious metal used, and the place and year of manufacture.

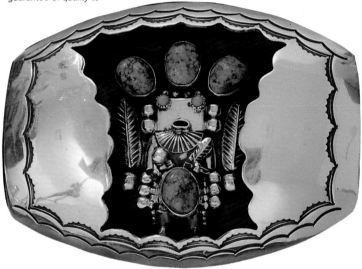

10cm; it is difficult to hammer accurately if the punch is too long, and difficult to hold the punch if it is too short. Anneal steel by heating it until it is bright red. Do not cool the hot steel in water at this stage; it will become too hard. Do not anneal brass, as it cannot easily be rehardened.

Saw, file, carve or engrave the decoration on one end of the punch. The punch should not contain deep crevices in which metal might jam, nor undercut edges that would prevent the punch being withdrawn after stamping. Check the impression by pushing the punch into plasticine. Continue working on the decoration until the plasticine impression is clearly defined. Sandpaper to remove file marks, and then polish with emery paper. File off the edges of the punch on the end to be hammered. This helps to prevent metal curling over after repeated hammer blows. Curled edges can be dangerous because they sometimes fly off during hammering.

Harden the steel by heating the decorated tip until it is bright red and then straight away quenching it in water. Besides becoming very hard, the steel will also become brittle and, therefore, will be liable to chip. Consequently, the steel must now be softened a little by tempering it. Sandpaper, then polish the punch with emery polishing paper. To keep the metal clean when tempering, rub a cake of soap over the top 5cm of the polished punch. Then direct a blow torch flame about 3cm from the top. Colors will soon be seen to travel out across the metal from the point at which the punch is heated. The first color to appear is a light straw yellow. It is followed by a dark straw yellow, then a golden yellow and a dark yellow. Watch the metal carefully while heating as the colors will travel quickly up the punch. As soon as the dark yellow color reaches the tip of the punch, remove the flame and quench the top to cool it. If the correct color is missed, re-harden and re-polish the punch before re-tempering it. After the tempering process is completed, sandpaper and polish the punch.

Impression stamping techniques

Anneal the metal to be stamped, and place it on a steel support, such as a block or stake. The shape of the support must match the shape of the metal to be stamped. Place the punch in contact with the metal, and hit the punch once with a heavy hammer; repeated hitting produces a blurred image. For a continuous line of punched decorations, reposition the punch after hammering, and hammer again. Continue the process until the decoration is complete, when the metal may need to be reshaped by beating it with a wooden mallet.

Embossing

An embossed image is stamped with a punch in such a way that it shows on both sides of the metal. Embossing is carried out either by punching the metal into a depression in a soft support, or by forcing metal into a hard, shaped support, called a die. Depending on the way the metal is forced into the die, the latter technique is called die embossing or die stamping. Repeated

MAKING AN IMPRESSION PUNCH

This punch is suitable for the stamped, double-domed bracelet project on page 129.
1 Mark four spots on the end of a tool steel rod with a scriber or spring-loaded center punch.
2 Drill the holes with a 1mm drill bit.
3 File away excess metal so that the holes are close to the edge of the punch. Sandpaper and polish the punch.

Tools and materials	

Heating equipment
Files
Dividers for measuring
1mm drill bit and drill
Cleaning and polishing
  equipment
	10cm x 5mm square
	  section tool steel
	Soap to reduce
	  oxidization on
	  polished steel

4 Harden and temper the punch: cover the punch in soap to prevent the steel oxidizing, then heat the end of the punch to red heat. Immediately plunge it in water: this hardens the steel but also makes it brittle. Repolish the punch. Tempering the punch softens the steel slightly and so prevents the risk of brittle metal shattering when hammered. Temper by heating about 5cm from the tip of the punch. Watch the colors very carefully. A pale yellow will appear and begin to travel towards the tip. Pale yellow will be followed by a darker straw colour, then golden yellow. As soon as the golden yellow reaches the tip, plunge the punch in water to cool the tip.

hammer blows are usually necessary for successful embossing, so the weight of the hammer is less critical than it is for impression stamping.

Making embossing punches
The technique for making embossing punches is similar to that for making impression punches, except that the characteristics of the punch are different.

You must be able to move the metal easily to a new position, so the punch should have smooth, rounded features. Avoid sharp edges or corners, as these will cut through the metal, rather than reshape it. As in the case of impression punches, the punch should be shaped so that it can be easily withdrawn after stamping. Check the punch by moistening it with one drop of thin machine oil and pushing it into plasticine. If, on withdrawal, the plasticine clogs the punch, it is likely that the punched metal will jam. Correct the shape until the punch withdraws easily and cleanly from the plasticine.

Embossing supports
The most suitable support for embossing is lead. A small lead block, called a lead cake, is a useful addition to the workshop. To make a lead cake, melt any odd scraps of lead in a small steel box or container by heating the box gently from underneath. If melting an old pipe, cut it open with a hacksaw, so that no air can be trapped inside: trapped air may cause an explosion as it rapidly expands. Skim any dross (rubbish) from the surface of the molten lead with a small piece of cardboard, then leave the lead to cool and solidify in the box. When solid, the lead cake can either be removed for use on its own, or

used in the box.

Never allow lead to touch precious metal, as it will contaminate the surface and cause pitting or holes to appear when the precious metal is heated. Place a layer of paper between the precious metal and the lead.

The end-grain of soft wood is also suitable as a support; a 10cm cube should be adequate. Timber yards often have cheap offcuts of suitable wood.

Punch embossing
For the technique of punch embossing, the punch is first used to make a depression in the soft support (either lead cake or end-grain of soft wood). Hold the punch on the support and hammer it to make a depression of 2mm to 3mm; several blows are usually necessary. No extra allowance need be made for the thickness of the metal to be embossed, as the soft support will move with the metal.

If precious metal is to be embossed on a lead support, lay a sheet of paper between the precious metal and the lead during the process to prevent the lead from contaminating the precious metal. Replace the paper whenever it becomes torn.

Beginners are advised to emboss on metal no more than 0.5mm thick. Anneal the metal and lay it over the hollow, ensuring that there is excess metal around the depression. The metal takes up the shape of the die by being stretched internally and partly pulled from the excess metal. A hollow of 3mm to 4mm requires excess metal of 2mm to 3mm in width surrounding it.

Hammer the punch to push the metal into the depression, annealing the metal whenever it becomes springy. Finally, either saw out the embossed shape, or flatten the flange of excess metal using a wooden mallet.

Making embossing dies
Carved brass or steel, or cast bronze are suitable materials for embossing dies. Epoxy resin is hard enough to provide about 100 embossings, but will not withstand large production runs.

As with punches, dies must not include deep crevices or undercut edges that would prevent the withdrawal of the embossed metal from the die. Beginners are advised to use dies no deeper than 4mm; deeper decorations are best avoided until the

MAKING A STAMPED DOUBLE-DOMED BRACELET

This project shows how to make a bracelet that resembles the gold bracelet *(left)* found at Pompeii, and dating from the first century AD. The uniformly sized domes suggest that a stamping process was used to make them. The techniques described are similar to those used by jewelers in ancient times.

Tools and materials

Doming block and punch
Heavy hammer
Soldering equipment
Polishing equipment
Impression punch
Metal sheet: 0.6mm thick and sufficient for the number of domes chosen
Metal wire: 1mm round. Allow 2cm for each decorative junction, 1.2cm for each jump ring, and 5cm for the catch

1

1 Pierce out a disc that will just fit into the top of one of the hemispherical depressions in a doming block. Place the well annealed disk in the doming block and, using a heavy hammer, strike the matching punch to push the disk into the hole. Ideally, the disk should be domed with a single blow. If not, slide the disc around in the hollow, while repeatedly hitting the punch. This is, in fact, the standard way of using a doming punch, since it is rare to find perfectly matched punches and hollows. Repeat the process until you have a sufficient number of domes.

2

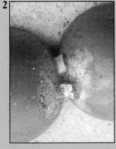

2 File a small "flat" on the edges of two domes at the place where they are to meet. This ensures that the join will be strong. Solder the two domes together with hard solder. Pair other domes in the same way.

3 Wind wire on a round rod to form the linking rings. If the former is rough, it will be difficult to slide the rings along it for sawing off. To avoid this problem, wrap a piece of paper around the former first.

4 Position the two horizontal rings on each pair of domes so that they pass through the centres of the vertical rings on the adjacent pair of domes. To solder the horizontal rings in the right place, support them on a scrap of metal, as shown. Be sure to keep the metal support clear of the soldered join. Butt the ends of the rings by easing them together with two pairs of pliers. File a small "flat" across the join at the openings and open the ring; place the "flat" against the dome. Join and solder the ring to the dome in one operation. On the vertical rings, file a small "flat" beside the openings and open the rings a little. One by one, solder the vertical rings to the domes while holding them in place with soldering tongs.

5 To make the decorations between the domes, solder two 1mm round wires together, then stamp them with the impression punch described on page 127.

6 Cut off pieces of the decorated strip. Curve them with half-round pliers. Solder the decorations in place between the domes.

7 For the catch, solder a square loop of wire to one side of the bracelet and a double wire hook to the other. Adjust the hook so that it clicks over the loop.

8 Polish all the units separately. Then hook each pair of vertical rings through a pair of horizontal rings on another unit. Close the rings with chain-nose pliers and solder. Take care not to solder adjacent links together. Polish the assembled bracelet.

3

4

5

8

To stamp into a lead die (right), first prepare the die by melting scraps of lead in a small steel box over the low heat of a stove or a Bunsen burner. If lead pipe is used, cut the pipe open to ensure that no air can become trapped as the metal melts. (Trapped air can cause explosions.) Skim dross (rubbish) from the surface of the molten lead with a small piece of cardboard and allow the lead to set. Carve, cut or file the required shape on steel to make the punch. If the punch is to be used often it is better to harden and temper it (see page 127). To make the die, hammer the punch into the lead. Mark the punch and lead so that the punch can be correctly lined up with the die. Place a sheet of metal across the hollow of the die. Line up the punch with the mark and hammer the punch to push the metal into the lead cake. Trim off excess metal.

The bronze mould or intaglio (below)was recently discovered in Corfu. Made in the sixth century BC, it shows two boxers with a prized tripod flanked by two horses on the top face and an owl, a dolphin, a mermaid and the death of Ajax on one side. Gold would be forced into the depressions by hammering leather or lead against the metal.

jeweler is familiar with the way that metals move when stamped. All dies need adequate material surrounding the hollow to ensure that the shape of the hollow does not distort during stamping. As a guide, allow at least 2cm of extra material beneath and around the hollow.

To make a brass or steel die, begin by making a model of the required shape in metal or wood.

To obtain a bronze die, a wax mold must first be prepared from the model. This is achieved by warming a block of casting wax and pushing the model into it (*see page 133*). Within a few seconds, the wax will set to the shape of the model. Few home workshops will have a blow torch large enough to melt the volume of bronze needed for the die, and it is usual to send the wax model to a bronze foundry for casting. Bronze foundries exist in most large towns to serve the needs of industry, architects and sculptors. The cast bronze will require the usual metal finishing processes of filing, sandpapering and polishing.

To make an epoxy resin die, first allow the liquid resin to set around the model, held in a container large enough to allow at least 2cm of resin to set below and around the model. Devise a way of supporting the model so that it penetrates the resin by not more than 4mm. It is helpful to mark the model, so that the resin can be poured to the correct level. Before pouring, powder the face of the model with talcum powder to prevent the wax from sticking to the resin. Mix the resin with its recommended hardener, pour the mixture into the container to the predetermined level and leave for 24 hours to set.

Die embossing

For die embossing, the metal to be decorated is pushed into the die, using a soft "carrier" material. The carrier consists of folded pads of lead sheet or leather.

Begin with metal about 0.5mm thick and remember to allow sufficient excess for the flow of metal into the die. Fold a pad of lead or leather, and lay it over the metal to be embossed. If using lead sheet with precious metal, protect the metal with paper. Hammer the pad to force the metal into the die, annealing as necessary. Continue until the shape is fully formed. Some leathers are inclined to break, and need to be replaced during embossing.

Die stamping

Die stamping is the most common embossing technique used in making jewelry. In this process, metal is sandwiched between a matching punch and die. Die stampers refer to the punch as the male part of the die, and to the hollow die as the female part.

The most common die stamping equipment consists of a set of domed punches and a brass or steel doming block, which has a series of hemispherical depressions cut into it. To use these tools for die stamping, choose a punch and hollow hemisphere that match, allowing only enough space for the thickness of metal that is to be stamped. The sharp edge around the hollow will mark protruding metal, so best results are achieved by using a disk of metal no larger than the top of the hollow. This flat metal disk is called a blank. A single, accurate hammer blow will push a 0.5mm thick blank of annealed metal into the hollow.

If large numbers of stampings are to be

Both the leaf and daisy motifs in this brooch (below)were stamped. The pre-stamped units were then assembled around the stone.

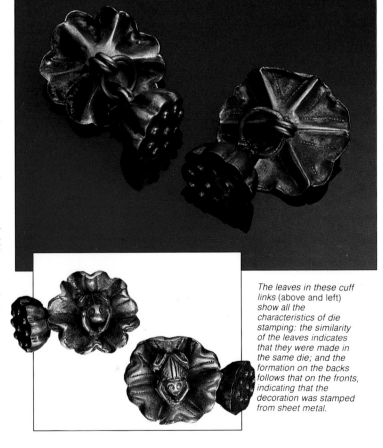

The leaves in these cuff links (above and left) show all the characteristics of die stamping: the similarity of the leaves indicates that they were made in the same die; and the formation on the backs follows that on the fronts, indicating that the decoration was stamped from sheet metal.

made, it is useful to cut large numbers of blanks. Industrial dies and punches usually shear the metal as well as shape it, so that no blanks are required. It is difficult for the beginner to produce dies and punches to shear metal, but it is easy to cut blanks in quantity. Purchase cutting punches to cut round blanks, and cut other shapes with blanking tools, which you can make yourself (*see below*).

Cutting Punches Round, hollow-ended steel cutting punches can be purchased from jewelry tool stores. These punches range in diameter from 2.5mm to 2cm and will cut annealed sheet gold, silver, copper and brass of up to 1.2mm thick. To begin with, use metal no more than 0.5mm thick.

Place the metal to be cut on a block of soft (annealed) brass. Do not cut onto steel as this will blunt the cutter. If brass is not avail-able, lead or wood may be used instead. Cutting onto lead takes longer than brass and produces a slightly domed blank; cutting onto hard wood is successful if the wood is evenly grained. Hold the cutting punch in contact with the metal, and hammer the punch until it shears the metal. This may require several blows. If the blank sticks inside the punch, it can usually be dislodged by rocking the punch slightly while tapping it.

Making blanking tools Cutting punches of various shapes can be carved from tool steel by the jeweler. The cutting edge should be chisel-shaped and filed to an angle of 45°. Harden the punch and temper until it is dark straw yellow in color.

If welding equipment is available, tools called blanking cutters can be made from steel strips 1mm thick and 5mm wide. Anneal the steel and, with pliers, bend the

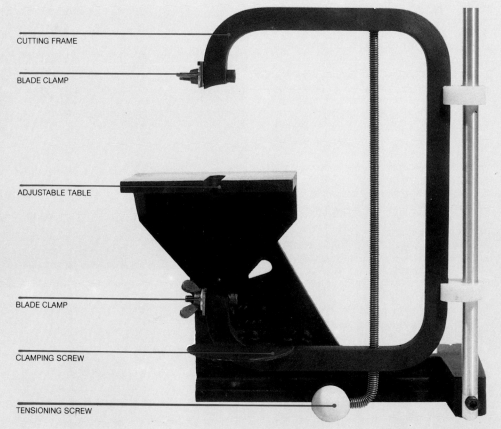

The R T Blanking tool cutter
This sawing table has been designed to cut a blanking tool accurately. Inaccurate cutting can result in pieces being bent instead of blanked; this sawing table ensures that the saw cut is always at the required angle. The blanking tool, once cut, is extremely versatile and can be used to cut metals from 0.1mm to 2mm thick as well as paper and plastics. For any jeweler wanting to produce many similar items, this tool is a great time-saver. The blanking tool is available only from Roger Taylor, and the Goldsmiths' technical report, giving precise details of correct cutting angles, is available from Roger Taylor and Goldsmiths' Hall (see list of suppliers).

CUTTING FRAME

BLADE CLAMP

ADJUSTABLE TABLE

BLADE CLAMP

CLAMPING SCREW

TENSIONING SCREW

strip into the outline of the shape to be cut. Then weld the ends together, making sure that the sides do not lean, as this will cause them to distort and collapse when struck. Working from the outside, file the cutting edge like a chisel to an angle of 45°. When this is completed, harden and temper it. To use the tool, place the metal to be cut on a soft brass block, place the cutter on the metal, and a steel plate on the cutter to protect the edges, then hammer the steel plate until the cutter has penetrated the metal.

The R T Blanking System By far the best type of blanking tool was invented in the late 1970s by London jeweler, Roger Taylor. It has shaped blades and cuts exactly like a pair of scissors. A punch and blanking die are formed by cutting the required shape from a single sheet of steel. Metal is sandwiched between the punch and die parts of the tool, and sheared by applying pressure with a hammer, press or vise. The punch and die are remarkably quick to make and use. For example, in just 40 minutes Roger Taylor made the tool and cut 100 butterfly shapes from silver 0.6mm thick. With such a system, it is economical to make a tool to cut only four or five identical blanks. Previously, blanking tools were worth making only if about 50 or more identical shapes were needed.

The R T Blanking System is patented but, to help jewelers wishing to use the technique, Roger Taylor and the Goldsmiths' Research Foundation have produced an excellent report that gives precise details of how to make and use the tools. The report, which is also a license to operate the system, is published by The Worshipful Company of Goldsmiths and is available from Goldsmiths' Hall in London.

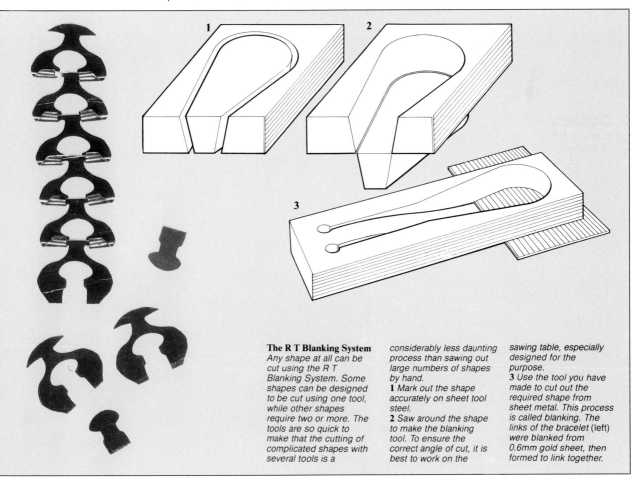

The R T Blanking System
Any shape at all can be cut using the R T Blanking System. Some shapes can be designed to be cut using one tool, while other shapes require two or more. The tools are so quick to make that the cutting of complicated shapes with several tools is a considerably less daunting process than sawing out large numbers of shapes by hand.
1 Mark out the shape accurately on sheet tool steel.
2 Saw around the shape to make the blanking tool. To ensure the correct angle of cut, it is best to work on the sawing table, especially designed for the purpose.
3 Use the tool you have made to cut out the required shape from sheet metal. This process is called blanking. The links of the bracelet (left) were blanked from 0.6mm gold sheet, then formed to link together.

CASTING

Casting is a way of forming an object by allowing a liquid, such as molten metal, to solidify in a shaped hollow called a mold. The mold shape is formed from a model of the item to be cast, or else carved. Casting allows the jeweler to produce shapes that might be difficult to construct by any other method; for example, in making chunky jewelry. The process also provides a way of making copies of the work, a factor that makes the technique ideal for mass production as well as for one-off pieces. Casting leaves metal with a dull surface, sometimes with scraps of surplus metal attached. So, various finishing processes, such as filing, sanding and polishing are essential after casting.

Designing for casting

Good results can be relied upon if the jewelry is specially designed for the casting process. Being porous, cast metal does not polish as brightly as compacted metal, and undecorated or smooth surfaces tend to show pitting, so suitable designs are likely to have decorated surfaces rather than plain ones. Cast metal is also inclined to be brittle, so strong, bulky designs are more appropriate than delicate, spindly forms.

The design should also take into account the fact that the metal must be able to flow unhindered into all parts of the mold. Once flowing, the metal will not easily run through offshoots that go against the main direction of the flow, and it will tend to solidify almost immediately in narrow channels, preventing molten metal from fully filling the mold.

As metal shrinks on cooling, the cast piece will be smaller than the mold. The amount of shrinkage depends on the casting process used and the alloying of the metal, but it can shrink as much as three per cent in length, that is, nine per cent in volume. If the size of the piece is critical, shrinkage must be anticipated at the design stage.

Casting techniques

The mold used for casting metal jewelry may be made from cuttlefish bone, charcoal, ceramic or plaster. The casting technique chosen depends on the object to be cast and the number of castings required.

A cuttlefish bone mold is appropriate for casting if an existing, rigid object is to be reproduced just once. Charcoal molds are

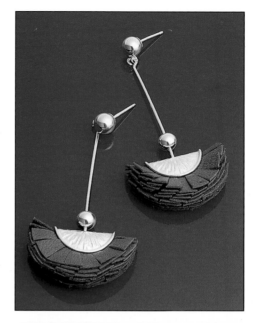

Casting provides a convenient method of making chunky pieces or unusual shapes that would be difficult to form in other ways. It is often used commercially, as the process is particularly well suited to mass production. The silver and leather earrings (left) are by Vivia Bremmer-Goldie and Peter Crump (UK). The stick pins (right) were cast in red, yellow and white gold by Julie Crossland (UK). The gold necklace (below), entitled "Baying at the Moon," is by Merry Kerr Woodeson (UK). Merry experimented with many wax shapes before selecting suitable ones for the necklace.

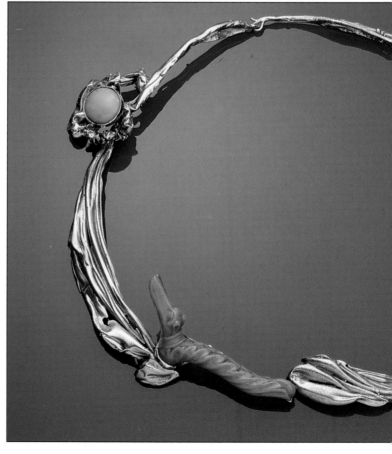

CUTTLEFISH CASTING

1 Flatten the surfaces of two pieces of cuttlefish bone by rubbing them on a flat sheet of sandpaper.
2 Push the model halfway into one cuttlefish surface. Push three locating pegs around the model (short lengths of matchstick are suitable).

Tools and materials

Cuttlefish
Matches
Binding wire
Scriber
Heating equipment
Crucible and handle
Borax
Cleaning and polishing equipment
Model
Metal for melting:
 silver, gold, brass or bronze

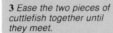

3 Ease the two pieces of cuttlefish together until they meet.
4 Separate them. Remove the model. Cut a pour hole with a knife. Drag a scriber across the surface to cut vent holes.
5 Relocate the two pieces of cuttlefish, using the pegs to ensure an accurate match. Tie the mold together with binding wire and stand it upright beside the heating area. Heat the metal with some borax in a crucible.
6 Pour the metal. When it is completely molten, the metal should pull into a mobile ball-shape and the surface appear to "roll."
7 After a few minutes, separate the two pieces of cuttlefish and remove the casting. File, sandpaper and polish the piece to finish it.

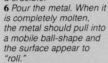

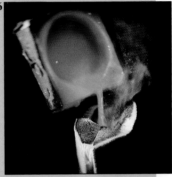

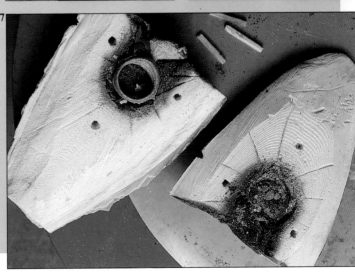

made by carving directly into the charcoal, so no model is necessary, and the same mold can be used to cast one or two similar shapes. Ceramic and plaster molds are made from wax models and used in a casting technique called the lost-wax process. This technique is suitable for producing single items or for mass production. The wax models may be individually constructed by the jeweler, or formed from models of another material in a preliminary wax casting process.

CHARCOAL BLOCK CASTING

1 Carve the shape directly in the flat surface of a charcoal block. Carve a dish-shaped crucible about l5mm from the shape. The crucible should be deeper than the shape so that molten metal does not flow into the shape before it is poured. Join the two with a pouring channel about 5mm wide. Cut vent tracks with a sharp point.

2 Bind a second flat-surfaced charcoal block on top of the first with binding wire, so that the crucible and part of the pouring channel are exposed but the shape to be cast is covered. Heat the metal in the crucible until it is molten. Then tip the charcoal blocks so that the metal flows into the mold.

3 After a few minutes, when the metal has solidified, separate the blocks and remove the casting. File, sandpaper and polish the piece to finish.

Tools and materials

Carving tools
Two natural willow charcoal blocks
Binding wire
Heating equipment
Borax
Cleaning and polishing equipment
Metal for melting:
silver, gold, brass or bronze

Cuttlefish casting

Cuttlefish bones are soft and fragile, yet heat resistant: on contact with molten metal, the surface will char, but not change in shape.

To make a mold, flatten the faces of two cuttlefish bones by rubbing them on a sheet of sandpaper. Gently push the hard model halfway into one bone surface, together with three or four short lengths of matchstick to act as locating pegs. Push the smooth face of the other cuttlefish bone against the other side of the model and ease the two faces together. Then separate them and remove the model. In one cuttlefish bone, cut about six air vents from the extremities of the hollow to the outside of the bone by drawing a sharp point across the surface. The vent need be no more than 1mm deep. Cut a funnel-shaped pour-hole through any part of the bone to allow molten metal to be poured into the hollow. Reassemble the mold, securing the two pieces together with binding wire. The locating pegs will ensure accurate repositioning of the two halves of the mold. With a blow torch, melt the metal in a crucible and pour the molten metal into the mold. After a few minutes, the metal will have hardened. Separate the mold, remove the hot casting with steel tweezers and allow it to cool.

Charcoal block casting

The natural willow charcoal blocks that are used as soldering supports are easily carved to make molds. Their resistance to heat allows the metal to be melted in a hollow adjacent to the mold. The block is then tilted so that the molten metal runs down a track leading to the mold. This convenient pouring system makes charcoal block casting relatively simple.

To make the mold, use carving gravers to cut the design into the flat face of a charcoal block. With a sharp point, score vent holes, no more than 1mm deep, from the carved hollow mold to the outside of the block. About 2cm from the mold, carve a shallow depression; this forms the crucible in which the metal is melted. Cut a track linking the crucible to the mold, for the metal to flow down.

Place another flat charcoal block over the mold, leaving the crucible and track exposed. Bind the blocks together with binding wire. With a blow torch, melt the metal in the crucible, and then, using large, steel tweezers, tilt the two blocks so that the metal flows down the track into the mold. Leave the blocks tilted for approximately one minute until the metal has solidified, then separate them, remove the hot casting with steel tweezers and allow to cool.

Lost-wax casting

In lost-wax casting, ceramic or plaster molds are formed around models made of wax. The wax is then melted and poured out, and metal is cast in the resultant molds. The molds can be used only once, but many wax models can be joined together and used to form a mold for mass production casting.

There are two main ways of producing the wax models: the jeweler may work directly on casting wax by carving, melting or by assembling separate components; alternatively, he or she may inject molten wax into a rubber mold and allow it to set. The rubber mold can be used to form identical waxes for the mass production of castings.

Working in wax Casting wax is available in blocks, sheets and wires, and also as pre-shaped components suitable for jewelry.

The wax is easily shaped with carving gravers or a scalpel, and a warm scalpel blade can be used to smooth out the surface. To weld wax components, warm the junctions with the scalpel blade until they melt into each other.

If the wax model is to be formed by casting, then a metal model must be made first to form the rubber mold in which the wax will be cast. A metal wire, about 2mm in diameter, is attached to the metal model; this will form the sprue (the passage through which the metal is poured after the rubber mold is set). This is then positioned in a steel frame with a hole in it for the sprue wire to protrude. Pieces of vulcanizing rubber sheet (specially prepared rubber that will withstand heavy pressure and heat) are stacked around the metal model. The frame containing the model and rubber is then subjected to heat and pressure in a vulcanizing press. The rubber melts and flows around the model to form a rubber mold with the metal sprue protruding. After cooling, the solid rubber mold is cut open with a scalpel blade; locating lugs are cut at the same time so that the mold always fits together in

Lost-wax casting
In lost-wax casting, the shape of the item to be cast is first formed in wax and mounted onto a conical base support on a short wax sprue. It is then surrounded by a cylindrical metal ring or flask, which is filled with a plaster/silica slurry called investment. After the investment has set, the base support is removed and the resulting mold heated slowly to red heat to melt out the wax, burn out residues and harden the investment. After partial cooling, molten metal is poured into the mold. Later, the investment is broken away and the casting cut from the sprue. If many items are to be cast at one time, the wax patterns are attached to a central wax sprue in a tree-like formation. The burn-out kiln below is surrounded by lost-wax casting accessories, together with some wax rings.

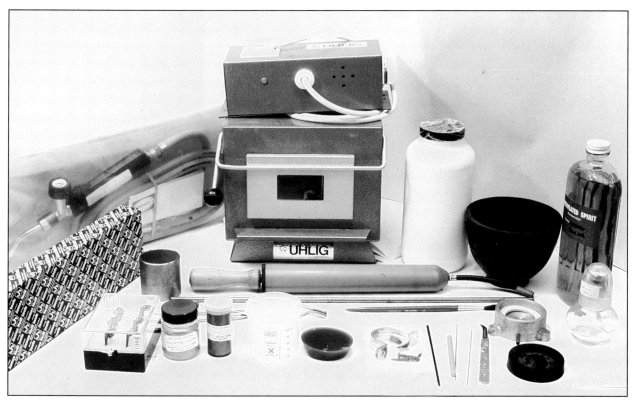

exactly the same way. The metal model is then removed, the rubber mold reassembled and liquid wax injected into the hole left by the sprue wire. After cooling, the rubber is opened to remove the set wax. In this way, numerous identical waxes can be produced from the same rubber mold.

Once the waxes have been produced, they are ready for use in the ceramic shell or plaster mold lost-wax processes.

David Reid ceramic shell casting In the mid-1970s in New Zealand, bronze caster David Reid developed and refined a new lost-wax casting technique. His process, based on the ceramic shell casting method

used by some sculptors and bronze foundries, gives quick, high quality results.

Make the wax model either by working directly on the wax or by injecting wax into a rubber mold. Attach a short wax sprue and a shallow wax dish to the model. The whole wax assembly must now be given a three-layer ceramic coating. The step-by-step instructions for the project on page 138 show how this is done.

When the shell mold formed around the wax is dry, up-end it on a wire mesh soldering support and heat with a blow torch. The wax will melt and flow out through the sprue hole. While the mold is still hot, place the metal to be melted in the crucible formed by

To make a rubber mold of a piece such as the Egyptian scarab (below), suspend the item on a wax rod in a small container and pour cold-set rubber into the container. When it is set, remove the model and wax rod. Then reassemble the rubber and pour in molten wax to form the wax model.

CERAMIC SHELL CASTING

1 Prepare a wax crucible and attach it to the wax scarab. To make the crucible, swill several coats of molten wax around the inside of a small, glazed cup. The set wax comes out easily.
2 Wash the wax in a solution of 10 parts wood alcohol to 1 part liquid detergent.
3 Mix a slurry of colloidal silica 1030 and molochite 200 to the consistency of heavy cream. Stir immediately and pour over the wax model.

4 Blow on the wet slurry to remove air bubbles.
5 Sprinkle the outside with molochite 30/80 grain.
6 Dry in front of a fan for 30 to 60 minutes: do not use heat as the wax may melt. It is important that this shell is completely dry before proceeding; test by stroking the shell with a finger. If the shell wipes off, it is still wet.
7 Pour pure colloidal silica over the shell.
8 Recoat the ceramic slurry. Drain and recoat with larger-grained

molochite 16/30. Dry the shell in front of the fan.
9 Dip in pure colloidal silica and repeat step 8. Below, the wax model and ceramic shell formed from 3 coats of molochite.
10 Invert the ceramic-covered wax on

Tools and materials

Heating equipment
Borax
Cleaning and polishing equipment
Fan or good draft
Wax for model
Wood alcohol and detergent for washing
Colloidal silica
Molochite 200
Molochite 30/80
Molochite 16/30
Metal for melting: silver, gold, brass or bronze

coating the wax dish. Melt the metal, so that the metal flows into it from the crucible. When the metal has solidified, break the shell off with a hammer.

Plaster mold casting This is the lost-wax method commonly used by commercial casting firms. An object or model is first formed in wax. A wax sprue, 2mm to 5mm long, is attached to the model, which is then set in a plaster and silica slurry called investment with the sprue protruding. The wax is melted out from the plaster and, while the plaster is still hot, molten metal is poured into the hole left by the wax. When the metal has solidified, the plaster is broken away.

If many items are to be cast at the same time, the wax models are attached to a central column of wax, and the resulting wax "tree" is set in plaster. The wax is melted out in a burn-out kiln, and molten metal is forced into the sprue hole left in the plaster. This is done by means of a vacuum or by centrifugal force in a rotating machine.

If large numbers of an item are to be cast, it is better to send the metal model to a commercial caster. With modern equipment and techniques, specialist casting firms are able to produce high quality results very inexpensively. Sending casting to a specialist is normal practice in a professional jewelry workshop.

a gauze. Direct a blow torch on the shell and melt out the wax quickly.
11 Continue heating until the shell is pure white and no black residue remains.
12 When the shell is cool, break away the rough edges from the crucible.
13 Load the cold crucible with metal and begin to heat.
14 Gently heat the mould and crucible until

completely red. Then raise the metal to red heat. Note: If you are using standard silver, cover the metal with a good layer of charcoal to prevent heavy oxidation of the silver, which would otherwise occur during the next heating. Apply further heat to the mold, then direct the flame onto the metal, so that it melts rapidly: the metal should flow straight into the mold. Remove the flame.

15 Leave for 10 minutes to cool and then tap the shell gently with a hammer, so that it breaks away from the cast piece.

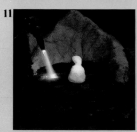

ENGRAVING

In engraving, metal is removed from the surface of the work with a steel cutting tool called a graver, leaving fine, sharp marks. Jewlers engrave metal to decorate a surface, or inscribe wording. The Vikings exploited the decorative qualities of engraving by covering entire surfaces with complicated images, patterns and lines. However, they did not restrict the ornamentation to engraving: a single piece might include engraving and carving, impression stamping and embossing. Remember this when designing jewelry, and never allow a restricted use of technique to limit the impact of the piece.

Preparing the graver

The graver consists of a steel shaft with a sharp cutting point at one end and a projecting point, or tang, at the other, which is fitted into a wooden handle. For general purpose engraving, purchase a 2.5mm square graver and a mushroom handle with a flat, cut-off section. A graver with a lozenge-shaped cross-section is sometimes used to engrave extremely fine lines, but this type of tool is much more difficult to use.

Before fitting the handle, the shaft will probably need shortening. To estimate the length that you need to remove, nestle the handle securely in the palm of your hand and hold the loose shaft with your forefinger and thumb, so that the cutting tip of the shaft protrudes about 2cm beyond your fingers. The handle should lie alongside the tang of the graver. About 3cm of the tang will fit into the handle; note any excess to be removed. Shorten the shaft at the tang end by clamping the shaft in a vise, with just the excess metal protruding. Strike it with one firm hammer blow. The metal should break off cleanly. If necessary, use a carborundum stone to re-grind the tang end to a point to make it easier to push into the handle. Heat the tang before fitting it to the handle, in the same way as for files. Align the shaft so that the cutting tip is on the same side as the flat in the handle.

The graver cuts best when the shaft is almost parallel to the metal, but when this is the case the user's hand tends to get in the way. To prevent this, the graver is modified in one of three ways: the shaft, or belly, of the graver is curved; the handle is attached at an angle; or the shaft is ground so that it

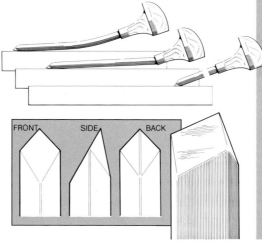

Preparing the graver
The cutting edge of a graver should be almost parallel with the metal. To achieve this. either bend the shaft, angle the handle or set the angle between the tip of the graver and the horizontal plane to 20°. Adjust the length of the shaft to the hand size and secure the cut-off mushroom handle as for files (see page 25).

FRONT   SIDE   BACK

changes direction at the point. The latter option is the one chosen by most professionals. Producing the correct cutting angle is called setting up the graver. After setting up, the graver is sharpened. The illustration on the right shows how to set up and sharpen the graver by using a small "India" stone.

Transferring the design

The technique chosen to transfer the design to the metal depends on whether a normal or reversed copy is required. The design is transferred in reverse for seals, so that the impression made by the seal in wax is the right way round. Sometimes a design is transferred to the metal in both normal and reversed form in order to produce symmetrical patterns.

To transfer a normal design onto metal, use the tracing paper and plasticine technique, as described in the section on sawing (*see page 20*). To transfer a reversed image, use thin, clear acetate sheet. Trace the design with a sharp scriber onto the acetate. Scrape graphite dust from a "lead" pencil into the scribed grooves in the acetate. Brush the dust across any unfilled grooves with the finger tip and shake off any excess graphite. Roll plasticine across the metal surface, so that it can be easily marked, and then place

Tools and materials

Square graver (2.5mm)
Mushroom handle with cut off
India stone for sharpening graver
Leather sandbag
Curved steel burnisher (for metal)
Piercing saw and blades
Cleaning and polishing equipment
Heating equipment
Transparent plexiglass: 2mm or 3mm thick *or*
Metal: 1mm thick
Ear fittings, if appropriate

Sharpening the graver
Place the graver face down in a spot of oil on an India stone. Ensure that the whole face is in contact with the stone and rub the face on the stone to sharpen the point. Resharpen when cutting becomes difficult.

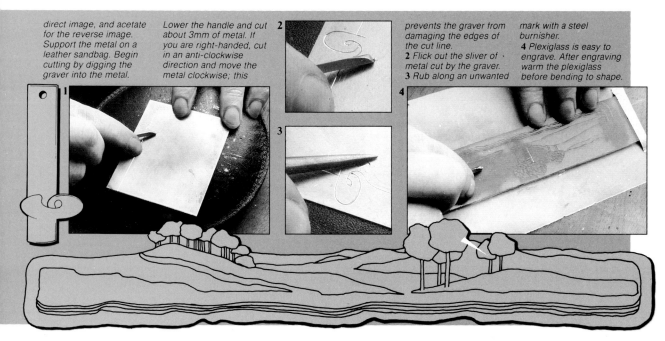

direct image, and acetate for the reverse image. Support the metal on a leather sandbag. Begin cutting by digging the graver into the metal.

Lower the handle and cut about 3mm of metal. If you are right-handed, cut in an anti-clockwise direction and move the metal clockwise; this

prevents the graver from damaging the edges of the cut line.
2 Flick out the sliver of · metal cut by the graver.
3 Rub along an unwanted

mark with a steel burnisher.
4 Plexiglass is easy to engrave. After engraving warm the plexiglass before bending to shape.

The technique of engraving is used for inscriptions, personal messages, heraldic devices and decoration. The cuff-links (below) include engravings of a monogram and a crest by George Lukes (UK). The engraving on the locket (bottom) is decorative.

the acetate pattern face down on the metal, rubbing the acetate with a straight burnisher. When the reversed design has been transferred, remove the acetate and scribe the marked lines into the metal.

Cutting the lines
If an item is to be given a polished finish, this should be done before engraving, as polishing buffs will destroy the fine, bright-cut quality of the lines.

Support the metal to be engraved on a leather sandbag (the 15cm diameter size is adequate for jewelry); placing the work on a raised surface makes it easier to hold and work on the metal. Holding the handle of the graver securely in the palm of your hand, use your thumb and forefinger to support the shaft 2cm from its tip. Dig the graver point into the metal exactly on a scribed line, and then lower your hand so that the shaft is as close as possible to the metal, while keeping the point firmly located in it. Ease the point 2mm to 3mm through the metal; a small curl of waste metal (swarf) will be pushed ahead of the graver. Flick out the swarf with the graver, and then re-insert the tool in the cut groove. Engrave the next 2mm to 3mm of the line, and again flick out the swarf. Continue cutting in this way until you have finished. It is easier to work in an anti-

clockwise direction (for a right-handed person) when engraving curves; if necessary, move the metal clockwise toward the graver. While engraving, remember to turn the work frequently to make certain that the cutting action is always in the same direction.

Correcting mistakes
A curved, oval steel burnisher is used for "earasing" mistakes in engraving. To remove, or at least disguise, an unintentional cut, rub the curved face of the burnisher along the unwanted line. This will encourage metal from the sides to fill the groove. Do not rub across the lines, as the burnisher will drop into the groove and may widen it.

Finishing engraving
During the engraving process, the metal surface may become slightly scratched. Any scratches must be removed as delicately as possible if the fine lines of the engraving are to be retained. Charcoal is useful for removing scratches as it is a very fine abrasive. Gently rub away the scratches with a small piece of charcoal, then re-polish the metal carefully by hand, using buff sticks, as described in the section on finishing (*see page 47*).

CARVING

In jewelry carving, gravers or special chisels are used to ease away the metal or other material, bit by bit, in small slivers. Because the tools and techniques are similar to those used in engraving, the reader should refer to the section on engraving (*see page 140*) for further information on topics covered only briefly here.

Gravers for carving

Gravers of various shapes are available for carving. The selection below is recommended for the beginner. Each one should be fitted with a round wooden handle.

Preparing the graver

The carving graver should nestle comfortably in the palm of your hand with the point protruding about 1.5cm to 2cm. Break off any excess metal and fix the handle.

To shape the cutting face of a carving graver, grind it on a small combination carborundum stone. For the repeated sharpening necessary during the carving process, use an Arkansas stone, which is very finely abrasive and will maintain a sharp cutting edge on the graver. The step-by-step instructions on page 141 show how to shape and sharpen a graver.

Marking the metal

Transfer the design to the material to be carved and scribe it clearly. Some carvers engrave the design prior to carving so that, as areas are carved away, some of the original guidelines remain. If too many lines are carved away, it may be necessary to re-transfer the design.

Carving the shapes

Use a sandbag to support the piece to be carved. Alternatively, secure the work in setter's cement on a block of wood (*see pages 82-3*).

Start the carving process by establishing the general form of the work. This process, called blocking out, entails lowering all deep areas until the levels of adjoining sections are correctly related. Do not try to finish any details at this stage; this can make it more difficult to judge the overall shape. Scoop

Carving a half-hoop ring
Taper-mill or forge the last 15mm of each end of a bar of metal 3mm square by 5cm long: the final length should be 6.5cm. Bend to create a ring. File the shank. Drill, then pierce out holes for the stones. Carve the top and side.

1 Carving with a chisel
Grind a cutting angle of about 45°. Dig the chisel into the work, lower it, then tap gently. A sliver of metal should rise before the chisel. If the angle is too small, the chisel will skate across the surface; if too great, the chisel will dig in.

2 Sharpening the graver
Grind only the front face of the graver at an angle of about 45°. Drop a spot of oil onto an Arkansas stone and press the face flat against the stone until the oil oozes out.

3 Carving gravers
From top to bottom: spitstick no.10 (1mm), half-round no.6 (0.6mm), bullstick no.19 (1.9mm), flat no.14 (1.4mm), multi-line no.18 (8-row, 1.8mm).

4 *These gold rings were hand-carved by Alan Craxford (UK).*

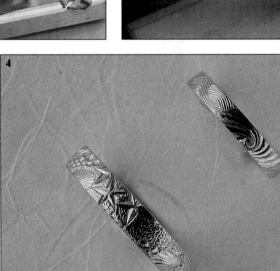

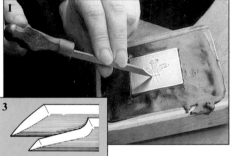

CARVING
A PENDANT
Transfer and pierce out the pattern. If the piece is large, rest it on a leather sandbag. Alternatively, secure it on a block of wood with setter's cement. Begin by establishing the overall form. Ensure that the relationship between the low and high areas is correct. For example, the feet should appear behind the dress, and the back arm should be lower than the front one and on the same level as the back leg. When you have established the relative positions of the sections, carve in the details — the folds of the material and the curls of the hair. Sandpaper and polish to finish.

Tools and materials

Carving tools with round handles as follows: spitstick no. 10, half-round no. 6, bullstick no. 19, flat no. 14, Arkansas stone for sharpening tools
Block of wood and setter's cement for

securing work
Piercing saw and blades
Cleaning and polishing equipment
Metal, **wood** or **plexiglass:** 2mm thick and sufficient for the pattern chosen

out the metal a little at a time by digging the tool into the surface, cutting a small sliver of metal and flicking it out.

Once the shape is clearly defined, begin adding the surface details. Finish smooth areas by holding the tool closer to the metal and gently skimming off high points. Polishing the side faces of the cutting edge with emery paper helps to achieve a bright finish.

Reflections from bright-cut surfaces sometimes make the work difficult to judge. To dull the reflections, dust the surface of the metal with talcum powder shaken from a small powder bag. To make the bag, lay four 15cm squares of finely woven cotton material, one on top of another. Empty three teaspoons of talcum powder in the middle, then gather up the corners of the material and bind them together with string to form a loose bag. Tapping the bag on the work will cause powder to penetrate the cotton and settle as a fine film on the surface of the metal. This will be sufficient to reduce the glare from the metal without obliterating its shape.

Chisel carving
Some professionals prefer to carve with chisels because they find that they can then work more quickly. However, most people find this process more difficult to learn than carving with gravers.

The chisels used for carving have no handles; they are hammered to cut the metal or other material. Chisel carvers normally make their own tools. These can be forged and filed from tool steel, polished, then hardened and tempered in the same way as impression punches. The chisels are sharpened on an "India" stone to form cutting edges similar to those on ordinary woodworking chisels.

Commercial gravers also can be sharpened and used for carving in the same manner as chisels. The soft tang will bend at the tip if hammered, so break off the tip of the tang, leaving a 1cm butt for striking with the hammer. Do not remove all of the tang; hammering directly onto the hardened metal of the shaft is likely to result in flying chips of steel.

To carve, position the chisel on the metal and tap it with a chasing hammer. It is not necessary to hit hard. Cut short, thin slivers of metal, rather than large chunks, so that cutting is fast yet controlled.

CHASING AND REPOUSSE

Chasing and repoussé are techniques for embossing metal. The design is produced a little at a time with many differently shaped punches, and may be developed from the front or the back of the metal to produce complex, overlapping and intertwined forms. Unlike work embossed by stamping, the metal can fold back on itself or drop into deep, narrow crevices.

Chasing refers to a design punched into metal from the front. Repoussé indicates that the design was worked from the back of the metal. In discussing chasing and repoussé, the two words are often abbreviated to "chasing," and the technician skilled in both chasing and repoussé is called a chaser.

Tools for chasing and repoussé

To chase, the jeweler needs chasing punches, a pitch bowl and a chasing hammer. There are four categories of chasing punch; each of them has a particular function:

1 Line tracers for outlining.
2 Blocking punches with full, rounded faces for creating depth.
3 Planishing punches with flatter faces for smoothing.
4 Matting punches with patterned faces for patterning or texturing.

These tools can be either home-made or purchased: the step-by-step instructions on page 146 show how to forge your own chasing punch.

A pitch bowl is used to support work and to hold it absolutely steady for chasing. A pitch bowl is a hemisphere of cast iron that rests on a leather ring. Pitch bowls are normally 20cm in diameter, which is quite adequate for most jewelry work. Almost fill the bowl with scrap iron or cement, and then top up the last 3cm with pitch mixture. To make the correct pitch consistency, mix two parts of pitch with one part of Plaster of Paris powder and add a thimble-sized knob of tallow.

A 4oz/115g chasing hammer is comfortable for most people. This type of hammer has a broad head, and the handle has a bulb-shaped end so that it moves easily in the hand when the head is bounced on the punch.

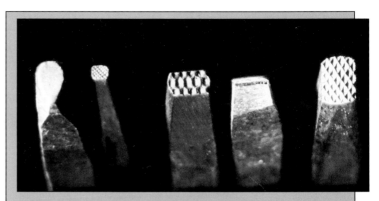

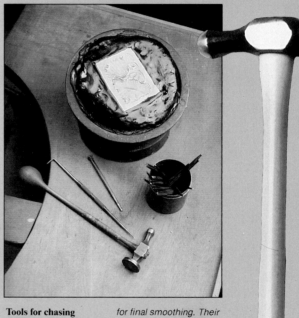

Tools for chasing and repoussé
Line tracers have narrow heads for outlining. They are straight for straight lines and curved for curved lines. The line chaser is usually the first tool used in chasing and blocking punches are usually the second. Blocking punches usually have full, rounded, cushion-shaped faces; they can be round, square, pear-shaped (first punch, top), pyramid-shaped (fourth punch, top), or even triangular in cross-section. Planishing punches have smooth, flatter faces and are used for final smoothing. Their cross-section should resemble the shape of the area to be planished. Matting tools have patterned faces and are used to texture surfaces (second, third and fifth punches, top). A pitch bowl in position on a leather-ring support stands next to a selection of chasing tools and a chasing hammer with a hand-made handle (above). The broad, flat face of the chasing hammer reduces the risk of mishitting the chasing punch and its bulb-ended handle facilitates the bouncing action required for chasing (right).

The chased gold charm (right) *was made in the early Roman Imperial period. The buckle (far right) was chased in niobium by Roy Flewin (UK) and the design is based on a Chinese jade carving. This piece is also shown in the pitch bowl on page 144. The central silver decoration of the leather and silver neckpiece (below) is by Susan Fortune (UK) is chased.*

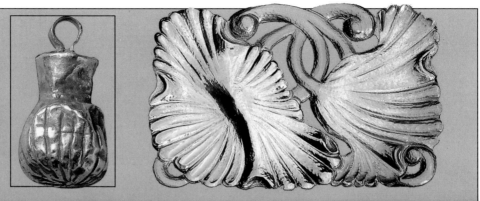

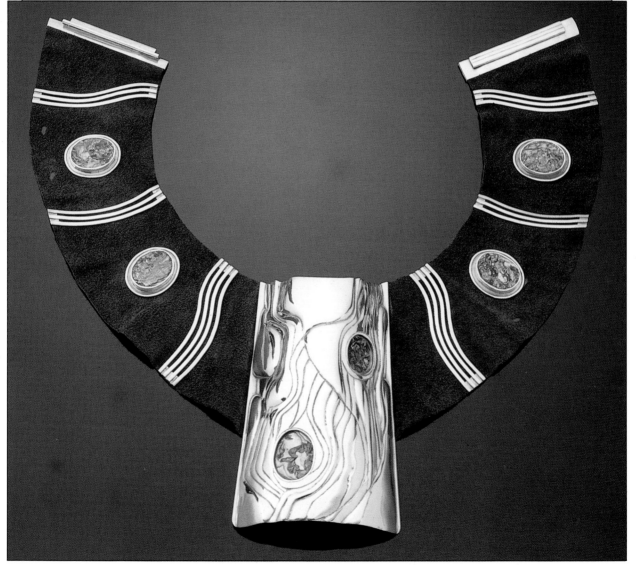

MAKING A LINE TRACING PUNCH

1 Hold the steel upright and direct the flame up the metal. Heat the end to red heat and forge the shape.

2 File the shape. Chamfer the edge of the end to be hammered; this helps prevent the hammered steel from curling over. Sandpaper and polish.

3 Coat the top 5cm of the punch with cake soap. Heat the end to bright red and immediately quench it in water; this hardens the steel but leaves it brittle. Counteract this by tempering. Direct the flame at a point about 3cm from the tip and watch the steel begin to change color. First the punch turns light straw in color, then, as heating continues, the light straw color moves toward the tip to be replaced by dark straw, then golden yellow. As soon as the golden yellow reaches the tip, quench the punch.

Tools and materials	
Heating equipment	5mm x 10cm of square
Heavy forging hammer	section tool steel
Steel block or anvil	Soap to reduce
Files	oxidization on
Cleaning and polishing	polished steel
equipment	

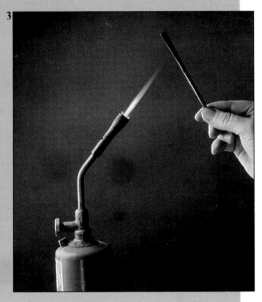

Chasing and repoussé techniques

Transfer and scribe the design on the metal. Before placing it on the pitch, warm the metal with the blow torch and wet the underside. This makes it easier to remove from the pitch. Soften the surface of the pitch by wafting the flame over it. Do not allow the pitch to bubble or burn. Position the metal on the pitch and, *with wet fingers*, push a little pitch over the edges of the metal to hold it in place. Then leave it, to allow the pitch to harden. If hot pitch should get on your hands, let it harden before peeling it off; attempting to pull off hot pitch may damage the skin.

Hold the punch like a pen in your left hand (if you are right-handed), keeping your forefinger straight. This will give maximum stability to the punch. If it is held by only the finger tips, it will be inclined to wobble when hit.

If the design is complex, begin by chasing the lines with a line tracer. Otherwise, begin work with the blocking tool. When chasing, develop the technique of moving the punch and hitting it simultaneously; this method will produce smooth depressions. Hitting a stationary punch results in abrupt dents. Ease the punch along while hammering, until the metal is resting in the required position. Then proceed gradually along one side of the piece, maneuvering the metal as required. When you have finished, turn the metal over and work from the other side. As soon as the metal becomes hard to shape, separate the metal from the pitch and re-anneal. Then re-soften the pitch, replace the metal and resume chasing.

Once the overall form of the piece has been established, add the finer details with the line tracer, working from the front and back, as necessary. Then use planishing punches to even out any unwanted bumps and leave the work with a shiny, hammered finish. The planished surface can be left as it is, textured or patterned with a matting punch, given a high polish, or rubbed with a Scotch stone to remove all punch marks and then polished.

Tools and materials

Pitch, pitch bowl and
  leather ring to
  support bowl
Chasing punches
Chasing hammer
Heating equipment to
  soften pitch
Piercing saw and
  blades
Metal: 0.5mm to
  0.8mm thick and
  sufficient for the
  pattern chosen.
Buckle or brooch
  fittings as appropriate

CHASING A FLOWER

1 *Soften the pitch with a soft flame: do not allow the pitch to bubble. Push the pitch into place with a steel dab.*

2 *Lower the metal onto the pitch, ensuring that no air bubbles are trapped under the metal. Push the pitch over the edges of the metal with wet fingers.*

3 *Transfer the design to the metal. If several identical pieces are to be made, make a mask from the pattern, and scribe around the mask.*

4 *Begin chasing with the line tracer. Holding the punch upright, as shown, bounce the hammer on the punch while moving the punch along the marked line. Next, push out the fluting of the flowers with a blocking punch.*

5 *Push plasticine into the depressions to check the shapes and depths of the fluting.*

6 *Finish the piece with a planishing punch.*

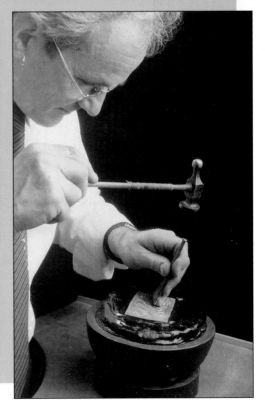

ADVANCED TECHNIQUES

So far, in order to give beginners the chance to acquire and practice new skills, many of the projects have concentrated on a single process. It is more usual for a piece of jewelry to include a variety of techniques and in the advanced projects, techniques introduced earlier in the book are combined together in the production of one piece. The techniques themselves remain as simple as when first tried, even though the piece appears more complicated and, as skills are mastered, personal approaches and combinations of techniques can be developed.

Aside from practicing basic skills, there are a number of other helpful hints for the successful making of jewellery. Planning is essential: consider both the design of the piece and the method and order of construction. Pitfalls can then be predicted and avoided — there is no satisfaction in struggling from one mishap to the next. Look for the simplest possible approach. Pieces that appear complicated are often assembled from simple, easy-to-construct elements: the elaborate garnet clusters on the page opposite are made up from flat, oval layers of stones. The layers are held together by pegs which pass from the top piece through holes in the second piece and are then bent over to hold the two pieces together. Pegs for the second layer then pass through holes in the third layer, and so on. This makes construction setting and polishing much easier. Each element is completed separately and all are brought together after polishing.

Do not forget the basic guidelines: work is likely to be more accurate if held steady; keep tools in good order — damaged tools are liable to damage work; when sawing, choose the right blade; when filing, select the largest file possible for the job; when soldering, always begin with hard solder, then use medium and finally easy; remove all marks before polishing; and work systematically and safely.

Tools and materials
By now you will have collected a range of tools and, provided the tools fall into the following main categories, few more should be needed for the advanced projects:

1 Tools for cutting
2 Tools for manipulating metal
3 Equipment for heating and soldering
4 Tools for cleaning and polishing

Suggested metal measurements are given with each project. These are guidelines and each jeweler should adjust the exact measurements to the stones and materials used.

Inlay and patination
Here, Dana Tinsley has
combined inlay and
patination to produce a
very individual effect.
Pages 150-1.

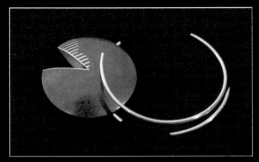

No-pressure settings
Ideal for stones too
fragile to withstand metal
being hammered over
them. Pages 158-9.

Coronet clusters
The jeweler will need a
wide range of technical
skills to construct these
advanced clusters.
Pages 166-7.

Single-stone ring
Pages 160-1
Three-stone ring
Pages 162-3
Built-up construction
Pages 164-5

Chain making
Pages 152-3

Linking and jointing
Pages 154-7

Inlay and patination

This brooch is made using a technique devised by American jeweller, Dana Tinsley: silver is inlaid in copper; both metals are textured by etching; and the copper is chemically darkened to contrast with the silver. For this work, use copper sheet about 1.2mm thick and silver strips that match the thickness of a saw blade.

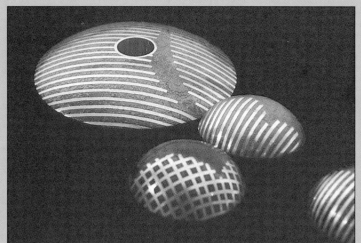

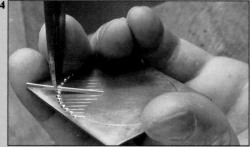

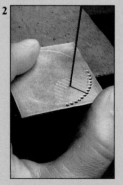

1 Scribe a circle in copper sheet and mark where the silver inlay is to be. Outside the circle, drill holes at the end of each inlay line to provide access for the saw blade.

2 Thread the blade through a hole and saw along the marked inlay line. Repeat for all other inlay lines.

3 Prepare silver strips to fit the sawn slots exactly. The strips can protrude a little above the surface of the copper but they should not fall below the surface. Hammer the end of each strip into the non-drilled end of its slot.

4 Trim to length with jeweler's shears.

5 Push the strip firmly into the metal with parallel pliers: repeat this process for all other slots.

6 To solder the inlay in place, first distribute pallions of solder evenly over the inlay area.

7 Heat the work with a soft flame to flow the solder around all inlay strips.

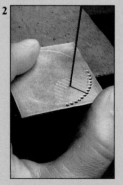

8 *Saw out the disk and file around the edge.*
9 *Dome the piece with a wooden doming punch, striking it with a wooden mallet. Hitting with a metal doming punch can produce stretching or unwanted marks.*
10 *The surface patination is achieved by etching some of the surface with acid and then coloring the copper. First, some parts of the surface are protected with a resist, a coating that prevents the acid used for etching from reaching the surface. The resist used in this case is powdered resin, which can be obtained from a printer's supplier. Make a small bag from an open-weave material like muslin. Load the resin in the bag, and shake it over the hot metal. The powder will fall randomly across the surface, leaving some metal exposed for etching and protecting other parts. Allow the metal to cool.*
11 *To etch the surface of the brooch, immerse the*

8

9

11

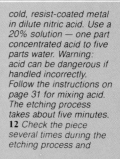

12

cold, resist-coated metal in dilute nitric acid. Use a 20% solution — one part concentrated acid to five parts water. Warning: acid can be dangerous if handled incorrectly. Follow the instructions on page 31 for mixing acid. The etching process takes about five minutes.
12 *Check the piece several times during the etching process and remove when the required surface effect is reached. After etching, wash the piece thoroughly in running water. To remove the resin after etching, scrub the surface with a bristle brush loaded with fine pumice powder. This will leave the silver bright.*
13 *For the coloring solution, dissolve a small piece (about 1cm cube) of liver of sulfur (potassium sulfide) in a cup of cold water. Add a few drops of ammonia if a slightly bluish tinge is preferred. It is important that the water is cold: if hot water is used, then the silver will be darkened too. Dip the work in the coloring solution and watch the copper darken. Remove it when the required depth of color is reached and wash the piece thoroughly under running water. If the silver has colored, re-scrub it with pumice. The color of the copper will not be affected by gentle rubbing.*

10

13

Chain making

Chain making is not difficult and, with patience, the jeweler can design individual and imaginative chains. The chain maker aims to produce links that require no filing and to solder them so that each moves freely and independently. A jig is used to make the chain links; a jig is a former that allows many links of the same size and shape to be formed with ease. Use the correct type of saw blade to cut the links so that no burrs are formed and the links will not have to be filed. Align the ends of the links accurately and use the minimum of solder to join them. Plan the work carefully so that, when assembled, the joins are hidden by adjacent links. Precise heat control should ensure that links are not inadvertently soldered together. Neighboring links can be painted with rouge to protect them from solder *(see page 154).*

1

2

3

4

5

Oval link chain
1 *Wind wire around an oval nail.*
2 *Saw off links with a 4/0 saw blade.*
3 *Solder half the links and connect these with unsoldered links.*
4 *Stand unsoldered links upright for soldering.*
5 *Or solder while holding adjoining links in tongs.*

Victorian-style chain
This chain consists of various kinds of links, some of which contain stones in rub-over settings with twisted wire decoration. The ornate links are enameled but would also look attractive if simply polished. Two specially made jigs are needed to form these links. Since six small leaves are required for each link, and it would take a considerable time to pierce them all by hand, the R T Blanking System should be used to make the leaves (see page 133). The back view (below and bottom) shows assembly details.

Fancy link chain
To make the jig, hammer one thick and three thin nails into wood and remove heads. Wind the wire around the nails to form the links; several links can be wound at once. Saw off the links and then solder. Each join should be concealed by another part of the link. Join fancy links to oval ones, as shown.

1 *A line drawing of the ornate link showed that it could be made most easily from two elements, each formed from a continuous wire. To save time, these elements should be shaped on the jigs shown rather than constructing the link by soldering together many pieces of wire by hand. Make the jigs from nickel silver strips 3mm wide by 1.2mm thick. Solder the shapes to nickel plates 1mm thick — nickel silver is used because it is reasonably strong, easy to work with, and retains a polished surface. Polish the jigs to remove marks which would otherwise be transferred to the links. It is worth spending some time making the jigs, as their accuracy determines the quality of the links formed on them.*
2 *Wind up the two wire elements of the link on the jigs.*
3 *File the diamond-shaped element of the link so that it merges smoothly with the curve of the other element. Solder the two together.*
4 *Solder the leaves and end rings in place; the leaves can be left flat, or shaped. Sandpaper and polish each link separately. Finally, assemble all the links and carefully repolish the whole chain (see page 45).*

Linking and jointing

Many items of jewelry need to be flexible in order to be comfortable. For example, if a tight wrist band is rigid, it is difficult to move the wrist. Flexibility can also prevent damage: earrings and other suspended decorations are less liable to break when knocked if they are jointed. Jointing may also be a decorative feature of the piece. There·are many ways of achieving flexibility and different techniques produce different types and degrees of flexibility. So bear in mind the amount and type of flexibility required when considering what kind of linking or jointing to use.

The watch shoulders are joined to the cases with hinges (left), while the suspended decorations (above) are linked with tiny round rings.

1 Saw vertical slots to fit the rectangular linking bar exactly.
2 Wedge the collets along the linking bar. Solder only one end of each collet to the bar. Drill the holes for the rivets through the collet

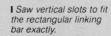

and linking bar at the unsoldered end of the collet. (Alternatively, drilling could be done after the links have been separated.)
3 Secure all rivets.
4 Saw out the bar from the inside of the collets.

Line jointing
This system allows each collet along a rectangular rod to rock slightly in a vertical plane. When viewed from the front, the collets always appear to be in a straight line. The rectangular rod should be strong and the slots in the collets must fit tightly. The same principle can also be applied to collets of other shapes.

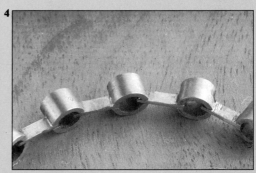

U-wire jointing
This system gives horizontal flexibility. The principle can be used for any collet shape.
1 Saw two horizontal slots. Draw down round wire to fit tightly into the slots. Bend a U-wire and hook it around one upright.
2 Wedge the U-wire into the next collet and solder carefully.

Ring-bar jointing

This system allows more vertical flexibility than the line-jointing system. Some horizontal flexibility can be introduced, without reducing the strength of the jointing, by widening the slot through which the ring fits. This principle can be applied to collets of any shape. This is a good jointing system for beginners because as long as the rings are strong enough it is not necessary to solder them after they have been closed over the bar. As a result, there is little risk of accidentally soldering together adjacent links.

1

2

3

1 Saw opposing vertical slots. Wind up rings to fit tightly into the slots. Position each ring as shown and solder.
2 File a horizontal groove. Solder the bar and file off the excess wire.
3 Hook the rings over the bar and close them.

Hints for fine soldering
1 Solder first joins with hard solder and last with easy solder.
2 Use the minimum amount of solder.
3 Ensure joins are absolutely clean and touching tightly.
4 Rouge powder mixed with water inhibits the flow of solder. Paint rouge on completed soldered joins, or on adjacent links, to prevent mishaps
5 Use a fine, hard flame.

Multi-flexibility

Sometimes a design requires flexibility over a metal surface. Such pieces often appear quite complicated but the principles used are usually simple and often based on primitive mechanical devices with loosely fitting joints. Often the most difficult aspect of this type of jointing is keeping everything in the right place. The easiest way to do this is to use plaster of Paris to hold the pieces in place until they have been jointed.

Borax the units and set them up in plasticine. Mix dental-grade plaster of Paris to a thick cream and pour over the units. When set, invert the work, remove the plasticine, and solder the joints. Then drop the still warm work in water to dislodge the plaster. In this way, a bar-bell joint through two half-rings (left) and a vertical and horizontal ring joint (below) can be made.

Hinges

Hinging is a common form of jointing. All the knuckles in a hinge must be in a straight line, otherwise the rivet will not pass through the holes or will bend to pass through misaligned holes and the hinge will not flex.
1 For the tiny hinges used in jewelry, saw a gap in the chenier, leaving a "bridge" to hold the two knuckles in line; saw out the bridge after soldering.
2 Alternatively, keep them in place with U-wires.

1

2

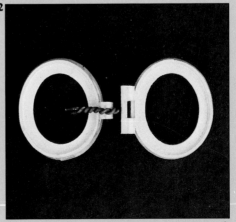

Linked earrings

The links are cut from a three-sided channel of metal, using a chenier cutter (right and below). Rectangular wire is used for the joints. Once the process of linking the channel has been mastered, make short lengths for earrings.

1 On a strip of metal 12mm wide x 0.8mm thick, file or engrave two right-angle shaped grooves 4mm from the outside edges and 0.4mm deep. Bend the metal up to make a three-sided channel and pull through a square draw plate.
2 Cut off units 4.5mm long with a chenier cutter.
3 Cut off units 1mm long.

To finish the earrings, solder on an ear post or a ring for an ear hook. Polish the links by hand with suede on a buff stick (below). The choker (right) has linked pendants 30cm long.

1   2   3   4   5   6   7   8

4 Saw 1mm off outside arms of the 1mm units.
5 Make U-shapes from rectangular wire 0.5 mm x1mm.
6 Paint the curves of the U-wires with rouge (see page 154). Hook through the1mm units.
7 Solder each 1mm unit in a 4.5mm unit.
8 Swivel down the arms of the U-wire.
9 Solder the protruding wires into the next unit.

9

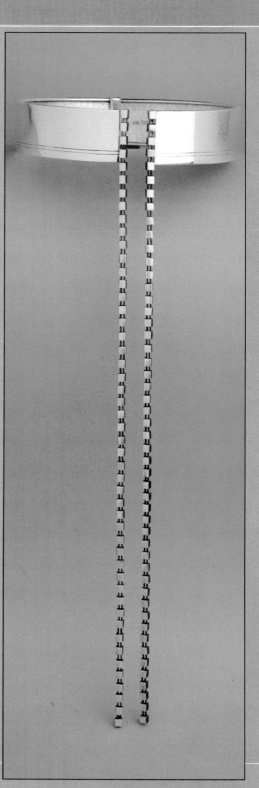

In most cases, simple jointing systems are effective. In the bracelet (left), the units are linked by simple rings that pass through holes drilled in the lower sections of the collets. Sometimes the jointing system is part of the design and clearly visible; in other pieces, the method of jointing is impossible to determine from the front. In the bracelet below, it is difficult to tell where the joints are from the front view and impossible to tell which type of joint has been used. The back view reveals that the bracelet has been made from units of different lengths hinged together and the side view shows the size of the hinges in relation to the thickness of the bracelet.

FRONT

SIDE

BACK

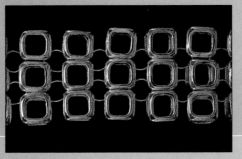

The U-wire jointing system gives the stone necklace (far left) such flexibility that it can be arranged in a tight S-shape. In the wire necklace (left and below left), wire rings pass loosely through holes on the inside of the cast box units. Such loose linking gives this piece enormous flexibility. Because each unit is linked to the surrounding units, they all retain their correct orientation. Such a system is not suitable for a single line of units, as the slack linking would make them inclined to twist.

"No-pressure" settings

Some stones and materials are fragile and will not withstand the pressure required for ordinary setting. The amber in this project, for example, has delicate, thin edges, so a special technique is used to set it. A collet is shaped to exploit the springiness of the metal. This collet is sprung around the stone and the set stone sprung into the piece.

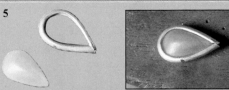

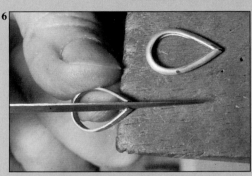

1 The collet is made from a U-shaped strip of metal. The stone measures 16mm x 12mm, so a strip 4mm wide x 0.5mm thick x 50mm long is suitable. The U-shaped cross-section of the collet makes it springy. Swage the strip by tapping a former onto it in a swage block.

5 Try the stone in the collet. If it does not fit, adjust the shape of the collet, or file the ends until they meet.
6 Bend up the collet base from a strip of metal 3mm wide x 0.6mm thick. This should fit around the inside edge of the collet and will hold the collet in the ring.
7 Tie the base strip to the collet with binding wire and then solder.
8 Next, make up the collet support from round wire; this will be part of the main section of the ring and the collet will spring into it. The collet base must fit tightly into the collet support. The round wire here is 2mm in diameter.

9 Reduce the height of the curved end of the collet base so that it is level with the collet support. Leave 5mm unfiled on either side of the point.
10 With round-nose pliers, curl over the two 5mm-long, higher sections at the pointed end. These curled "ears" will tuck under the round-wire collet support.
11 At the curved end of the collet, file a shallow groove in the collet base, directly under the collet. This weakens the collet base a little so that it can be pushed easily over the collet support in the next step.
12 Accuracy is essential at this stage if the collet is to spring properly into the ring. Tuck the "ears" of the collet base under the round-wire collet

2 Snip a point on the end of the strip.
3 Draw the strip through a round draw plate to partially close the U-shape.
4 Bend the annealed U-shaped strip to fit the stone. Work gently to avoid crushing the U-shape. If it opens slightly, reshape with pliers.

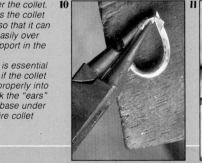

support and push the collet tightly into the support. With a setter's pusher or a burnisher, push the metal at the curved end of the collet base over the round wire. Push over only 8mm of metal across the curve, so that the collet can be snapped in and out of position. If too much metal is pushed over, the collet will be secured permanently.

13 Insert a knife between the collet and the round-wire support. Twist the knife to ease out the collet. If it comes out too easily, replace it and push over more metal from the back; if it will not come out at all, ease metal away from the wire. Refit the collet in the support wire. When pushed into place, the collet should make a distinct "snap." The snap must be made to work at this stage — if it does not work now it will certainly not work later.

14 To make the pattern for the next part of the ring, first measure the outside of the wire with a strip of paper. Then sketch a curve to fit the finger and cut it out of paper. Fit the paper pattern on the finger and adjust if necessary.

15 Pierce the pattern from metal 1mm thick.

16 Bend it to fit under the outside edge of the round-wire support. Solder the point.

12

13

14

15

16

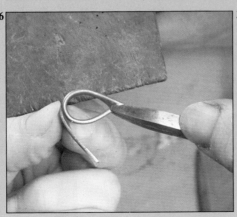

17

18

19

20

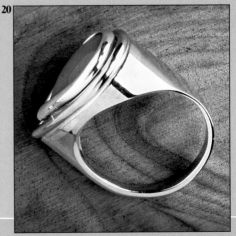

17 The shank should be half round at one end and triangular at the other. Hammer a length of 2mm round wire into the appropriate grooves in a swage block. (File grooves in a steel bar to make a suitable block.)

18 Bend up the shank, adjust its length, and solder it in place.

19 Bind the round wire in place and solder.

20 Spring the stone into the collet and then snap the collet into the ring.

Single-stone settings

The single-stone ring remains popular as an engagement ring. The metal section is usually light but strong.

For the collet, anneal a strip of metal 6mm wide x 0.9mm thick. Allow a length of about 30cm for each collet.

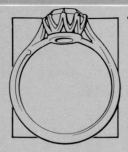

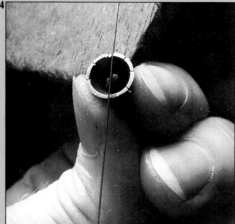

4

5 Around the base, file V-shaped grooves with a three-square needle file.
6 File the front of the V-shapes so that the metal curves down to a point at the base of each prong. The V-shapes are called nick-ups.

1 Wedge the annealed strip for the collet against the joint of a pair of parallel pliers. Curve the strip with grooved half-round pliers.
2 Wind up a collet as shown. Overlap the strip. Check that the edge of the stone falls halfway across the thickness of the collet wall. Saw through the double thickness of metal and solder the join.

7 With a twist of binding wire (size 32), wire the collet to a small, flat plate, l.2mm thick. Holding the work by means of the binding wire, solder each point to the flat plate with one tiny pallion of solder.

8 Drill through the base plate in the middle of the collet. File the outside of the base plate to match the angle of the collet walls and in line with the tops of the prongs. The plate should protrude 0.5mm from the rounded nick-ups to protect the collet from wear.
9 Experienced jewelers hold the collet in their fingers to saw out the prongs. Beginners may find it easier to use a "handle." Sharpen the end of a pencil or dowel rod, coat the end in setter's cement (or shellac), and warm the cement and metal. Wedge the point of the stick through the hole in the base plate and push cement over the base of the collet to hold it in place.
10 Saw straight down between the prongs; leave prongs 1.2mm wide. Saw out the sloping curves at the bottom. File.
11 For the shank, mark off 7mm from each end of some 2.5mm square wire (36mm makes a ring of size "M"). Thin out the section by forging.

3 Make the collet round by hitting it with a collet punch in a collet plate. If it is lopsided, tap the punch through the collet on the back of the collet plate.
4 Mark out six prongs with the saw. Plan the work so that the solder will be cut out and not fall along the prong. Mark the prong positions down the sides of the collet and onto the base.

 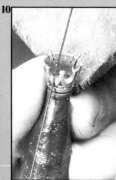

12 *Swage the thinner section to make it half round. The bar should now be 52mm long.*

13 *To bend the thick ends, first cover a lead cake with paper to protect the metal in the ring from contamination by lead. Then place a steel bar across one end of the work and hammer.*

14 *Bend the rest of the shank with half-round pliers and solder the ends. Tap the ring on a mandrel to make it round.*

11

15

12

13

16

15 *Saw through the soldered join. On both ends, mark 1mm out from the inside of the shank and extend a line 4mm back from the cut. Saw along these lines.*

16 *Bend up the "lift-ups" so that they curve smoothly into the collet. File back the lower supports so that they fit the collet exactly.*

17 *Wire the collet in place as shown. Holding the binding wire, solder the shank to the collet. Then solder one lower support. Check that the collet looks straight from all angles. Solder the remaining three points. File a curve on the inside of the collet base plate (finger bezel). Finish the ring and set the stone.*

14

17

Three-stone settings

The principles involved in making three-stone, five-stone and seven-stone rings are identical. As for single-stone rings, the purpose of the metal is to display the stones, so the metal should be light and recede beneath the stones when viewed from the top. The stones should be displayed across the top and if, say, five stones are to be fitted across a small shank, the outside collets should be higher than the middle ones. If this is not done, the stones will be hidden between the fingers.

3 Mark one prong down the center of each side of the middle collet; mark a prong at each end of the line of collets. The double metal between the collets will form ear pieces rather than prongs. On each outside collet, mark a prong midway between the ear piece and the end prong. File the nick-ups at the base of each prong or ear piece.

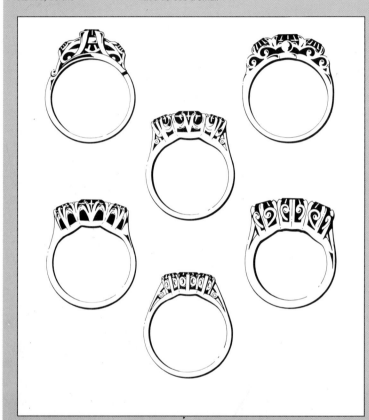

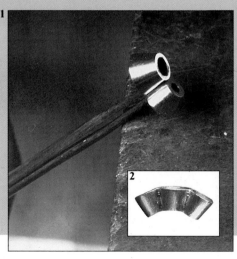

3

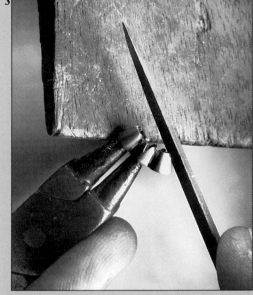

4

4 From metal 1mm thick, curve the finger bezel to the ring size.
5 Check that the base of the collets fits the finger bezel. Wire the finger bezel in place and solder. Drill the center of each collet and file the outside to shape.

1 Make individual collets in the same way as for the single-stone ring. Half the collet wall should be visible around the outside of the stones. File a flat surface down the solder join of all three collets. On one collet, file a second "flat" opposite: the wall thickness should be reduced by half where the "flat" is filed. Hold together the "flats" of two collets and solder.
2 Solder the third collet to the other two. File the inside curve to match the curve of the finger.

1

2

5

6 *Saw out beside the two end prongs only. Construct and fit the shank (see page 160). With the shank in place, it is easier to hold the ring when cutting the other prongs.*

6

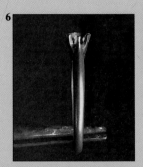

7 *Saw out the other prongs, making sure that the width of each one and the depths of the scallops are consistent. Do not leave the prongs too narrow at this stage — more metal will be lost when the piece is filed, sandpapered and polished. Using prong settings and including nick-ups helps to reduce the amount of metal in the piece and can result in considerable cost saving. Removing metal also allows light to reach the back of colored stones, enhancing their appearance and allowing access for cleaning behind them.*
8 *File up the prongs.*
9 *Sandpaper and polish.*

7

8

9

It is probably best to send the ring to an experienced setter, since the setting of the three-stone ring involves a combination of setting techniques. Each stone is held partly by prongs and partly by ear pieces. The latter are set in the same way as rub-over settings. Grains raised along the intervening sections give the stones further support.

Cross-over shanks
1 *Make a shank four sizes too big for the final ring size. Bend the S-curve as shown.*
2 *File the shank so that the half-round section at the back blends into the front curves. For elegance, file the curves thinner where they will meet the collets.*
3 *Saw out the shank to accommodate the collets and wire the collets in place. Solder, file and polish the ring ready for setting.*

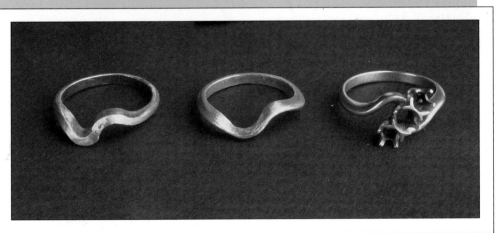

Built-up construction

Most pieces of jewelry consist of many elements that have to be fitted together and one of the problems for the jeweler is to keep all the parts in the right place while soldering. Balancing sometimes works but the most common method is to hold sections together with twists of soft iron binding wire. Another method is to set the parts in plaster of Paris (quick-setting dental grade is best) — after soldering, the plaster is broken away. Alternatively, charcoal chips, such as those used in fish-tank filters, can be packed around the work to support parts that rest at awkward angles or different heights while they are soldered. Sometimes, parts of a piece are completed separately and assembled after setting and final polishing by means of rivets, hinges or joints on the back of the piece. Most items of jewelry that appear extremely complicated are, in fact, assembled from many quite simple components.

1 *The silver ring in this project has six oval-faceted garnets, 7mm x 5mm, a central round cabochon garnet, 8mm in diameter, and six half-pearls, 4mm across. Begin by making the collets for all the garnets from a strip of metal 3mm x 0.7mm thick: the stones should drop inside the collets. Make the collets for the pearls from a strip 2mm wide x 0.7mm thick.*

2 *Make the twist decorations from 0.5mm round wire.*

3 *Solder the twists to the bases of the collets.*

4 *Next, make the stone support to hold the collets and decorations in place. Pierce the open pattern from sheet silver 1.2mm thick. The support has a decorated edge that protrudes about 1mm beyond the base of the collets. Calculate the diameter of the support from the sizes of the collets.*

5 *Except for the edge decoration, the pierced pattern on the support plate serves mainly to reduce the amount of metal used. Support plates sometimes bear monograms or messages.*

6 *Make the twelve, 2mm-round daisy*

decorations. Several methods could be used: a stamp could be made; or a setter's milligrain wheel could be used to make a strip of balls, which would then be wound into rings. For the method shown here, make chenier 2mm in diameter from a strip 0.6mm thick. Mark eight divisions on the end.

7 File them to form pyramids.

8 Ball them with a setter's grain tool.

9 Form a ball by melting a scrap of silver and

solder it to the center of the daisy.

10 Slightly dome the support plate with a doming punch in a doming block. With pliers, curve two opposite edges so that they follow the curve of the finger. Wire the central collet in place and solder it to the support plate. Then wire the six oval collets evenly around the central collet and solder them. Solder the daisy decorations in pairs first, then solder the pairs between the oval collets. The daisy decorations sit on top of the twisted wire surrounds. Finally, solder the pearl collets between the twisted wire surrounds and in front of the daisy decorations.

11 Pierce out the two shank decorations from silver sheet 1.2mm thick. Secure the decoration in setter's cement. Engrave, then carve the shapes shown.

12 Bend the decoration with half-round pliers.

13 Shape the shank from D-section wire 3mm wide. Wire the two side decorations in place and solder them to the shank.

14 The finger bezel bridges the gap between the shank and the top decoration and makes a comfortable rest for the decoration. To make the finger bezel, bend a strip of metal 1.2mm thick x 4mm wide into an oval that will rest beneath the top decoration. Solder the shank to the finger bezel.

15 File out the inside of the finger bezel in line with the curve of the shank.

16 File the top side of the finger bezel to fit under the top decoration.

17 Wire the top support in place and solder. Sandpaper and polish. Secure the ring in setter's cement and set all the stones in rub-over settings: begin with the central stone, then set the oval garnets and finally the pearls. Finish the ring with a final polish.

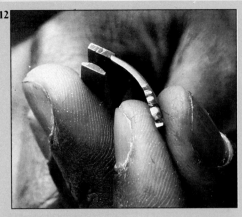

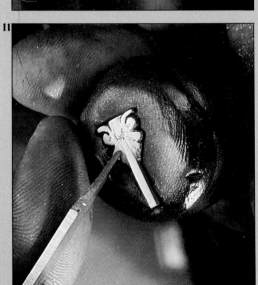

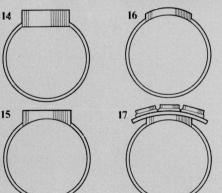

Coronet clusters

Coronet cluster rings are made up to fit the stones, so purchase the stones first. Lay them out in plasticine, then measure the length and width of metal needed.

1 *Scribe the positions for the stones on metal 1.2mm thick. Mark the position for each stone.*

2 *Measure to check that all stones are evenly spaced around the center stone. Accuracy is essential.*

3 *Saw around the outside of the marked stone positions. Dome up the metal.*

4 *Slide the metal around inside the hollow of the doming block, tapping it from all angles to ensure even doming.*

5 *Spot the center of each stone position and drill through.*

6 *Thread a blade through an outside hole and open out the hole, angling the cut as shown to prevent the stone from falling out. The girdle (edge) of the stone should just rest on the edge of the hole. Open out alternate holes, then go back and open out the rest.*

7 *Open out the center hole so that the girdle of the stone just rests on the edge of the hole.*

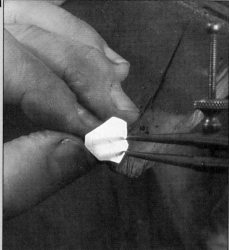

8 *Make prongs from a rectangular strip of metal 0.6mm x 1mm. Cut slots for the prongs in between the stones. Prongs can be used between all the stones, or between each pair, depending on the*

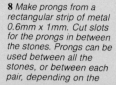

arrangement or the number of stones. Wedge in the prongs at a slight angle, then solder them.

9 *To make the support wall for the stone plate, curve a flat strip of metal*

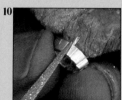

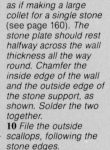

3mm wide by 1.2mm thick, then bend it round as if making a large collet for a single stone (see page 160). The stone plate should rest halfway across the wall thickness all the way round. Chamfer the inside edge of the wall and the outside edge of the stone support, as shown. Solder the two together.

10 *File the outside scallops, following the stone edges.*

11 *Cut the prongs into the wall. Follow the process described for the prongs of the single-stone ring (see page 160).*

12 *Mark the nick-ups with a saw.*

13 *File the nick-ups with a three-square needle file and round off their fronts.*

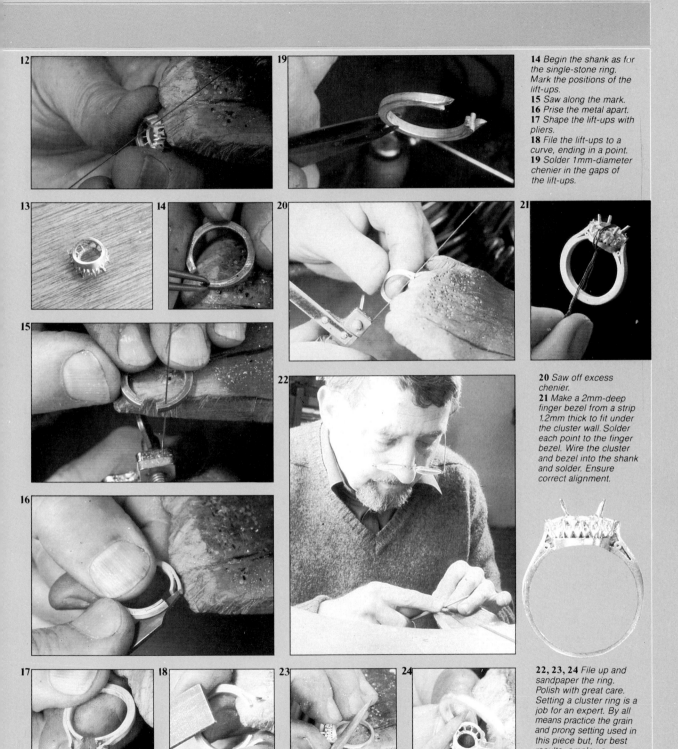

14 Begin the shank as for the single-stone ring. Mark the positions of the lift-ups.
15 Saw along the mark.
16 Prise the metal apart.
17 Shape the lift-ups with pliers.
18 File the lift-ups to a curve, ending in a point.
19 Solder 1mm-diameter chenier in the gaps of the lift-ups.

20 Saw off excess chenier.
21 Make a 2mm-deep finger bezel from a strip 1.2mm thick to fit under the cluster wall. Solder each point to the finger bezel. Wire the cluster and bezel into the shank and solder. Ensure correct alignment.

22, 23, 24 File up and sandpaper the ring. Polish with great care. Setting a cluster ring is a job for an expert. By all means practice the grain and prong setting used in this piece but, for best results, employ a professional setter.

HALLMARKING

Pure gold, silver, and platinum are too soft to withstand everyday wear. To make them harder, they are alloyed with other metals of relatively little value. With experience, you may be able to judge the purity of the metal. The only reliable indication, however, is the hallmark: a series of impressions punched in the metal at an official Assay Office after testing. Besides showing the type and purity of the precious metal used, most hallmarks also identify the Assay Office involved, the year in which the piece was marked, and its sponsor (the person who makes or controls the making of the item and arranges for it to be hallmarked). Repairs, alterations, and additions to items of precious metal may also be hallmarked. No formal system of marks exists in the USA, so jewelers usually use their own stamps. Articles exported to the UK are hallmarked on arrival, at one of the four Assay offices. Hallmarks stamped on articles imported into the UK are completely different to those stamped on British-made articles *(see far right).*

How hallmarks developed

Marks indicating the quaiity of precious metal have been found on items dating from Roman times. In Britain, laws controlling such markings were first passed in 1238 and applied only to gold and silver items made in London. An Act of 1300 extended these controls to items made anywhere in Britain and its dominions and remained in force until 1856, although various other regulations were introduced in the intervening period.

The early Acts defined standards of fineness for gold and silver, and the Act of 1300 also introduced a leopard's head mark for items assayed in London. This became known as the hallmark — the mark of the London Goldsmiths' Guild's Hall, where both gold and silver items were assayed. Provision for a maker's mark came soon after this, first for gold items and, in 1423, for silver. The 1423 Act also allowed items to be assayed and marked in various other towns in Britain and eventually the term "hallmark" came to be applied to the whole series of impressions made in assayed metal. After 1784, a mark showing the sovereign's head was used to indicate that excise duty had been paid on the gold or silver but this practice ceased in 1980. The hallmarking of platinum items commenced in Britain in 1975.

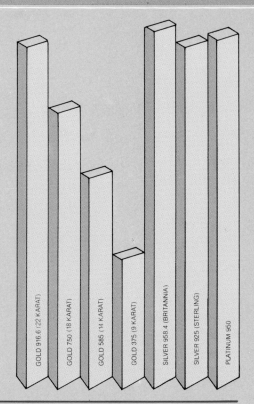

The proportion of precious metal in an alloy is now measured in parts per thousand by weight. Previously, the number of parts, called karats, of precious metal in 24 parts of the alloy was used. For example, 22 k gold is an alloy in which 22/24, or just over 916 parts in 1000, are pure gold. Since 1975, the standard mark for 22 k gold has been 916. The diagram (right) shows the legal standards used for describing objects made from precious metals. The standard mark applied to an object after assaying is a guarantee not only that the article has been made or sold by the sponsor whose initials it bears but also that the alloy contains at least the specified proportion of precious metal. If the alloy is below the minimum standard of fineness shown for that particular precious metal, then not only will it not be hallmarked but it will be returned as scrap.

(Bar chart labels, left to right): GOLD 916.6 (22 KARAT) · GOLD 750 (18 KARAT) · GOLD 585 (14 KARAT) · GOLD 375 (9 KARAT) · SILVER 958.4 (BRITANNIA) · SILVER 925 (STERLING) · PLATINUM 950

THE COMPONENTS OF A HALLMARK

SPONSOR'S MARK   STANDARD MARK   ASSAY OFFICE   DATE LETTER

YZ · 750 · £

STANDARD MARK

		ON BRITISH ARTICLES	ON IMPORTED ARTICLES
GOLD	91.6 PER CENT (22 KARAT)	916	916
	75.0 PER CENT (18 KARAT)	750	750
	58.5 PER CENT (14 KARAT)	585	585
	37.5 PER CENT (9 KARAT)	375	375
SILVER	95.8 PER CENT (BRITANNIA)		958
	92.5 PER CENT (STERLING)		925
PLATINUM	95.0 PER CENT		950

TABLES

ASSAY OFFICE MARK

	ON BRITISH ARTICLES			ON IMPORTED ARTICLES		
	GOLD	SILVER	PLATINUM	GOLD	SILVER	PLATINUM
LONDON						
BIRMINGHAM						
SHEFFIELD						
EDINBURGH						

DATE LETTERS ON BRITISH AND IMPORTED ARTICLES

1983	1984	1985	1986	1987

CONVENTION HALLMARKS

	18 KARAT GOLD	14 KARAT GOLD	9 KARAT GOLD
COMMON CONTROL MARK	750	585	375
FINENESS MARK	750	585	375

	SILVER †	PLATINUM
COMMON CONTROL MARK	925	950
FINENESS MARK	925	950

Marks indicating a standard of silver below sterling (925) are not approved hallmarks in the United Kingdom.

A hallmark comprises five marks: the sponsor's mark indicates the manufacturer or sponsor of the article; the standard mark defines the precious metal content of the alloy from which the article is made; the Assay Office mark identifies the particular office in which the piece was tested and marked — London, Birmingham, Sheffield and Edinburgh are the four British Assay Offices; and the date letter indicates the year in which the article was hallmarked. A special system of internationally recognized hallmarks has been agreed by signatory countries of the International Convention — Austria, Finland, Ireland, Norway, Portugal, Sweden, Switzerland and the United Kingdom. The Convention marks consist of a sponsor's mark, a common control mark, a fineness mark (showing the standard in parts per 1000) and an Assay Office mark. In many countries, including the USA, there is no official system for marking items made from precious metal, so the makers usually stamp their own marks in the metal to specify its fineness.

The tables on this page provide the jeweler with useful information at a glance. Determine the size and quality of the silver or gold you wish to use by referring to the table at bottom, and the size of the diamond by scanning the table below right. For information on melting temperatures, specific gravity, color, annealing details, appropriate solders and further useful hints on gold, silver and many other metals, turn to the table on page 17. Once you have decided on the size of precious stone or pearl you require, you may wish to refer to the table on page 98 for details on the color, transparency, hardness and cut of different precious stones before mounting and setting it. The formula below makes it easy for the jeweler to calculate the cost of copying a piece in another metal.

Calculating costs
If you wish to copy an already constructed piece in another metal, calculate the cost as follows. First weigh the piece, then use the table on page 17 to find the specific gravities (SG) of the two metals. Calculate the weight of the copy by using the formula below:

$$\frac{\text{weight of original} \times \text{SG of copy}}{\text{SG of original}}$$

To get the cost, multiply by the cost per gram of the metal.

WEIGHTS FOR PRECIOUS STONES AND PEARLS

The metric karat of 200 milligrams is the unit used for precious stones other than pearls, which are generally reckoned by grains, which are quarter-karats (ie 50 milligrams).

4 grains = 1 metric karat
1 metric karat = 200 milligrams
5 metric karats = 1 gram

DIAMOND SIZES

Weight	Diameter
0.02 karat	1.7 mm
0.03 karat	2.0 mm
0.04 karat	2.2 mm
0.05 karat	2.4 mm
0.06 karat	2.6 mm
0.07 karat	2.7 mm
0.08 karat	2.8 mm
0.09 karat	2.9 mm
0.10 karat	3.0 mm
0.11 karat	3.1 mm
0.12 karat	3.2 mm
0.14 karat	3.3 mm
0.16 karat	3.5 mm
0.18 karat	3.7 mm
0.20 karat	3.8 mm
0.22 karat	3.9 mm
0.25 karat	4.1 mm
0.30 karat	4.4 mm
0.33 karat	4.6 mm
0.35 karat	4.7 mm
0.40 karat	4.8 mm
0.45 karat	5.0 mm
0.50 karat	5.2 mm
0.75 karat	6.0 mm
1.00 karat	6.5 mm
1.25 karats	7.0 mm
1.50 karats	7.5 mm
1.75 karats	7.9 mm

Weights of metals of a specific thickness

Thickness of metal mm	Sheet Weight in g per cm² st. silver	9 k gold	18 k gold	Round wire Weight in g per metre st. silver	9 k gold	18 k gold
0.30	0.31	0.34	0.47	0.73	0.80	1.10
0.40	0.42	0.45	0.62	1.29	1.42	1.96
0.55	0.57	0.62	0.87	2.44	2.68	3.70
0.70	0.73	0.79	1.09	3.95	4.35	6.00
0.90	0.94	1.02	1.40	6.53	7.19	9.91
1.10	1.14	1.24	1.71	10.48	10.74	14.81
1.30	1.35	1.47	2.03	13.63	15.00	20.68
1.50	1.56	1.70	2.34	18.15	19.97	27.54
1.65	1.72	1.86	2.57	24.70	27.18	37.48
2.10	2.18	2.37	3.27	72.59	79.89	110.14
3.20	3.33	3.62	4.99	82.59	90.89	125.32

GLOSSARY

Annealing The process of heating and then cooling metal to make it softer and thus easier to work with. The required temperature for annealing, the duration of heating, and the rate of cooling vary according to the metal used.

Arkansas stone A fine abrasive stone.

Baguette A gemstone cut so that the shape of the top (table) is narrow and rectangular. It takes its name from the long French baguette loaf.

Base metal Non-precious metal, such as aluminum, copper, iron, and nickel.

Blanks Flat shapes cut from sheet metal.

Borax A flux commonly used when soldering jewelry. A special form of borax is produced for use by jewelers, which is easier to dissolve and melt than ordinary borax.

Buff stick A wooden rod with sandpaper or emery paper wound around it. The buff stick is used for sandpapering objects prior to the first polish.

Cameo A gemstone with a design cut in low relief.

Chasing The process of punching a relief design in metal from the front.

Chenier Thin metal tube, often used for making hinges in jewelry. It can also form other parts of a piece.

Collet A metal band that surrounds and supports a stone.

Cotter pin A double D-wire pin used to secure items. The pin is passed through a hole and the ends are spread to hold it in place.

Culet The small facet on the base of some brilliant cut stones.

Dowel rod A round, wooden rod used by jewelers to make round buff sticks.

Draw plate A hardened steel plate with a series of holes of various sizes. Wire is drawn through the plate to reduce its thickness, or to change its shape. Draw plates are commonly available with round, square, or triangular holes.

Electroforming The process of forming metal objects by using an electric

current to deposit the metal in a mold. The mold must be coated with a substance that conducts electricity. Electroforming is sometimes used to reproduce antique pieces; the process is also used for creating new individual pieces, and for mass production.

Electroplating The process of depositing a layer of metal on an object by means of an electric current. Jewelry made from base metal is often electroplated with silver or gold to enhance its appearance. Items made from plastic or other non-metallic substances can be electroplated if they are first coated with a substance that conducts electricity.

Electrum A naturally occurring pale yellow alloy of gold and silver. The proportions of the metals vary but this alloy usually contains more gold than silver.

Engraving The process of cutting away the surface of a substance, using a sharp steel tool called a graver. Lines are often engraved in a metal surface to form a decoration or inscription. Cameos and intaglios are made by engraving gemstones.

Etching The controlled corrosion of a surface with acid. In jewelry, the process is used to form surface decoration on metal: some parts of the surface are protected by an acid-resisting substance, while others are eaten away by the acid.

Facet A flat surface ground on a cut gemstone.

Filigree A decoration of fine wire, usually gold or silver, and often twisted or braided. The wire is often soldered to a sheet metal base; filigree without a base is called openwork. False filigree is an imitation formed by punching wire into the back of sheet metal, or by casting from a true filigree original.

Findings Mass-produced jewelry components, such as catches, joints, and clips, which are commonly used, even on hand-made jewelry. When such components are made by hand, they are sometimes called fittings.

Finger bezel The base of a collet in a ring, shaped to fit the finger.

Fire stain The black coating that forms on silver when it is heated. The coating consists of copper oxide and is formed by the copper in the impure silver combining with oxygen in the air.

Flux A substance used in soldering to ensure that the solder flows. Any oxide present on the metal tends to prevent the solder from flowing. The flux is applied to the parts to be soldered and prevents air from reaching them. As a result, no oxide is formed, so the solder is able to flow and join the metal. Borax is the flux commonly used by jewelers.

Forging The process of hammering metal to change its shape.

Former A steel shape for supporting metal while it is being hammered.

Gallery (1) A wire fixed to the back of jewelry to raise the level of the metal so that there is sufficient clearance below for the stones.

Gallery (2) A mass-produced decorative metal strip, often with a series of elongated holes across the center, usually known as a closed gallery. Open galleries are made by cutting a closed gallery along the middle of the holes to produce a series of U-shapes on each piece. An open gallery can be used as a ready-made prong setting, the arms of the "U"s forming the prongs.

German silver *See* nickel silver

Gilding The process of applying a thin layer of gold or gold alloy to another material. This may be done by attaching gold leaf, or by painting on an amalgam of mercury and gold and then heating to vaporize the mercury.

Gilding metal A gold-colored alloy consisting mainly of copper and zinc. It is used to make inexpensive jewelry and is usually gilded.

Gimp A coil of very fine wire used to protect the ends of threads on which beads or pearls are strung. The ends are passed through gimps so that they cannot wear away by rubbing on the catch of the jewelry.

Girdle The widest circumference of a gemstone. The girdle forms the boundary between the crown (top) and the pavilion (base).

Grain (1) A unit of weight, common to both the Troy and Avoirdupois systems. Four grains are equal to one karat, the unit of weight for precious stones and pearls.

Grain (2) A tiny ball of metal (*see* granulation).

Granulation The decoration or texturing of a surface by the application of tiny balls (grains) of gold or silver. Various techniques have been developed for making and attaching the grains. A recent method involves dropping molten gold onto a stone slab to form the granules and then welding them to the piece with resin.

Hallmark A series of impressions made in an item of gold, silver or platinum. The hallmark is an official guarantee of the fineness of the metal.

Intaglio An object with a hollowed-out design, the flat surround being the highest part. The opposite of a cameo, an intaglio is sometimes known as hollow relief. In jewelry, intaglio designs are usually made in gemstones and sometimes in metal.

Investment Fine-grade plaster used in the casting process.

Jig A tool used to form several items of identical shape.

Karat (1) A unit of weight, now standardized as being equal to one-fifth of a gram; this is equal to 3.086 grains Troy. The weight of gemstones is usually expressed in karats.

Karat (2) A measure of the fineness of gold or gold alloy. The number of karats is the number of parts by weight of pure gold in 24 parts of the metal. Pure gold is, therefore, described as 24 karat, and 14 kt gold is an alloy that contains 14 parts of pure gold in 24 parts of the alloy.

Lapidary A craftsperson who cuts, engraves, and polishes gemstones other than diamonds. The term is also applied to the craft.

Lapping The process of polishing flat metal surfaces with a flat felt buff.

Lead cake A block of lead used to support metal while it is being hammered.

Malleability The property, usually of a metal, of being easily hammered, rolled, or pressed to shape without fracturing.

Mandrel A tapered steel rod on which rings are shaped.

Marquise Any gemstone with a boat-shaped girdle. The curved sides meet at a point at each end of the stone.

Nickel silver An alloy of copper, nickel, and zinc (but no silver). It is also known as German silver and is used in costume jewellery and for articles that are to be silver plated.

Paste Glass used in jewelry, usually to imitate gemstones.

Pavé setting A style of setting in which many stones are set very close together, covering the metal like miniature paving.

Pickle A solution used during construction to clean flux and oxides from metal after heating — for example, after soldering. Pickle is also used to clean finished jewelry. Dilute sulfuric acid is often used as a pickle.

Piercing saw A saw with a blade narrow enough to be threaded through a drilled hole so that a pattern can be cut out from sheet metal or other material.

Pinchbeck An alloy of copper and zinc made to resemble gold.

Planishing The process of hammering metal with a polished hammer to obtain an even surface.

Rabbiting The process of joining two or more pieces of metal with a piece of chenier by spreading it over each side of the metal.

Repoussé A relief design punched into thin metal from the back.

Rolled gold A base metal with a thin coating of gold fused to it. Sheets of rolled gold are made by fusing a layer of gold to the base metal and then rolling it to the required thickness: one or both sides of the base metal may be covered with gold. So-called rolled gold wire is made by enclosing a core of base metal in a gold tube and drawing it down through a draw plate.

Rouge Jeweler's rouge is red iron oxide, a fine abrasive used for the final polishing stages of precious metals.

Scotch stone A block of abrasive stone.

Shank The part of a ring that passes around the finger.

Soldering The process of joining metal, using an alloy called solder. The solder is designed to melt at a temperature lower than the metal it is intended to join. The work and solder are heated until the solder melts. On cooling, it solidifies to form a firm joint. The terms easy, medium, and hard solder describe solders with progressively higher melting points. Thus, some joints can be made at a relatively low temperature without melting earlier joints made with a higher-melting-point solder.

Split pin *See* cotter pin.

Sprue The unwanted piece of metal attached to a casting and formed by the access channel in the mold.

Stamping The process of forming a pattern in sheet metal, using a punch bearing the complete design. The pattern is formed by a single blow and the process is suitable for mass production.

Stoning The process of abrading with a grindstone.

Swaging The process of making a piece of metal U-shaped by hammering it directly into a U-shaped groove in a metal block.

Tempering The process of heating metal after hardening to reduce its brittleness.

Tensile strength The stress that must be applied to a material to break it.

Tripoli A coarse abrasive used in the first stages of polishing metal.

Vulcanizing press A press used for compressing hot rubber to form molds for casting.

Work hardening The hardening of a metal caused by hammering or bending, which often makes the metal too hard to work with until it has been softened by annealing.

INDEX

USEFUL ADDRESSES

This section includes some of the main suppliers, and others who will supply goods by mail. It also lists publications that will help you locate your nearest supplier, and organizations that will advise you.

UK

INFORMATION

The Worshipful Company of Goldsmiths
Goldsmiths' Hall
Foster Lane
London EC2V 6BN

Gemmological Association of Great Britain
Saint Dunstan's House
Carey Lane
London EC2V 8AB

Crafts' Council
8 Waterloo Place
London SW1Y 4AU

British Crafts' Centre
43 Earlham Street
London WC2H 9LD

GALLERIES

Aspects
3 Whitfield Street
London W1P 5RA

British Crafts' Centre

Crafts' Centre and Design Gallery
Leeds City Art Gallery
The Headrow
Leeds LS1 3AA
West Yorkshire

Crafts' Centre
Royal Exchange Theatre
St Ann's Square
Manchester M2 7DD

Crafts' Council Gallery
12 Waterloo Place
London SW1Y 4AU

Electrum Gallery
21 South Molton Street
London W1Y 1DD

Oxford Gallery
23 High Street
Oxford OX1 4AH

Victoria and Albert Museum
Cromwell Road
South Kensington
London SW7 2RL

MAGAZINES

Crafts' Council

Goldsmiths' Technical Reports and *Goldsmiths' Gazette* from:
The Worshipful Company of Goldsmiths

British Jeweller
27 Frederick Street
Birmingham B1 3HJ

The Retail Jeweller
Northwood House
93-99 Goswell Road
London EC1V 7QA

EQUIPMENT AND TOOLS' SUPPLIERS

Charles Cooper
Knights House
23-27 Hatton Wall
Hatton Garden
London EC1N 8JJ

Frank Pike
15 Hatton Wall
Hatton Garden
London EC1N 8JE

H S Walsh & Sons Ltd
12-16 Clerkenwell Road
London EC1M 5PQ

243 Beckenham Road
Beckenham
Kent BR3 4TS

BULLION DEALERS

J Blundell & Sons Ltd
199 Wardour Street
London W1V 4JN

D Pennellier & Co Ltd
28 Hatton Garden
London EC1N 8DB

Johnson Matthey Metals Ltd
43 Hatton Garden
London EC1N 8EE

Vittoria Street
Birmingham B1 3NZ

173/5 Arundel Gate
Sheffield S1 1JY

101 Grafton Street
Dublin 2
Republic of Ireland

SPECIAL METALS

Goodfellow Metals Ltd
Cambridge Science Park
Milton Road,
Cambridge CB4 4DJ

PRECIOUS AND SEMI-PRECIOUS STONES

R Holt & Co Ltd
98 Hatton Garden
London EC1N 8NX

SPECIALIST MATERIALS AND SERVICES

Ceramic shell casting

H R A Bronze
Coldharbour Works
245a Coldharbour Lane
London SW9 8RR

R T Blanking System
Tools exclusively from:
Taylor Designs
132 Abbotts Drive
North Wembley
Middlesex

Goldsmiths' Technical Report from:
Taylor Designs and
The Worshipful Company of Goldsmiths

SETTERS

Corbier Setting Co
48 Hatton Garden
London EC1N 8EX

POLISHERS

Sinclair Ltd
23 Hatton Garden
London EC1N 8BQ

ASSAY OFFICES

Goldsmiths' Hall
Gutter Lane
London EC2V 8AQ

Newhall Street
Birmingham B3 1SB

137 Portobello Street
Sheffield S1 4DR

15 Queen Street
Edinburgh EH2 1JE

USA

INFORMATION

The Jewelry Institute of America
40 Sims Avenue
Providence
RI 02909

PRECIOUS METALS

Hauser and Miller Co
4011 Forest Park Boulevard
St Louis
Missouri 63108

Hoover and Strong
10700 Trade Road
Richmond
Virginia 23236

Leach and Garner Co
608 Fifth Avenue
New York
New York 10020

REFRACTORY METALS

Reactive Metals Studio
P O Box 425
Jerome
Arizona 86331

EQUIPMENT & TOOLS' SUPPLIERS

Allcraft Tool & Supply Co Inc
100 Frank Avenue
Hicksville
New York 11801

Rio Grande Albuquerque
6901 Washington N E
Albuquerque
New Mexico 87109

Anchor Tool & Supply Co Inc
231 Main Street (*or* P O Box 265)
Chatham
New Jersey 07928

Frei & Borel
119 3rd Street
Oakland
California 94607

William Dixon Co
750 Washington Avenue
Carlstadt
New Jersey 07072

Paul H Gesswein & Co Inc
225 Hancock Avenue
Bridgeport
Connecticut 06605

C R Hill Co
2734 W11 Mile Road
Berkley
Michigan 48072

I Schor Co
71 Fifth Avenue
New York
New York 10003

The L S Starrett Co
121 Crescent Street
Athol
Massachusetts 01331

4949 West Harrison Street
Chicago
Illinois 60644

5946 East Washington Boulevard
Los Angeles
California 90040

Swest Inc
(Formerly Southwest Smelting and Refining Co)
10803 Composite Drive
Dallas
Texas 75220

431 Isom Road
San Antonio
Texas 78206

1725 Victory Boulevard
Glendale
California 91201

Myron Toback
23 West 47th Street
New York
New York 10036

TSI Inc
(Technical Specialities International)
Nickerson Street Business Park
101 Nickerson Street
Seattle
Washington 98119

SPECIALIST MATERIALS & SERVICES

Paul H Gesswein's Co Inc
255 Hancock Avenue
Bridgeport
Connecticut 06605

Billanti Casting Co
64 West 48th Street
New York
New York 10036

C A Brown Inc
315 Wellington Avenue
Cranston
Rhode Island 02901

R T Blanking System
Tools available from UK only

Goldsmiths' Technical Report from:
The Jewelry Institute of America

POLISHERS

The Lea Manufacturing Co
237 East Aurora Street
Waterbury
Connecticut 06720

LAPIDARY EQUIPMENT

Grieger's Inc
900 S Arroyo Parkway
Pasadena
California 91109

MINERAL GEMSTONES

Grieger's Inc
900 S Arroyo Parkway
Pasadena
California 91109

The Lapidary Journal
Box 80937
San Diego
California 92138

ACKNOWLEDGMENTS

The pictures on these pages were produced by courtesy of the following:
Half-title Annie Sherburne (piece), Tony Lumb (photograph)
6 Joel Degen (l); **8** David Watkins (l), Joel Degen (tr,cr,b); **9** Ramon Puig Cuyas (tr), Alan Craxford (br); **10** Electrum Gallery (l,tr,cr); **11** David Watkins (tl), Electrum Gallery (ct), Setsu Sato (c), Joel Degen (br), Joel Degen and the British Crafts' Centre (b1); **12** Mary Evans' Picture Library; **14** Electrum Gallery (t), Reema Pachachi (bl), Joel Degen (br); **15** Joel Degen (ct,tr), Electrum Gallery (cr), Barry and Sally Milburn (bl); **16** Electrum Gallery (tl), Crafts' Council Collection (tr), Joel Degen (cr,br); Electrum Gallery (bl,cb); **18** Trustees of the British Museum (t); **19** Joel Degen (t,b); **23** Jerry Young (b); **26** Robin Kyte (tl); **27** Trustees of the British Museum (tr); **35** Trustees of the British Museum (tl), Electrum Gallery (tr), Joel Degen (b); **39** Joel Degen (tl); **41** Royston Henry Osborne (br); **43** Joel Degen (c,bl,br); **52** British Crafts' Centre (t); **56/7** Bert Kitchen (b); **64** Cartier Collection, Paris (t); **65** E T Archives (t); **69** Electrum Gallery (l,r); **70** British Crafts' Centre (t,bl); **72** Joel Degen (b); **73** David Ward (t), Joel Degen (b); **74** De Beers; **76** Michael Freeman (t), Joel Degen (b); **78/9** Michael Freeman (cb); **85** Robin Kyte (tl); **87** Joel Degen (tr); **97** Electrum Gallery (b); **108** Joel Degen (t), Sarah Letts (ct), Setsu Sato (c); **109** Joel Degen (t); **112** Sarah Letts; **116** Phil Barnes (t,bl); **120** Joel Degen (c,b); **121** Joel Degen (tl,cr,br), Pauline Gainsbury (cl); **126** Manley Photo-Tuscon (t); **128** Trustees of the British Museum (r); **130** Ashmolean Museum (b); **132/3** Roger Taylor, Taylor Designs; **135** Julie Crossland (tl); **137** Medina Art Castings Ltd; **149** Dana Tinsley (tl); **168/9** Joint Committee of the Assay Offices of Great Britain/Broadfield Advertising.

All other photographs are the property of Quill Publishing Limited.

Key: (t) top; (b) bottom; (l) left; (r) right; (c) center

While every effort has been made to acknowledge all copyright holders, we apologize if any omissions have been made.